I0764146

OPINIONS OF THE PRESS.

From the Baltimore American.

"We have examined with pleasure a very useful work, entitled, A TEXT BOOK OF GEOMETRICAL DRAWING, just published by our townsman, Mr. Wm. Minifie, Architect, and Teacher of Drawing, in the Central High School of Baltimore. The work is designed for the use of Mechanics and Schools, and has also been prepared for those who desire to instruct themselves. For this purpose, the author has taken care to employ the most simple terms in his definitions, as well as his problems, and has illustrated his lessons for drawing Buildings, Machinery, &c., with fifty-six Steel Plates, containing over two hundred Diagrams. This work is designed to supply a want which the author experienced in his course of instruction; and is the result of a well-digested plan which he found promotive of great benefit among his scholars. With a judgment that does not always accompany talent, the author has adapted his lessons to their practical application in every-day business, and thus while the scholar learns the art of Mechanical Drawing, he also learns what is equally essential, its adaptation to all useful purposes. We regard Mr. Minifie's work as one likely to confer great benefits on the rising generation, as a knowledge of what it teaches is of consequence to every one—to the mechanic who reduces the art to practice, and to the merchant or the capitalist who tests the mechanic's skill by its application to his work.

From the Baltimore Sun.

"MINIFIE'S DRAWING.—A Baltimore book of the first class. A text book designed unquestionably to take rank among the most valuable acquisitions of the art. The author exhibits in the details of the work the familiarity of a master with his subject; and, while with a dexterous hand simplifying his theme by the avoidance of technicalities as much as possible and the use of plain language, he adds to the attractiveness of the study, and lures the pupil by facilitating the way to the highest attainments in the art. It will command beyond doubt an extensive popularity."

From the Baltimore Western Continent.

"We are gratified to see a book of such sterling merit issued from a Baltimore publication house. All the externals are carefully attended to. The engravings are all on steel, executed with great neatness and precision. The paper is white, the type so clear that it is a real gratification to read it, and the binding solid and substantial. It may be thought strange that we mention such traits as these, but after reading books carelessly printed and so loosely bound that they fall to pieces on the first perusal, such advantages as we have alluded to can be better appreciated.

"To come to the subject matter of the book. The lessons are (as they should be in a text book intended to be used not only by drawing masters, but also by those who wish to teach themselves the art of Mechanical Drawing,) progressive, beginning at the simplest rudiments, and gradually advancing to the higher and more complicated problems. During every stage of his advance, the student is furnished with numerous illustrations. He is required to do nothing of which a model is not supplied; and he is taught to study these models intelligently by a very clear and copious explanation of the necessary processes required, and a full definition of all the technical terms which are applicable to the figures presented to him. Linear Drawing, the division of Angles, the formation of Polygons, the principles of Circles, the use of the various Mathematical Instruments, the construction of the different Curvilinear figures take up the early lessons. The work then passes to the consideration of Solids and their Sections, more particularly those of the Cone and the Cylinder. This, of course, completes the study of the principles of the art. The student, if he have bestowed on his lessons the necessary attention and care, has now mastered the *alphabet of drawing*.

"At this point of the course comes in the practical application of the knowledge already acquired. The rules are first applied to Building, to the laying of boards, the construction of arches, the drawing of plans and elevations of houses and the delineation of the various mouldings used in architecture. Machinery next takes its turn, and then we have a treatise on Isometrical Drawing, preparatory to Perspective. The former is, in most works on this subject, included in the latter.

"The pupil is now fully prepared to enter upon the study of Perspective. The principles of this important branch of drawing are laid down, and several examples given. We were pleased to find that Mr. Minifie has paid attention to the theory of Vanishing Points, and giving rules for determining their position, a matter too often left by writers on Perspective to the blind arbitration of chance. The theory of Shadows, which is properly a corollary to Perspective closes the volume.

"In taking leave of Mr. Minifie's book, we would heartily commend it to all persons who desire to acquire a knowledge of the important art of Mechanical Drawing. This forms a distinct and separate branch of art of the greatest practical importance to the builder, the machinist and indeed to all artizans, who work by plans laid down on a flat surface. The want of a work on this department of Graphics, thorough and at the same time easily intelligible, has long been felt. This want we believe to be fully supplied by the volume before us, which contains all the rules necessary to make a finished draughtsman of plans and models. *He who, having thoroughly mastered this book, cannot make any of the ordinary drawings of this kind, may well despair of ever being able to accomplish such a result."*

From the Boston Post.

"The title of this beautiful volume, does not present a sufficiently elevated idea of its character, usefulness, or outward elegance. It is, in the first place, one of the most handsomely printed works that we have ever seen, and in respect to illustrations is far superior to any scientific book which has ever come from the American press. *It is fully equal to the most expensive of the English publications of its class.*

"It is intended both for Schools and individuals without a master, and it includes, therefore, the definitions and rules of Geometry familiarly explained, and very many of the practical problems, beginning with the most simple, and embracing descriptions as void of technicalities as possible. The whole is illustrated by fifty-six Steel Plates, containing more than two hundred Diagrams. Plan Drawing, Sections and elevations of Buildings and Machinery are fully discussed and illustrated; and to these are added an introduction to Isometrical Drawing, and an essay on Linear Perspective and Shadows. The work is very intelligibly and systematically written, and we must repeat, that the illustrations are most beautifully engraved. A strong, substantial binding is a fitting finish to the internal excellence of the volume. We would call the attention of *school committees* and *mechanics* of all branches to the book under notice. It is evidently intended to be a standard one, and from what we know of the wants of both juvenile and adult students of Geometrical Drawing, is just the thing for both classes."

From the Boston Journal.

"The plan of this work is a good one—something of the kind is much wanted at this time—and so far as we are able to judge, the want is well supplied by the work before us, which is eminently practical in its character, and will be found useful to the *Mechanic*, the *Engineer* and the *Architect.* It is well adapted, not only for private self-instruction, but as a text book of drawing to be used in our High Schools and Academies, where this useful branch of the fine arts has been hitherto too much neglected."

Second Notice.

"This publication is not a new candidate for public favor. No better evidence of its utility is required, than the fact that it has, within less than one year reached its second edition. It is eminently practical in its character, and is admirably calculated to smooth the path of the youthful Engineer and Architect, to the attainment of one of the most important branches of study in his profession. We do not hesitate to pronounce it after a careful examination, a *useful and truly valuable book.*"

From the Boston Chronotype.

"An elementary practical text book on Perspective and Drawing as applied to objects of utility, such as Buildings, Machines, Surveys, &c., has been a great desideratum. All the works we have seen, are either too superficial and elementary, or too scientific and extensive. Here is one adapted to meet the wants of a large class of learners and practical mechanics, which contains all the scientific principles that are ordinarily needed, with a plenty of practical problems. To be able to use mathematical instruments and correctly to delineate any object, in true perspective, or as it actually appears, is a most useful and valuable faculty to any one, and considering the ease with which the art may be acquired with proper teaching, it is wonderful that it is not more taught. It ought to be a part of every common school education.

"A text book like this, which unites beauty, simplicity and science, bringing the most useful applications of the art of drawing within the reach of all, is truly a valuable gift to the cause of education."

From the Boston Atlas.

"Minifie's Mechanical Drawing Book.—This is the title of a new work issued from the press of Wm. Minifie & Co. of Baltimore. It seems to be eminently well adapted as a text book, for the use of Schools, and students in Engineering, Architecture and Mechanics. When it becomes known, it will without doubt, be extensively used in Schools and Colleges, as well as for private self-instruction."

From the Boston Daily Advertiser.

"The rules for drawing figures of every description on a plain surface, or in Perspective, by the simplest methods, are clearly given, based on mathematical principles. The definitions and descriptions have the merit of being both *precise* and *intelligible*, and the work appears to be well adapted as a text book for High Schools, or a practical manual for architects."

From the Boston Daily Bee.

"From the excellent manner in which the work is produced, and the high standing of its Author in the scientific world, we can with confidence recommend it to the *attention* of our Mechanics and Artists. No book of the kind ever went before the public with higher commendations than the one in question; and none ever won higher praise from the American Press."

From the Washington National Intelligencer.

"A TEXT BOOK OF GEOMETRICAL DRAWING.—This is the title of a work recently published in Baltimore, by an architect of established reputation there. The origin of it Mr. Minifie explains in his preface to have been in the necessities of the pupils to whom, as Professor in the High School, he gives instruction and lectures on Mechanical Drawing and the applications of Geometry, and for whom no one existing text book, furnished the solution of problems, which are of daily practical occurrence, and which, for that very reason, are apt to be passed over, as too simple for exposition by those who apply themselves to the more recondite topics of Mathematics. In this respect, Mr. Minifie has gone far to remedy the deficiency; and while he does not assume to have originated any thing new, he has presented in a small and cheap compass, and in a judicious and instructive arrangement, what otherwise had to be searched for in a dozen volumes or more. For the young Mechanic, therefore, in furnishing the rules and proportions of laying out and fitting work, *this single book is a library.*

"Such completeness is not purchased, either by an undesirable or unintelligible brevity; but by a sedulous restriction on the part of the author to the aim with which he set out. This was the enabling of an ordinarily intelligent Mechanic to represent on paper or on a board, either work that *had been,* or work that *had to be* executed in solid materials. Here, mere theory is unnecessary, further than to show the reasonableness of the several processes, and to assist the memory in retaining the sequence of the several steps; but distinct and literal rules, referred throughout to accompanying Diagrams, are copiously given for every thing, from the marking off a mitre-joint to the development of the metal roofing of hemispherical domes, and from the erection of a perpendicular to the Perspective Drawing of extensive buildings.

"The style and order of arrangement seems to have arisen from a practical intimacy with the subject; *those difficulties are chiefly dwelt on which are likely to arise in actual working cases, and with actual workmen;* and these are so treated, with minute and particular rules, accompanied with abundant and perspicuous drawings, as to render the book quite adapted to the purpose of self-instruction. Indeed, one who patiently and carefully goes through it could not be said, so far as principles and methods are concerned, any longer to want a master, while, as regards neatness of execution, the plates are quite sufficient to serve as models for the learner.

"On the whole, we have good authority for saying that so useful and so cheap a book for all who are concerned in the arts of building and design, has not appeared for a long time."

From the Washington News.

"In every department of business or condition of life drawing is not an accomplishment, but an indispensable necessity. With the inventive genius of our people, the art of drawing would be eminently useful, tending as it would, to advance the Mechanic and manufacturing arts. We esteem what is important for men to know as men, should be learned by children in school. To teachers we commend Minifie's Drawing Book; and to our hardy Mechanics who have not time to devote to the study of long mathematical demonstrations, the book will be found eminently practical and useful."

From the New York Scientific American.

"It is the best work on Drawing that we have ever seen, and is especially a text book of Geometrical Drawing for the use of Mechanics and Schools. No young Mechanic, such as a MACHINIST, ENGINEER, CABINET MAKER, MILLWRIGHT or CARPENTER, should be without it. It is illustrated with fifty-six Steel Plates, and contains more than two hundred Diagrams. The author, Mr. Minifie, shows that he is master of his subject in all its various branches, which he has illustrated with Plans, Sections, Elevations, Perspective and Linear Views of Buildings and Machinery. SUCH BOOKS—ARE BOOKS.

"The price is very moderate, considering the quality, the sterling worth and style of the work."

Second Notice—21st February, 1850.

"The first edition of this great work was disposed of in a short time, the second is now ready. The author has improved its appearance very much, while the matter stands far above any similar work ever published."

From the New York Farmer and Mechanic.

"A VALUABLE SCIENTIFIC WORK.—We cannot forbear noticing more particularly an excellently arranged, highly practical, and exceedingly valuable work recently published by Messrs. William Minifie & Co. at Baltimore, being a TEXT BOOK OF GEOMETRICAL DRAWING, and admirably calculated for the use of *Mechanics, Schools* and *Academies.* In this work the various rules and definitions of Geometry are familiarly explained with great distinctness, and the practical problems arranged, gradually progressing from the most simple to the more complex, dispensing with the long and tedious detail of technicalities in description, so objectionable in many other works on the subject.

"The volume also contains some of the best illustrations for drawing Plans, Sections and Elevations of Machinery, and Buildings that we have seen; including an introduction to Isometrical Drawing, and an essay on Linear Perspective and shadows; and is beautifully illustrated with nearly sixty Steel Engravings. Mr. Minifie, the author, is an Architect of distinction, and a popular teacher of Drawing in the Central High School of Baltimore, and certainly in this work has given a proof of talents of a high order.

"The usefulness and capabilities of the application of the rules contained in this book, to the usual practical every-day business of life, is one of its best recommendations, and we believe its value will only require to be known, to cause it to be most extensively adopted in Schools and Colleges, as well as for private instruction. We most cheerfully commend it as a valuable acquisition to the libraries of all our mechanical readers."

Second Notice—February 14th, 1850.

"We cannot too highly recommend so useful a work to the favorable notice of those who have not yet availed themselves of an opportunity to procure the *best Mechanical Drawing Book,* which has yet been published."

From the American Rail Road Journal.

"MINIFIE'S TEXT BOOK OF MECHANICAL DRAWING.—We are happy to call the attention of our readers to this work. It is recommended by artists and gentlemen who are best qualified among us to judge correctly of its merits, as being the *most thorough and complete work of the kind ever published in this country*, and as indispensable to those whose business requires a knowledge of the principles of Geometrical Drawing or Sketching, and as a suitable guide and companion to amateurs in this delightful art. It has received universal commendation from the press, and we believe it fully merits all that has been said in its praise."

From the Eureka, New York.

"The author is well known as a teacher of Architectural and Mechanical Drawing in Baltimore, and has in this produced a work treating of the principles of Geometry applicable in drawing, the use of instruments, &c. The book contains also an excellent introduction to the principles of Isometrical drawing, of linear perspective and shadows. All the subjects treated, are copiously illustrated by fine steel engravings, and so described that those seeking this kind of instruction, by their unassisted exertions, will find here a valuable treatise. It is got up in a style highly creditable to the publishers."

From the Philadelphia Public Ledger.

"This will be found a most excellent text book, by an accomplished teacher of Architectural and Mechanical Drawing. The problems are all selected with a view to their practical application in the every-day business of the Engineer, Architect and Artizan.

From the Pennsylvania Inquirer.

"One of the most comprehensive works of the kind ever published, and cannot but possess great value to Builders. The style is at once elegant and substantial."

From the Philadelphia North American.

"The volume before us forms the second edition of the original octavo, which we spoke of in high terms at its first appearance a year ago. We feel very safe in renewing our praise. The work is a valuable one, full and scientific, yet *adapted peculiarly to the purposes* of *practical men.*"

From McMakin's Model Journal, April 7.

"It is, indeed, in all respects, a very excellent and a very timely book."

From the Richmond Daily Whig.

"We regard it as a book evincing great thoroughness in the subject on which it treats; one which must supply a deficiency which has long been felt, and one which must prove an invaluable assistant, either to the theoretical teacher or the practical artizan. It is a book also for self-instruction. The drawings are very numerous, and the plates admirably executed."

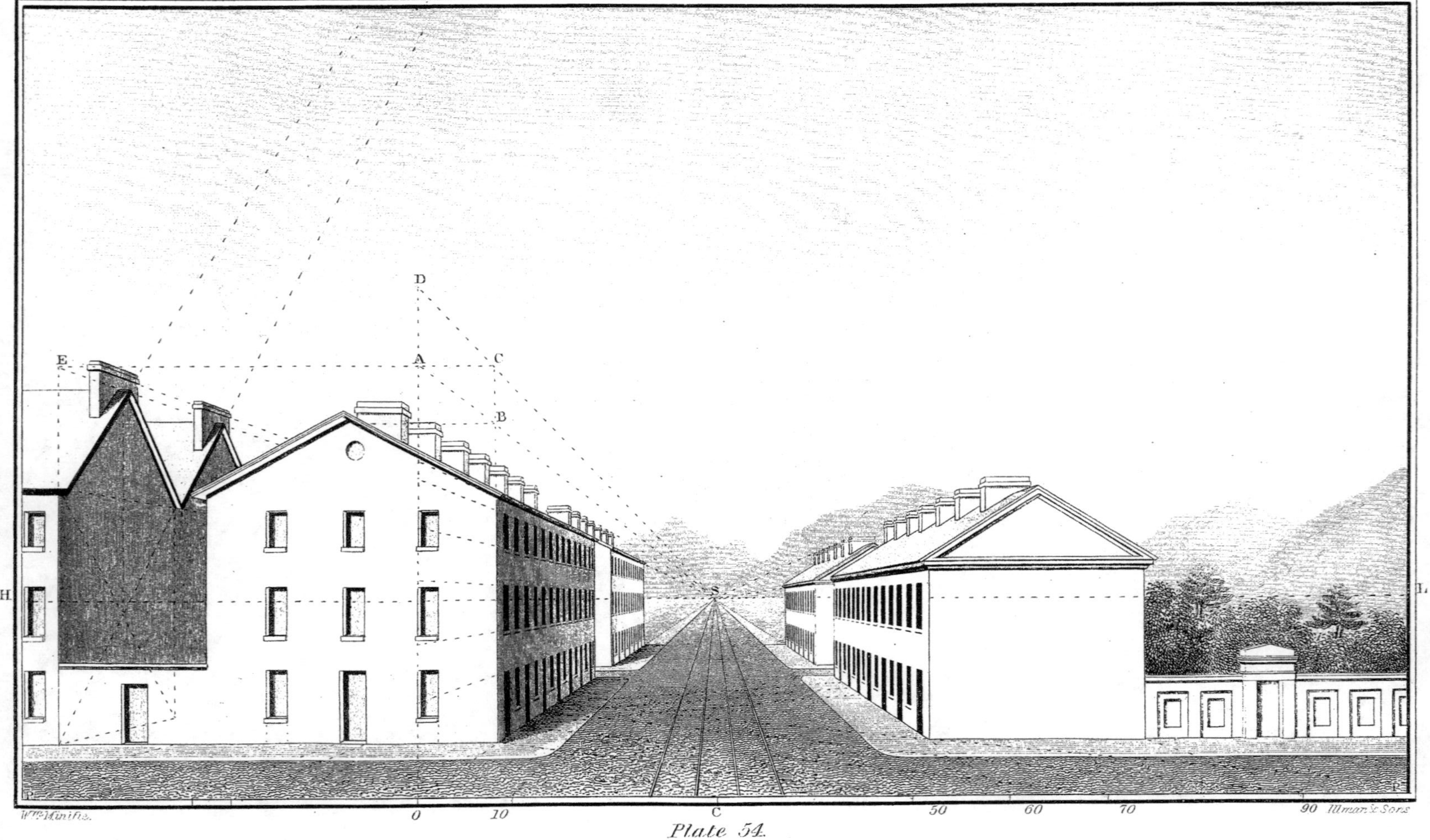

Plate 54.
PERSPECTIVE.

A

TEXT BOOK

OF

GEOMETRICAL DRAWING,

FOR THE USE OF

Mechanics and Schools,

IN WHICH

THE DEFINITIONS AND RULES OF GEOMETRY ARE FAMILIARLY EXPLAINED, THE PRACTICAL PROBLEMS ARE ARRANGED FROM THE MOST SIMPLE TO THE MORE COMPLEX, AND IN THEIR DESCRIPTION TECHNICALITIES ARE AVOIDED AS MUCH AS POSSIBLE;

WITH ILLUSTRATIONS FOR DRAWING PLANS, SECTIONS AND ELEVATIONS OF

BUILDINGS AND MACHINERY:

AN

INTRODUCTION TO ISOMETRICAL DRAWING,

AND AN

ESSAY ON LINEAR PERSPECTIVE AND SHADOWS:

THE WHOLE ILLUSTRATED WITH

FIFTY-SIX STEEL PLATES,

Containing over Two Hundred Diagrams.

BY

WM. MINIFIE, Architect,

AND

TEACHER OF DRAWING IN THE CENTRAL HIGH SCHOOL OF BALTIMORE.

THIRD EDITION.

PUBLISHED BY WM. MINIFIE & CO.

NO. 114 BALTIMORE STREET,

BALTIMORE.

1851.

STEREOTYPED AT THE

BALTIMORE TYPE AND STEREOTYPE FOUNDRY.

FIELDING LUCAS, JR., PROPRIETOR.

JOHN D. TOY, PRINTER.

PREFACE.

Having been for several years engaged in teaching Architectural and Mechanical drawing, both in the High School of Baltimore and to private classes, I have endeavored without success, to procure a book that I could introduce as a text book; works on Geometry generally contain too much theory for the purpose, with an insufficient amount of practical problems; and books on Architecture and Machinery are mostly too voluminous and costly, containing much that is entirely unnecessary for the purpose. Under these circumstances, I collected most of the useful practical problems in geometry from a variety of sources, simplified them and drew them on cards for the use of the classes, arranging them from the most easy to the more difficult, thus leading the students gradually forward; this was followed by the drawing of plans, sections, elevations and details of Buildings and Machinery, then followed Isometrical drawing, and the course was closed by the study of Linear perspective and shadows; the whole being illustrated by a series of short lectures to the private classes.

I have been so well pleased with the results of this method of instruction, that I have endeavored to adopt its general features in the arrangement of the following work. The problems in constructive geometry have been selected with a view to their practical application in the every-day business of the Engineer, Architect and Artizan, while at the same time they afford a good series of lessons to facilitate the knowledge and use of the instruments required in mechanical drawing.

The definitions and explanations have been given in as plain and simple language as the subject will admit of; many persons will no doubt think them too simple. Had the book been intended for the use of persons versed in geometry, very many of the explanations might have been dispensed with, but it is intended chiefly to be used as a *first book in geometrical drawing*, by persons who have not had the benefit of a mathematical education, and who in a majority of cases, have not the time or inclination to study any complex matter, or what is the same thing, that which may appear so to them. And if used in schools, its detailed explanations, we believe, will save time to the teacher, by permitting the scholar to obtain for himself much information that he would otherwise require to have explained to him.

But it is also intended to be used for *self-instruction*, without the aid of a teacher, to whom the student might refer for explanation of any difficulty; under these circumstances I do not believe an explanation can be couched in too simple language. With a view of adapting the book to this class of students, the illustrations of each branch treated of, have been made progressive, commencing with the plainest diagrams; and even in the more advanced, the object has been to instil principles rather than to produce effect, as those once obtained, the student can either design for himself or copy from any subject at hand. It is hoped that this arrangement will induce many to study drawing who would not otherwise have attempted it, and thereby render themselves much more capable of conducting any business, for it has been truly said by an eminent writer on Architecture, "that one workman is superior to another (other circumstances being the same) directly in proportion to his knowledge of drawing, and those who are ignorant of it must in many respects be subservient to others who have obtained that knowledge."

The size of the work has imperceptibly increased far beyond my original design, which was to get it up in a cheap form with illustrations on wood, and to contain about two-thirds of the number in the present volume, but on examining some specimens of mathematical diagrams executed on wood, I was dissatisfied with their want of neatness, particularly as but few students aim to excel their copy. On determining to use steel illustrations I deemed it advisable to extend its scope until it has attained its present bulk, and even now I feel more disposed to increase than to curtail it, as it contains but few examples either in Architecture or Machinery. I trust, however, that the objector to its size will find it to contain but little that is absolutely useless to a student.

In conclusion, I must warn my readers against an idea that I am sorry to find too prevalent, viz: that drawing requires but little time or study for its attainment, that it may be imbibed involuntarily as one would fragrance in a flower garden, with little or no exertion on the part of the recipient, not that the idea is expressed in so many words, but it is frequently manifested by their dissatisfaction at not being able to make a drawing in a few lessons as well as their teacher, even before they have had sufficient practice to have obtained a free use of the instruments. I have known many give up the study in consequence, who at the same time if they should be apprenticed to a carpenter, would be satisfied if they could use the jack plane with facility after several weeks practice, or be able to make a sash at the end of some years.

Now this idea is fallacious, and calculated to do much injury; proficiency in no art can be obtained without attentive study and industrious perseverance. Drawing is certainly not an exception; but the difficulties will soon vanish if you commence with a determination to succeed; let your motto be PERSEVERE, never say "it is too difficult;" you will not find it so difficult as you imagine if you will only give it proper attention; and if my labors have helped to smooth those difficulties it will be to me a source of much gratification.

WM. MINIFIE.

BALTIMORE, 1st March, 1849.

ILLUSTRATIONS.

PRACTICAL GEOMETRY.

PLATE I.

DEFINITIONS OF LINES AND ANGLES.

1. A Point is said to have position without magnitude; and it is therefore generally represented to the eye by a small dot, as at *A*.
2. A Line is considered as length without breadth or thickness, it is in fact a succession of points; its extremities therefore, are points. Lines are of three kinds; *right lines, curved lines,* and *mixed lines.*
3. A Right Line, or as it is more commonly called, *a straight line,* is the shortest that can be drawn between two given points as *B*.
4. A Curve or Curved Line is that which does not lie evenly between its terminating points, and of which no portion, however small, is straight; it is therefore longer than a straight line connecting the same points. Curved lines are either regular or irregular.
5. A Regular Curved Line, as *C*, is a portion of the circumference of a circle, the degree of curvature being the same throughout its entire length. An *irregular curved line* has not the same degree of curvature throughout, but varies at different points.
6. A Waved Line may be either regular or irregular; it is composed of curves bent in contrary directions. *E* is a regular waved line, the inflections on either side of the dotted line being equal; a waved line is also called a line of *double curvature* of *contrary flexure,* and a *serpentine* line.
7. Mixed Lines are composed of straight and curved lines, as *D*.
8. Parallel Lines are those which have no inclination to each other, as *F*, being every where equidistant; consequently they could never meet, though produced to infinity.

If the *parallel lines* *G* were produced, they would form two concentric circles, viz: circles which have a common centre, whose boundaries are every where parallel and equidistant.

9. INCLINED LINES, as *H* and *I*, if produced, would meet in a point as at *K*, forming an angle of which the point *K* is called the vertex or angular point, and the lines *H* and *I* the legs or sides of the angle *K;* the point of meeting is also called the summit of an angle.

10. PERPENDICULAR LINES.—Lines are perpendicular to each other when the angles on either side of the point of junction are equal; thus the lines *N. O. P* are perpendicular to the line *L M.* The lines *N. O. P* are called also *vertical lines* and *plumb lines,* because they are parallel with any line to which a plummet is suspended; the line *L. M* is a *horizontal* or *level line;* lines so called are always perpendicular to a plumb line.

11. VERTICAL and HORIZONTAL LINES are always perpendicular to each other, but perpendicular lines are not always vertical and horizontal; they may be at any inclination to the horizon provided that the angles on either side of the point of intersection are equal, as for example the lines *X. Y* and *Z.*

12. ANGLES.—Two right lines drawn from the same point, diverging from each other, form an angle, as the lines *S. Q. R.* An angle is commonly designated by three letters, and the letter designating the point of divergence, which in this case is *Q,* is always placed in the middle. Angles are either *acute, right* or *obtuse.* If the legs of an angle are perpendicular to each other, they form a right angle as *T. Q. R,* (mechanics' squares, if true, are always right angled;) if the sides are nearer together, as *S. Q. R,* they form an acute angle; if the sides are wider apart, or diverge from each other more than a right angle, they form an obtuse angle, as *V. Q. R.*

The magnitude of an angle does not depend on the length of the sides, but upon their divergence from each other; an angle is said to be greater or less than another as the divergence is greater or less; thus the obtuse angle *V. Q. R* is greater, and the acute angle *S. Q. R* is less than the right angle *T. Q. R.*

Plate I.
DEFINITIONS OF LINES AND ANGLES.
A
B
C
D
E
F
G
H
I
K
L
M
N
O
P
Q
R
S
T
V
X
Y
Z

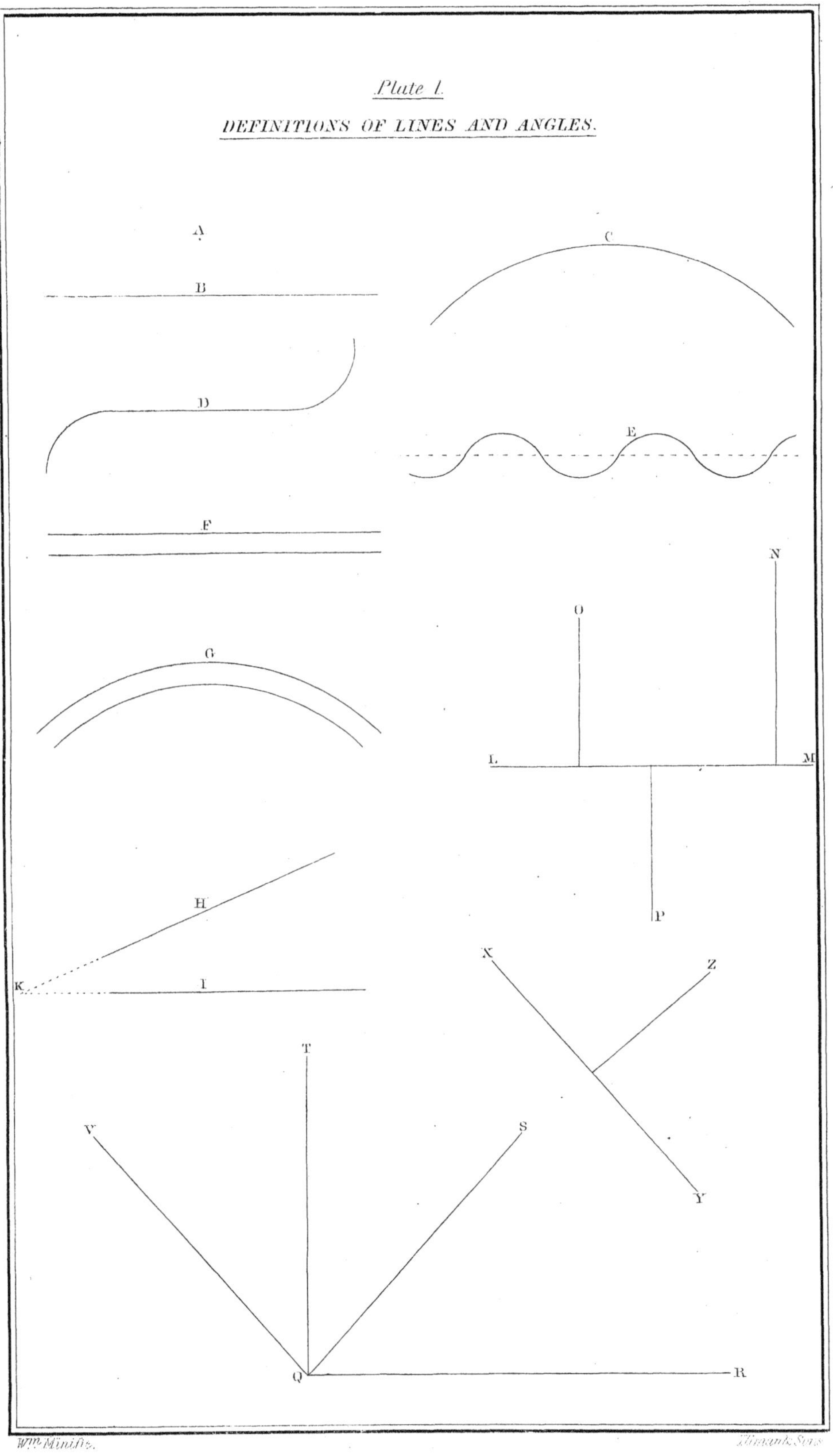

Wm Minifie.

Plate 2.

DEFINITIONS. PLANE RECTILINEAR SUPERFICIES.

TRIANGLES OR TRIGONS.

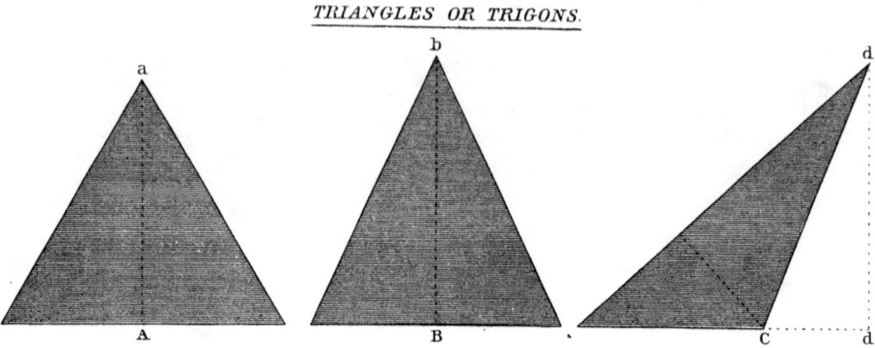

QUADRILATERALS, QUADRANGLES OR TETRAGONS.

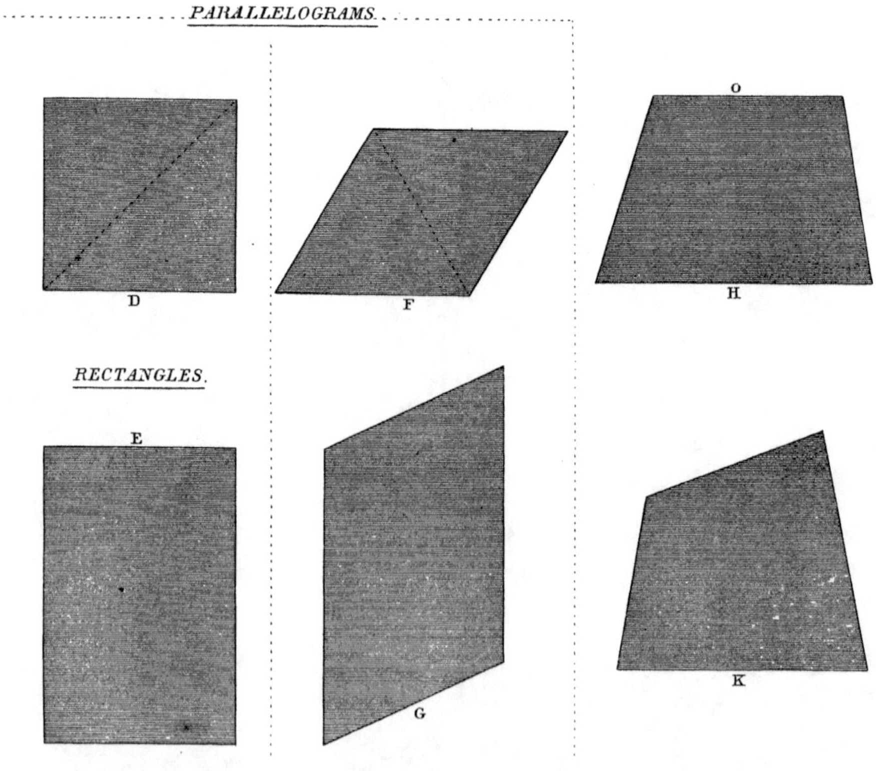

PARALLELOGRAMS.

O

D

F

H

RECTANGLES.

E

G

K

Wm. Minifie.

Illman & Sons

PLATE II.

PLANE RECTILINEAR SUPERFICIES.

13. A SUPERFICIES or SURFACE is considered as an extension of length and breadth without thickness.

14. A PLANE SUPERFICIES is an enclosed flat surface that will coincide in every place with a straight line. It is a succession of straight lines, or to be more explicit, if a perfectly straight edged ruler be placed on a plane superficies in any direction, it would touch it in every part of its entire length.

15. When surfaces are bounded by right lines, they are said to be RECTILINEAR or RECTILINEAL. As all the figures on plate second agree with the above definitions, they are PLANE RECTILINEAR SUPERFICIES.

16. Figures bounded by more than four right lines are called POLYGONS; the boundary of a polygon is called its PERIMETER.

17. When SURFACES are bounded by three right lines, they are called TRIANGLES or TRIGONS.

18. AN EQUILATERAL TRIANGLE has all its sides of equal length, and all its angles equal, as *A*.

19. AN ISOSCELES TRIANGLE has two of its sides and two of its angles equal, as *B*.

20. A SCALENE TRIANGLE has all its sides and angles unequal, as *C*.

21. AN ACUTE ANGLED TRIANGLE has all its angles acute, as *A* and *B*.

22. A RIGHT ANGLED TRIANGLE has one right angle; the side opposite the right angle is called the *hypothenuse;* the other sides are called respectively the base and perpendicular. The figures *A*. *B*. *C*, are each divided into two right angled triangles by the dotted lines running across them.

23. AN OBTUSE ANGLED TRIANGLE has one obtuse angle, as *C*.

24. If figures *A* and *B* were cut out and folded on the dotted line in the centre of each, the opposite sides would exactly coincide; they are therefore, *regular triangles.*

25. Any of the sides of an equilateral or scalene triangle may be called its BASE, but in the Isosceles triangle the side which is

2

unequal is so called, the angle opposite the base is called the VERTEX.

26. THE ALTITUDE of a Triangle is the length of a perpendicular let fall from its vertex to its base, as *a. A.* and *b. B,* or to its base extended, as *d. d,* figure *C.*

The *superficial contents* of a Triangle may be obtained by multiplying the altitude by one half the base.

27. When surfaces are bounded by four right lines, they are called QUADRILATERALS, QUADRANGLES or TETRAGONS; either of the figures *D. E. F. G. H* and *K* may be called by either of those terms, which are common to all four-sided right lined figures, although each has its own proper name.

28. When a Quadrilateral has its opposite sides parallel to each other, it is called a PARALLELOGRAM; therefore figures *D. E. F* and *G* are parallelograms.

29. When all the angles of a Tetragon are right angles, the figure is called a RECTANGLE, as figures *D* and *E.*

If two opposite angles of a Tetragon are right angles, the others are necessarily right too.

30. If the sides of a Rectangle are all of equal length, the figure is called a SQUARE, as figure *D.*

31. If the sides of a Rectangle are not all of equal length, two of its sides being longer than the others, as figure *E,* it is called an OBLONG.

32. When the sides of a parallelogram are all equal, and the angles not right angles, two being acute and the others obtuse, as figure *F,* it is called a RHOMB, or RHOMBUS; it is also called a DIAMOND, and sometimes a LOZENGE, more particularly so when the figure is used in heraldry.

33. A parallelogram whose angles are not right angles, but whose opposite sides are equal, as figure *G,* is called a RHOMBOID.

34. If two of the sides of a Quadrilateral are parallel to each other as the sides *H* and *O* in fig. *H,* it is called a TRAPEZOID.

35. All other Quadrangles are called TRAPEZIUMS, the term being applied to all Tetragons that have no two sides parallel, as *K.*

NOTE. The terms TRAPEZOID and TRAPEZIUM are applied indiscriminately by some writers to either of the figures *H* and *K;* by others, fig. *H* is called a *Trapezium* and fig. *K* a *Trapezoid,* and this appears to be the more correct method; but as Trapezoid is a word of comparatively modern origin, I have used it as it is most generally applied by modern writers, more particularly so in works on Architecture and Mechanics.

36. A Diagonal is a line running across a Quadrangle, connecting its opposite corners, as the dotted lines in figs. *D* and *F*.

Note.—I have often seen persons who have not studied Geometry, much confused, in consequence of the number of names given to the same figure, as for example fig. *D*.

1st. It is a *plane Figure*—see paragraph 14.
2nd. It is *Rectilineal*, being composed of right lines.
3rd. It is a *Quadrilateral*, being bounded by four lines.
4th. It is a *Quadrangle*, having four angles.
5th. It is a *Tetragon*, having four sides.
6th. It is a *Parallelogram*, its opposite sides being parallel.
7th. It is a *Rectangle*, all its angles being right angles.

All the above may be called *common names*, because they are applied to all figures having the same properties.

8th. It is a *Square*, which is its *proper name*, distinguishing it from all other figures, to which some or all of the above terms may be applied.

All of them except 7 and 8, may also be applied to fig. *F*, with the same propriety as to fig. *D*; besides these, fig. *F* has four proper names distinguishing it from all other figures, viz: a *Rhomb*, *Rhombus*, *Diamond* and *Lozenge*.

If the student will analyze all the other figures in the same manner, he will soon become perfectly familiar with them, and each term will convey to his mind a clear definite idea.

PLATE III.

DEFINITIONS OF THE CIRCLE.

1st. A Circle is a plane figure bounded by one curve line, every where equidistant from its centre, as fig. 1.

2nd. The *boundary line* is called the Circumference or Periphery, it is also for convenience called a *Circle*.

3rd. The Centre of a circle is a point within the circumference, equally distant from every point in it, as *C*, fig. 1.

4th. The Radius of a circle is a line drawn from the centre to any point in the circumference, as *C. A*, *C. B* or *C. D*, fig. 1.

The plural of Radius is Radii. All radii of the same circle are of equal length.

5th. The Diameter of a circle is any right line drawn through the centre to opposite points of the circumference, as *A. B*, fig. 1.

The length of the diameter is equal to two radii; there may be an infinite number of diameters in the same circle, but they are all equal.

6th. A SEMICIRCLE is the half of a circle, as fig. 2; it is bounded by half the circumference and by a diameter.

7th. A SEGMENT of a circle is any part of the surface cut off by a right line, as in fig. 3. Segments may be therefore greater or less than a semicircle.

8th. An ARC of a circle is any portion of the circumference cut off, as *C. G. D* or *E. G. F*, fig. 3.

9th. A CHORD is a right line joining the extremities of an arc, as *C. D* and *E. F*, fig. 3. The diameter is the chord of a semicircle. The chord is also called the SUBTENSE.

10th. A SECTOR of a circle is a space contained between two radii and the arc which they intercept, as *E. C. D*, or *O. C. H*, fig. 4.

11th. A QUADRANT is a sector whose area is equal to one-fourth of the circle, as fig. 5; the arc *D. E* being equal to one-fourth of the whole circumference, and the radii at right angles to each other.

12. A DEGREE.—The circumference of a circle is considered as divided into 360 equal parts called DEGREES, (marked °) each degree is divided into 60 minutes (marked ′) and each minute into 60 seconds (marked ″); thus if the circle be large or small, the number of divisions is always the same, a degree being equal to 1-360th part of the whole circumference, the semicircle equal to 180°, and the quadrant equal to 90°. The radii drawn from the centre of a circle to the extremities of a quadrant are always at right angles to each other; a right angle is therefore called an angle of 90°. If we bisect a right angle by a right line, it would divide the arc of the quadrant also into two equal parts, each part equal to one-eighth of the whole circumference containing 45°; if the right angle were divided into three equal parts by straight lines, it would divide the arc into three equal parts, each containing 30° Thus the degrees of the circle are used to measure angles, and when we speak of an angle of any number of degrees, it is understood, *that if a circle with any length of radius, be struck with one foot of the dividers in the angular point, the sides of the angle will intercept a portion of the circle equal to the number of degrees given.*

NOTE.—This division of the circle is purely arbitrary, but it has existed

Plate 3.

DEFINITIONS OF THE CIRCLE.

1. CIRCLE.

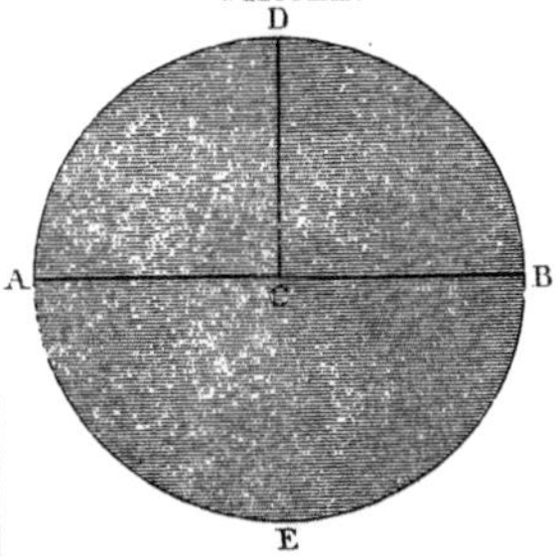

2. SEMICIRCLE.

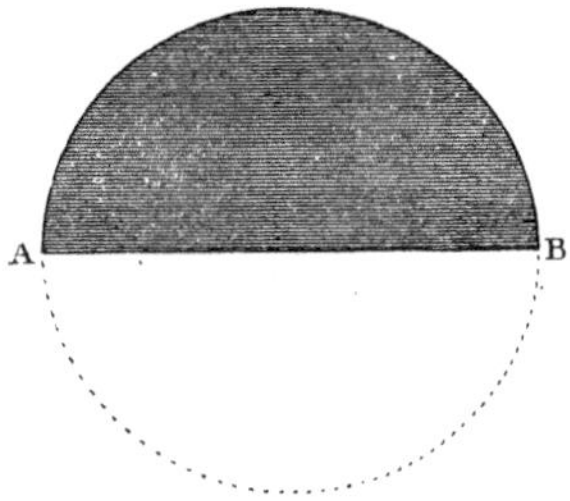

3. SEGMENTS.

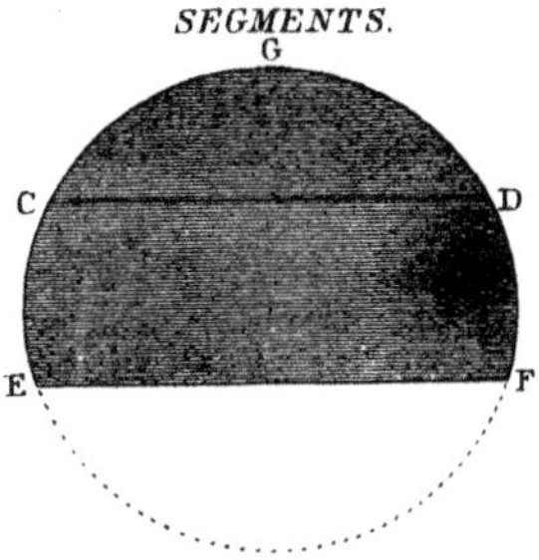

4. SECTORS.

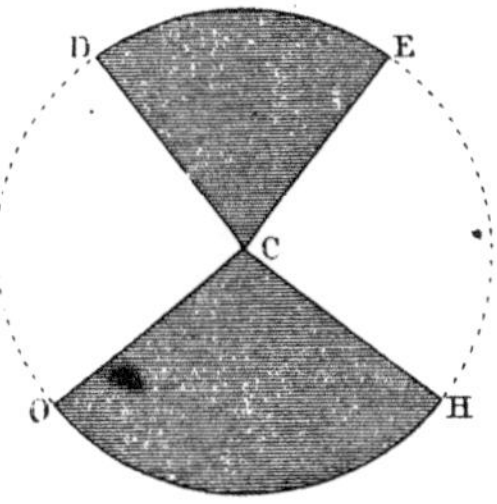

5. QUADRANT.

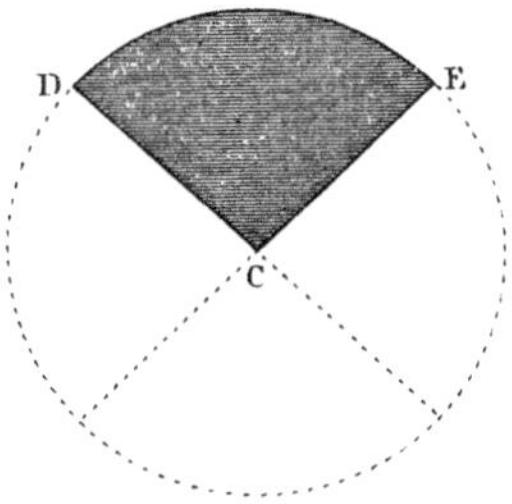

6. COMPLEMENT.

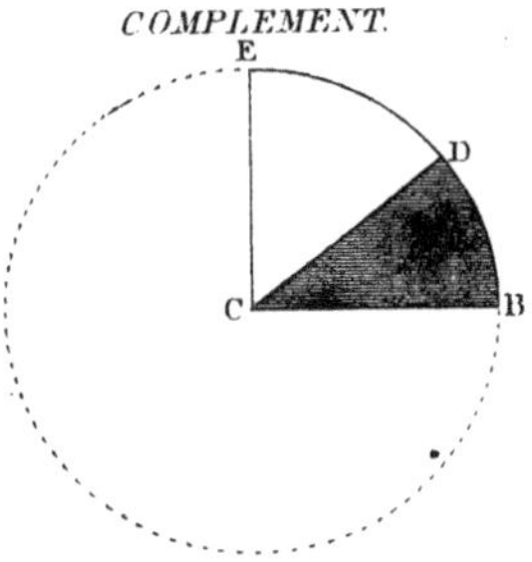

7. SUPPLEMENT.

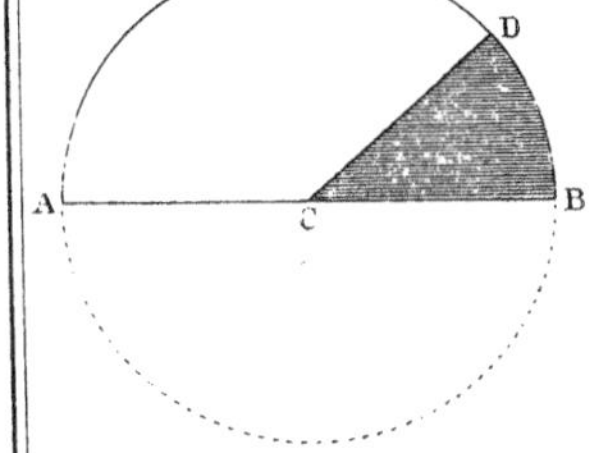

8. TANGENT &c.

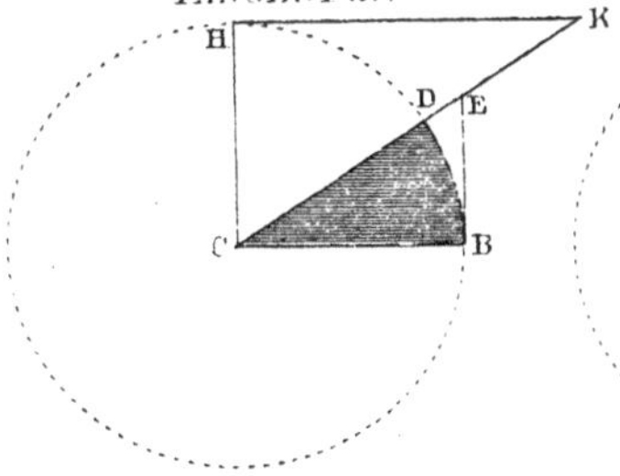

9. SINE.

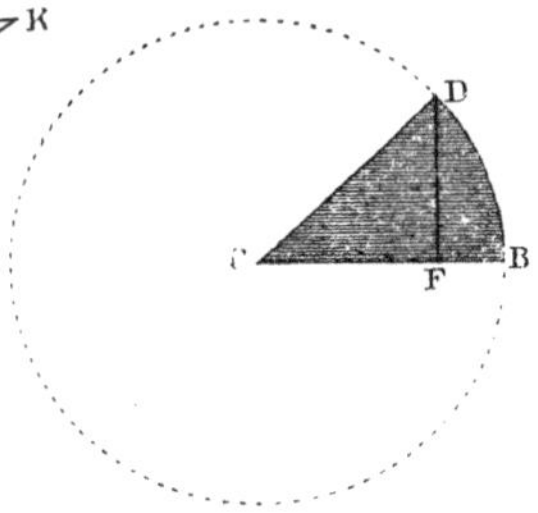

10. CO-SINE.

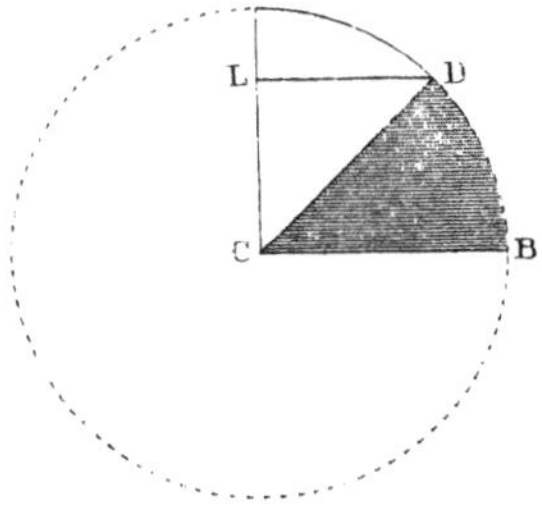

11.

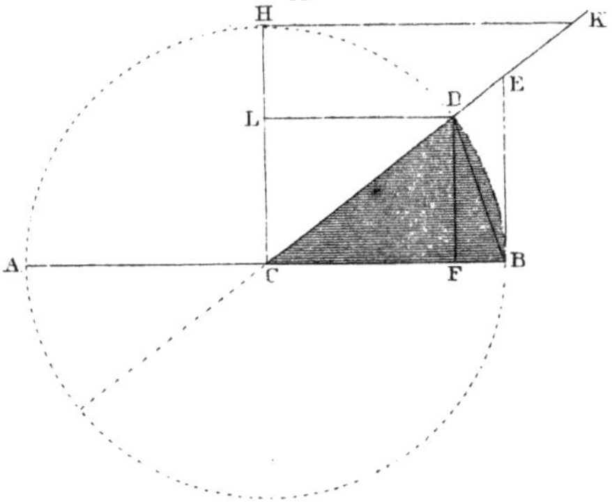

from the most ancient times and every where. During the revolutionary period of 1789 in France, it was proposed to adopt a decimal division, by which the circumference was reckoned at 400 *grades;* but this method was never extensively adopted and is now virtually abandoned.

13. The COMPLEMENT of an *Arc* or of an *Angle* is the difference between that arc or angle and a quadrant; thus *E. D* fig. 6 is the complement of the arc *D. B*, and *E. C. D* the complement of the angle *D. C. B.*

14. The SUPPLEMENT of an *Arc* or of an *Angle* is the difference between that arc or angle and a semicircle; thus *D. A* fig. 7, is the supplement of the arc *D. B*, and *D. C. A* the supplement of the angle *B. C. D.*

15. A TANGENT is a right line, drawn without a circle touching it only at one point as *B. E* fig. 8; the point where it touches the circle is called the point of contact, or the tangent point.

16. A SECANT is a right line drawn from the centre of a circle cutting its circumference and prolonged to meet a tangent as *C. E* fig. 8.

NOTE.—SECANT POINT is the same as *point of intersection*, being the point where two lines cross or cut each other.

17. The CO-TANGENT of an arc is the tangent of the complement of that arc, as *H. K* fig. 8.

NOTE.—The shaded parts in these diagrams are the given angles, but if in fig. 8, *D. C. H* be the given angle and *D. H* the given arc, then *H. K.* would be the tangent and *B. E* the co-tangent.

18. The SINE of an arc is a line drawn from one extremity, perpendicular to a radius drawn to the other extremity of the arc as *D. F* fig. 9.

19. The CO-SINE of an arc is the sine of the complement of that arc as *L. D* fig. 10.

20. The VERSED SINE of an arc is that part of the radius intercepted between the sine and the circumference as *F. B* fig. 9.

21. In figure 11, we have the whole of the foregoing definitions illustrated in one diagram. *C. H—C. D—C. B* and *C. A* are *Radii; A. B* the *Diameter; B. C. D* a *Sector; B. C. H* a *Quadrant.* Let *B. C. D* be the given *Angle*, and *B. D* the given *Arc*, then *B. D* is the *Chord*, *D. H* the *Complement*, and *D. A* the *Supplement* of the arc; *D. C. H* the *Complement* and *D. C. A* the *Supplement* of the given angle; *B. E* the *Tangent* and *H. K* the *Co-tangent*, *C. E* the *Secant* and *C. K* the *Co-secant*, *F. D* the *Sine*, *L. D* the *Co-sine* and *F. B* the *Versed Sine.*

PLATE IV.

TO ERECT OR LET FALL A PERPENDICULAR.

PROBLEM 1. FIGURE 1.

To bisect the right line A. B *by a perpendicular.*

1st. With any radius greater than one half of the given line, and with one point of the dividers in *A* and *B* successively, draw two arcs intersecting each other, in *C* and *D*.
2nd. Through the points of intersection draw *C. D,* which is the perpendicular required.

PROBLEM 2. FIG. 2.

From the point D *in the line* E. F *to erect a perpendicular.*

1st. With one foot of the dividers placed in the given point *D* with any radius less than one half of the line, describe an arc, cutting the given line in *B* and *C.*
2nd. From the points *B* and *C* with any radius greater than *B. D,* describe two arcs, cutting each other in *G.*
3rd. From the point of intersection draw *G. D,* which is the perpendicular required.

PROBLEM 3. FIG. 3.

To erect a perpendicular when the point D *is at or near the end of a line.*

1st. With one foot of the dividers in the given point *D* with any radius, as *D. E,* draw an indefinite arc *G. H.*
2nd. With the same radius and the dividers in any point of the arc, as *E,* draw the arc *B. D. F,* cutting the line *C. D* in *B.*
3rd. From the point *B* through *E* draw a right line, cutting the arc in *F.*

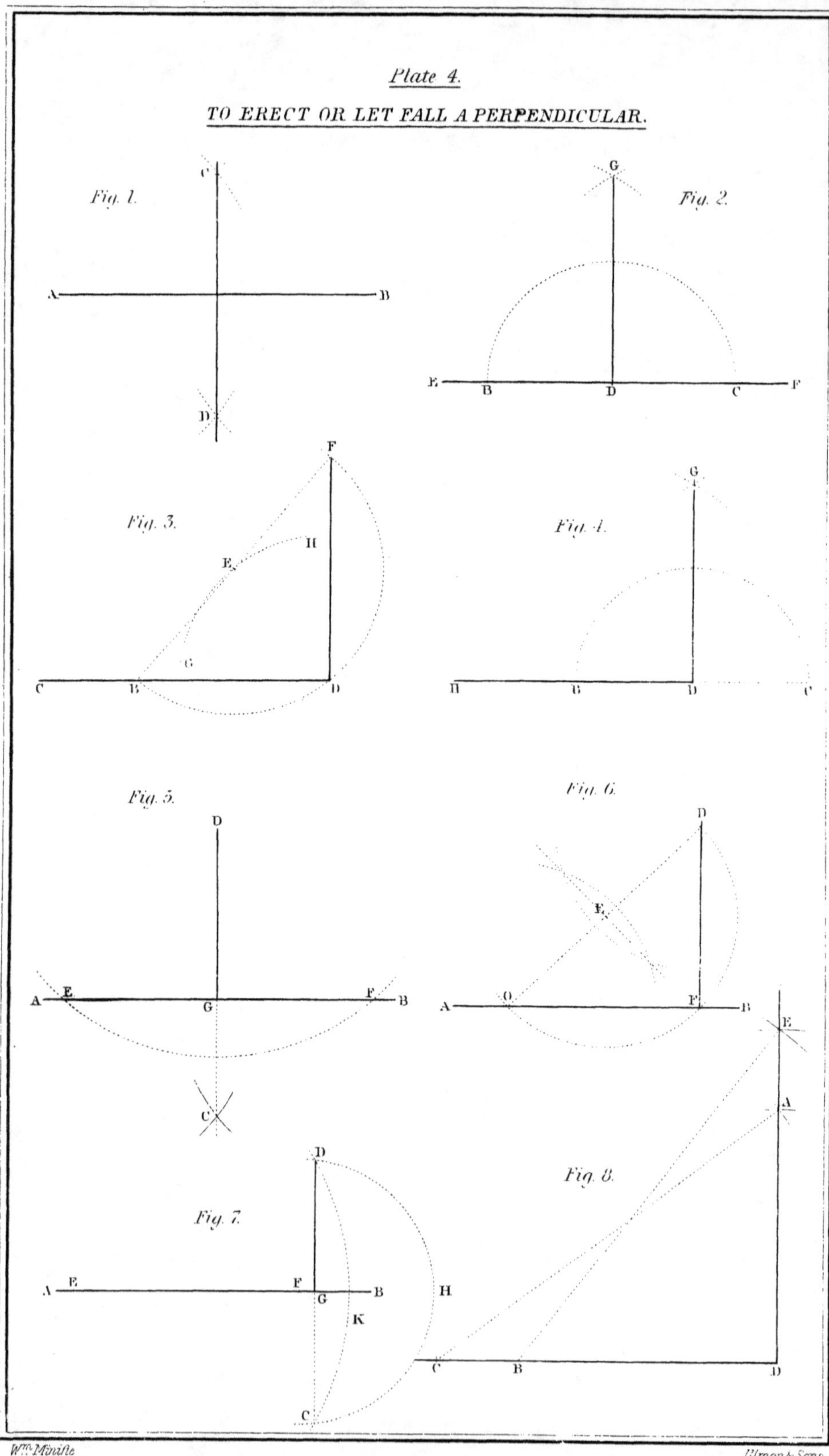

Wm. Minifie

Illman & Sons

4th. From *F* draw *F. D*, which is the perpendicular required.

NOTE.—It will be perceived that the arc *B. D. F* is a semicircle, and the right line *B. F* a diameter; if from the extremities of a semicircle right lines be drawn to any point in the curve, the angle formed by them will be a right angle. This affords a ready method for forming a "*square corner*," and will be found useful on many occasions, as its accuracy may be depended on.

PROBLEM 4. FIG. 4.

Another method of erecting a perpendicular when at or near the end of the line.

Continue the line *H. D* toward *C*, and proceed as in problem 2; the letters of reference are the same.

PROBLEM 5. FIG. 5.

From the point D *to let fall a perpendicular to the line* A. B.

1st. With any radius greater than *D. G* and one foot of the compasses in *D*, describe an arc cutting *A. B* in *E* and *F*.
2nd. From *E* and *F* with any radius greater than *E. G*, describe two arcs cutting each other as in *C*.
3rd. From *D* draw the right line *D. C*, then *D. G* is the perpendicular required.

PROBLEM 6. FIG. 6.

When the point D *is nearly opposite the end of the line.*

1st. From the given point *D*, draw a right line to any point of the line *A. B* as *O*.
2nd. Bisect *O. D* by problem 1, in *E*.
3rd. With one foot of the compasses in *E* with a radius equal to *E. D* or *E. O* describe an arc cutting *A. B* in *F*.
4th. Draw *D. F* which is the perpendicular required.

NOTE.—The reader will perceive that we have arrived at the same result as we did by problem 3, but by a different process, the right angle being formed within a semicircle.

PROBLEM 7. FIG. 7.

Another method of letting fall a perpendicular when the given point D *is nearly opposite the end of the line.*

1st. With any radius as *F. D* and one foot of the compasses in the line *A. B* as at *F*, draw an arc *D. H. C.*

2nd. With any other radius as *E. D* draw another arc *D. K. C*, cutting the first arc in *C* and *D*.

3rd. From *D* draw *D. C*, then *D. G* is the perpendicular required.

NOTE.—The points *E* and *F* from which the arcs are drawn, should be as far apart as the line *A. B* will admit of, as the exact points of intersection can be more easily found, for it is evident, that the nearer two lines cross each other at a right angle, the finer will be the point of contact.

PROBLEM 8. FIG. 8.

To erect a perpendicular at D *the end of the line* C. D. *with a scale of equal parts.*

1st. From any scale of equal parts take three in your dividers, and with one foot in *D*, cut the line *C. D* in *B*.

2nd. From the same scale take four parts in your dividers, and with one foot in *D* draw an indefinite arc toward *E*.

3rd. With a radius equal to five of the same parts, and one foot of the dividers in *B*, cut the other arc in *E*.

4th. From *E* draw *E. D*, which is the perpendicular required.

NOTE 1st. If four parts were first taken in the dividers and laid off on the line *C. D*, then three parts should be used for striking the indefinite arc, at *A*, and the five parts struck from the point *C*, which would give the intersection *A*, and arrive at the same result.

2nd. On referring to the definitions of angles, it will be found that the side of a right angled triangle opposite the right angle is called the Hypothenuse; thus the line *E. B* is the hypothenuse of the triangle *E. D. B.*

3rd. The square of the hypothenuse of a right angled triangle is equal to the sum of the squares of both the other sides.

4th. The square of a number is the product of that number multiplied by itself.

Example. The length of the side *D. E* is 4, which multiplied by 4, will give for its square 16. The length of *D. B* is 3, which multiplied by 3, gives for the square 9. The products of the two sides added together give 25. The length of the hypothenuse is 5, which multiplied by 5, gives also 25.

5th. The results will always be the same, but if fractional parts are used in the measures, the proof is not so obvious, as the multiplication would be more complicated.

6th. 3, 4 and 5 are the least whole numbers that can be used in laying down this diagram, but any multiple of these numbers may be used; thus, if we multiply them by 2, it would give 6, 8 and 10; if by 3, it would give 9, 12 and 15; if by 4—12, 16 and 20, and so on. The greater the distances employed, other things being equal, the greater will be the probable accuracy of the result.

7th. We have used a scale of equal parts without designating the unit of measurement, which may be an inch, foot, yard, or any other measure.

8th. As this problem is frequently used by practical men in laying off work, we will give an illustration.

Example. Suppose the line *C. D* to be the front of a house, and it is desired to lay off the side at right angles to it from the corner *D.*

1st. Drive in a small stake at *D*, put the ring of a tape measure on it and lay off twelve feet toward *B.*

2nd. With a distance of sixteen feet, the ring remaining at *D*, trace a short circle on the ground at *E.*

3rd. Remove the ring to *B*, and with a distance of twenty feet cut the first circle at *E.*

4th. Stretch a line from *D* to *E*, which will give the required side of the building.

PLATE V.

CONSTRUCTION AND DIVISION OF ANGLES.

PROBLEM 9. FIG. 1.

The length of the sides of a Triangle A. B., C. D. *and* E. F *being given, to construct the Triangle, the two longest sides to be joined together at* A.

1st. With the length of the line *C. D* for a radius and one foot in *A*, draw an arc at *G.*

2nd. With the length of the line *E. F* for a radius and one foot in *B*, draw an arc cutting the other arc at *G.*

3rd. From the point of intersection draw *G. A* and *G. B*, which complete the figure.

Problem 10. Fig. 2.

To construct an Angle at K *equal to the Angle* H.

1st. From *H* with any radius, draw an arc cutting the sides of the angle as at *M. N.*
2nd. From *K* with the same radius, describe an indefinite arc at *O*.
3rd. Draw *K. O* parallel to *H. M.*
4th. Take the distance from *M* to *N* and apply it from *O* to *P*.
5th. Through *P* draw *K. P*, which completes the figure.

Problem 11. Fig. 3.

To Bisect the given Angle Q *by a Right Line.*

1st. With any radius and one foot of the dividers in *Q* draw an arc cutting the sides of the angle as in *R* and *S*.
2nd. With the same or any other radius, greater than one half *R. S*, from the points *S* and *R*, describe two arcs cutting each other, as at *T*.
3rd. Draw *T. Q*, which divides the angle equally.

Note.—This problem may be very usefully applied by workmen on many occasions. Suppose, for example, the corner *Q* be the corner of a room, and a washboard or cornice has to be fitted around it; first, apply the bevel to the angle and lay it down on a piece of board, bisect the angle as above, then set the bevel to the centre line, and you have the exact angle for cutting the mitre. This rule will apply equally to the internal or external angle. Most good practical workmen have several means for getting the cut of the mitre, and to them this demonstration will appear unnecessary, but I have seen many men make sad blunders, for want of knowing this simple rule.

Problem 12. Fig. 4.

To Trisect a Right Angle.

1st. From the angular point *V* with any radius, describe an arc cutting the sides of the angle, as in *X* and *W*.
2nd. With the same radius from the points *X* and *W*, cut the arc in *Y* and *Z*.
3rd. Draw *Y. V* and *Z. V*, which will divide the angle as required.

Plate 5.

CONSTRUCTION AND DIVISION OF ANGLES.

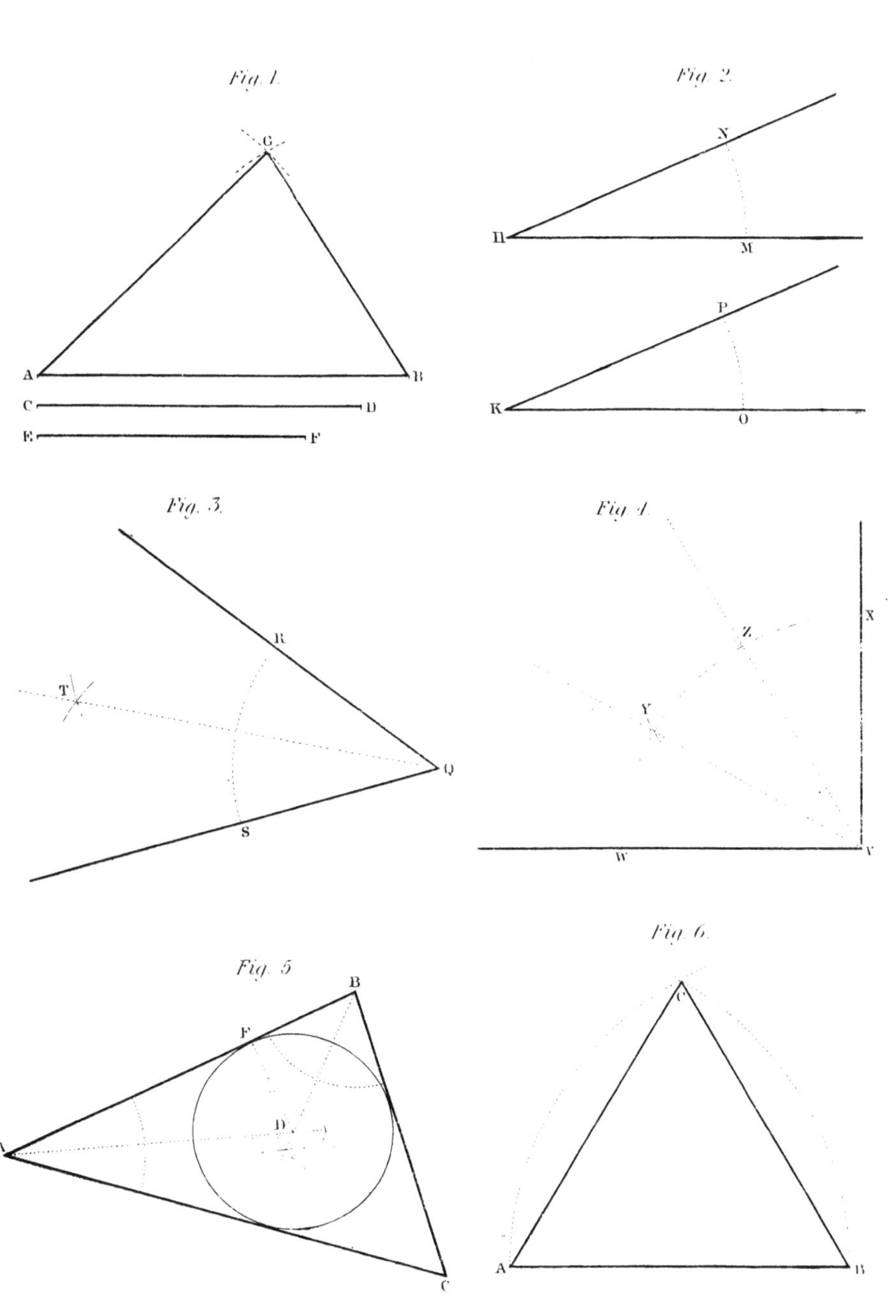

Wm. Minifie [illegible]

PROBLEM 13. FIG. 5.

In the triangle A. B. C, *to describe a Circle touching all its sides.*

1st. Bisect two of the angles by problem 11, as *A* and *B*, the dividing lines will cut each other in *D*, then *D* is the centre of the circle.

2nd. From *D* let fall a perpendicular to either of the sides as at *F*, then *D. F* is the radius, with which to describe the circle from the point *D*.

PROBLEM 14. FIG. 6.

On the given line A. B *to construct an Equilateral Triangle, the line* A. B *to be one of its sides.*

1st With a radius equal to the given line from the points *A* and *B*, draw two arcs intersecting each other in *C*.

2nd. From *C*, draw *C. A* and *C. B*, to complete the figure.

PLATE VI.

CONSTRUCTION OF POLYGONS.

A polygon of	3	sides	is called a	Trigon.
"	4	"	"	Tetragon.
"	5	"	"	Pentagon.
"	6	"	"	Hexagon.
"	7	"	"	Heptagon.
"	8	"	"	Octagon.
"	9	"	"	Enneagon or Nonagon.
"	10	"	"	Decagon.
"	11	"	"	Undecagon.
"	12	"	"	Dodecagon.

1st. When the sides of a polygon are all of equal length and all the angles are equal, it is called a regular polygon; if unequal, it is called an irregular polygon.

2nd. It is not necessary to say a regular Hexagon, regular Octagon, &c.; as when either of those figures is named, it is always supposed to be regular, unless otherwise stated.

PROBLEM 15. FIG. 1.

On a given line A. B *to construct a square whose side shall be equal to the given line.*

1st. With the length *A. B* for a radius from the points *A* and *B*, describe two arcs cutting each other in *C.*
2nd. Bisect the arc *C. A* or *C. B* in *D.*
3rd. From *C,* with a radius equal to *C. D,* cut the arc *B. E* in *E* and the arc *A. F* in *F.*
4th. Draw *A. E, E. F* and *F. B,* which complete the square.

PROBLEM 16. FIG. 2.

In the given square G. H. K. J, *to inscribe an Octagon.*

1st. Draw the diagonals *G. K* and *H. J,* intersecting each other in *P.*
2nd. With a radius equal to half the diagonal from the corners *G. H. K* and *J,* draw arcs cutting the sides of the square in *O. O. O,* &c.
3rd. Draw the right lines *O. O., O. O,* &c., and they will complete the octagon.

This mode is used by workmen when they desire to make a piece of wood round for a roller, or any other purpose; it is first made square, and the diagonals drawn across the end; the distance of one-half the diagonal is then set off, as from *G* to *R* in the diagram, and a guage set from *H* to *R* which run on all the corners, gives the lines for reducing the square to an octagon; the corners are again taken off, and finally finished with a tool appropriate to the purpose. The centre of each face of the octagon gives a line in the circumference of the circle, running the whole length of the piece; and as there are eight of those lines equidistant from each other, the further steps in the process are rendered very simple.

Plate 6.

CONSTRUCTION OF POLYGONS.

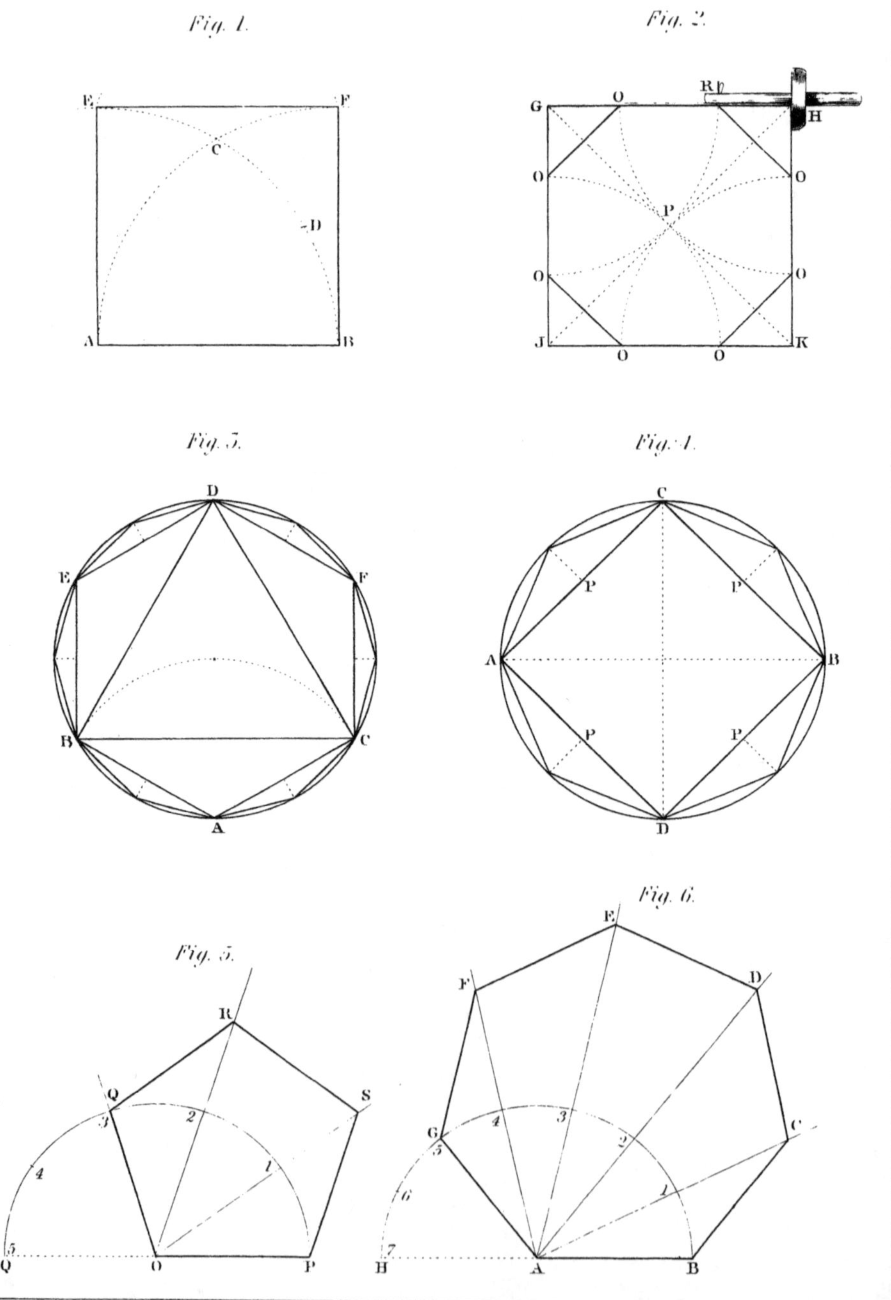

Wm. Minifie. Illman & Sons

PROBLEM 17. FIG. 3.

In a given circle to inscribe an Equilateral Triangle, a Hexagon and Dodecagon.

1st. For the TRIANGLE, with the radius of the given circle from any point in the circumference, as at *A*, describe an arc cutting the circle in *B* and *C*.

2nd. Draw the right line *B. C*, and with a radius equal *B. C*, from the points *B* and *C*, cut the circle in *D*.

3rd. Draw *D. B* and *D. C*, which complete the triangle.

4th. For the HEXAGON, take the radius of the given circle and carry it round on the circumference six times, it will give the points *A. B. E. D. F. C*, through them, draw the sides of the hexagon. The radius of a circle is always equal to the side of an hexagon inscribed therein.

5th. For the DODECAGON, bisect the arcs between the points found for the hexagon, which will give the points for inscribing the dodecagon.

PROBLEM 18. FIG. 4.

In a given Circle to inscribe a Square and an Octagon.

1st. Draw a diameter *A. B*, and bisect it with a perpendicular by problem 1, giving the points *C. D*.

2nd. From the points *A. C. B. D*, draw the right lines forming the sides of the square required.

3rd. For the OCTAGON, bisect the sides of the square and draw perpendiculars to the circle, or bisect the arcs between the points *A. C. B. D*, which will give the other angular points of the required octagon.

PROBLEM 19. FIG. 5.

On the given line O. P *to construct a Pentagon,* O. P *being the length of the side.*

1st. With the length of the line *O. P* from *O*, describe the semicircle *P. Q*, meeting the line *P. O*, extended in *Q*.

2nd. Divide the semicircle into five equal parts and from *O* draw lines through the divisions 1, 2 and 3.

3rd. With the length of the given side from *P*, cut *O* 1 in *S*, from *S* cut *O* 2, in *R*, and from *Q* cut *O* 2 in *R*; connect the points *O*. *Q*. *R*. *S*. *P* by right lines, and the pentagon will be complete.

PROBLEM 20. FIG. 6.

On the given line A. B *to construct a Heptagon,* A. B *being the length of the side.*

1st. From *A* with *A*. *B* for a radius, draw the semicircle *B*. *H*.
2d. Divide the semicircle into seven equal parts, and from *A* through 1, 2, 3, 4 and 5, draw indefinite lines.
3rd. From *B* cut the line *A* 1 in *C*, from *C* cut *A* 2 in *D*, from *G* cut *A* 4 in *F*, and from *F* cut *A* 3 in *E*, connect the points by right lines to complete the figure.

Any polygon may be constructed by this method. The rule is, to divide the semicircle into as many equal parts as there are sides in the required polygon, draw lines through all the divisions except two, and proceed as above.

Considerable care is required to draw these figures accurately, on account of the difficulty of finding the exact points of intersection. They should be practised on a much larger scale.

PLATE VII.

PROBLEM 21. FIG. 1.

To find the Centre of a Circle.

1st. Draw any chord, as *A*. *B*, and bisect it by a perpendicular *E*. *D*, which is a diameter of the circle.
2nd. Bisect the perpendicular *E*. *D* by problem 1, the point of intersection is the centre of the circle.

FIGURE 2.

Another method of finding the Centre of a Circle.

1st. Join any three points in the circumference as *F*. *G*. *H*.
2nd. Bisect the chords *F*. *G* and *G*. *H* by perpendiculars, their point of intersection at *C* is the centre required.

Plate 7.

PROBLEMS RELATING TO THE CIRCLE.

Fig. 1.

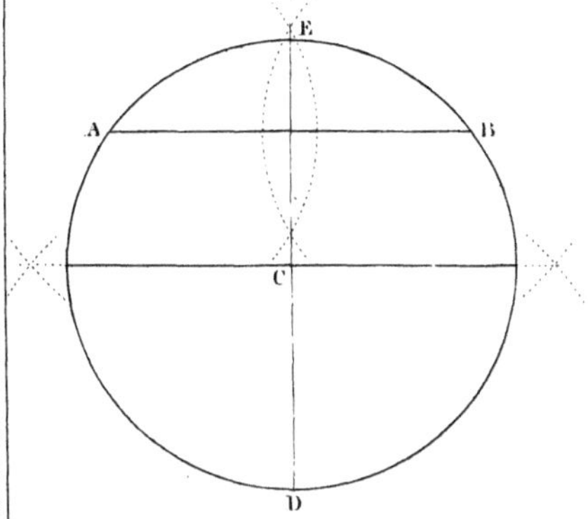

Fig. 2.

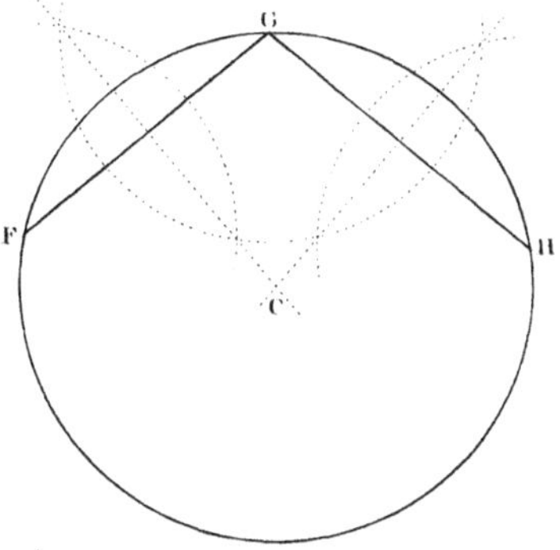

Fig. 3.

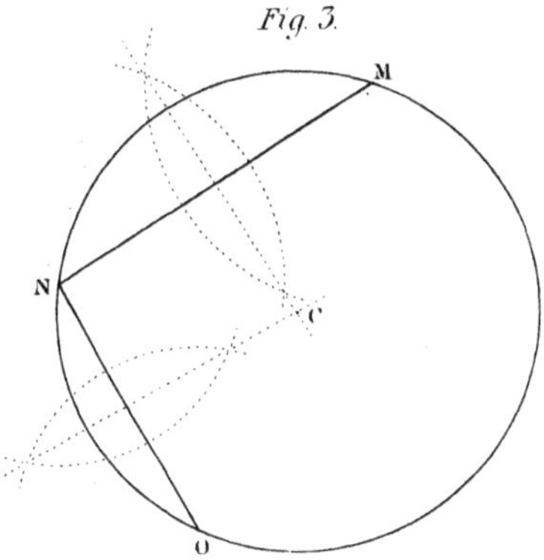

Fig. 4.

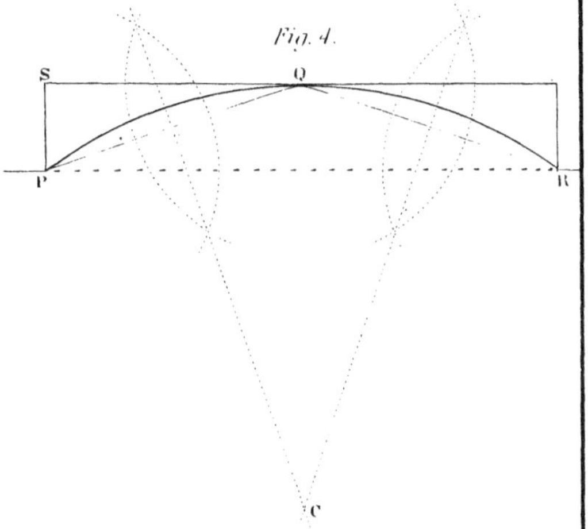

Fig. 5.

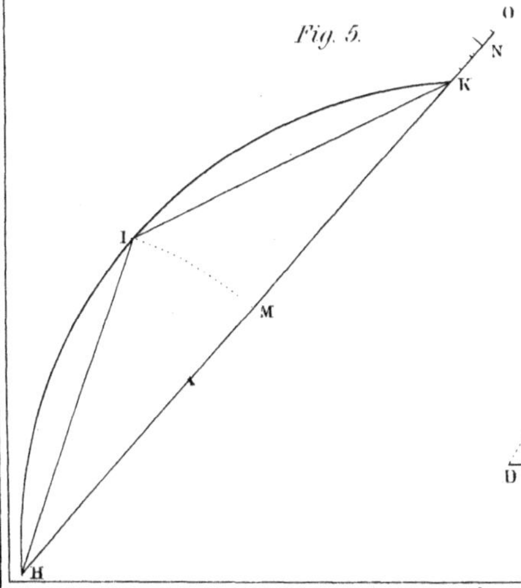

Fig. 6.

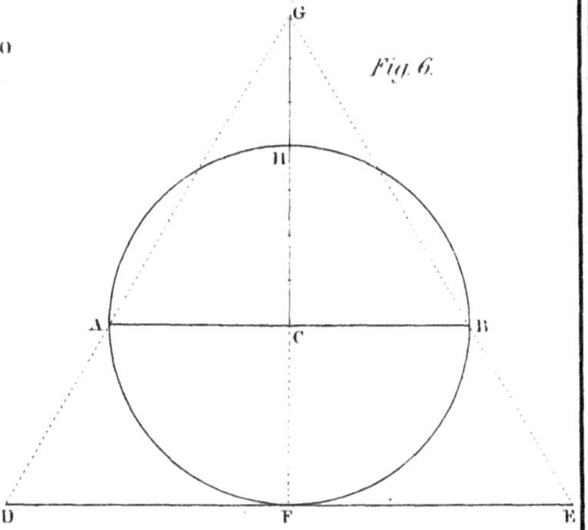

Wm. Minifie.

Illman & Sons

PROBLEM 22. FIG. 3.

To draw a Circle through any three points not in a straight line, as M. N. O.

1st. Connect the points by straight lines, which will be chords to the required circle.
2nd. Bisect the chords by perpendiculars, their point of intersection at *C* is the centre of the required circle.
3rd. With one foot of the dividers at *C*, and a radius equal to *C. M*, *C. N*, or *C. O*, describe the circle.

PROBLEM 23. FIG. 4.

To find the Centre for describing the Segment of a Circle.

1st. Let *P. R* be the chord of the segment, and *P. S* the rise.
2nd. Draw the chords *P. Q* and *Q. R*, and bisect them by perpendiculars; the point of intersection at *C*, is the centre for describing the segment.

PROBLEM 24. FIG. 5.

To find a Right Line nearly equal to an Arc of a Circle, as H. I. K.

1st. Draw the chord *H. K*, and extend it indefinitely toward *O*.
2nd. Bisect the segment in *I*, and draw the chords *H. I* and *I. K*.
3rd. With one foot of the dividers in *H*, and a radius equal to *H. I*, cut *H. O* in *M*, then with the same radius, and one foot in *M*, cut *H. O* again in *N*.
4th. Divide the difference *K. N* into three equal parts, and extend one of them toward *O*, then will the right line *H. O* be nearly equal to the curved line *H. I. K*.

PROBLEM 25. FIG. 6.

To find a Right Line nearly equal to the Semicircumference A. F. B.

1st. Draw the diameter *A. B*, and bisect it by the perpendicular *F. H*; extend *F. H* indefinitely toward *G*.
2nd. Divide the radius *C. H* into four equal parts, and extend three of those parts to *G*.
3rd. At *F* draw an indefinite right line *D. E*.

4th. From *G* through *A*, the end of the diameter *A. B*, draw *G. A. D*, cutting the line *D. E* in *D*, and from *G* through *B* draw *G. B. E*, cutting *D. E* in *E*, then will the line *D. E* be nearly equal to the semicircumference of the circle, and the triangles *D. G. E* and *A. G. B* will be equilateral.

NOTE.—The right lines found by problems 24 and 25, are not mathematically equal to the respective curves, but are sufficiently correct for all practical purposes. *Workmen* are in the habit of using the following method for finding the length of a curved line :—

They open their compasses to a small distance, and commencing at one end, step off the whole curve, noting the number of steps required, and the remainder less than a step, if any; they then step off the same number of times, with the same distance, on the article to be bent around it, and add the remainder, which gives them a length sufficiently true for their purpose: the error in this method amounts to the sum of the differences between the arc cut off by each step, and its chord.

PLATE VIII.

PARALLEL RULER AND APPLICATION.

FIGURE 1.

The parallel ruler figured in the plate consists of two bars of wood or metal *A. B* and *C. D*, of equal length, breadth and thickness, connected together by two arms of equal length placed diagonally across the bars, both at the same angle, and moving freely on the rivets which connect them to the bars; if the bar *A. B* be kept firmly in any position and the bar *C. D* moved, the ends of the arms connected to *C. D* will describe arcs of circles and recede from *A. B* until the arms are at right angles to the bars, as shewn by the dotted lines; if moved farther round, the bars will again approach each other on the other side.

The bars of which the ruler is composed, being parallel to each other, it follows, that if either edge of the instrument is placed parallel with a line and held in that position, another line may be drawn parallel to the first at any distance within the range of the instrument. This is its most obvious use; it is generally applied to the drawing of inclined parallel lines in mechanical drawings, vertical and horizontal lines being more easily drawn with the square, when the drawing is attached to a drawing board.

Plate 8.

PARALLEL RULER.

and its Application

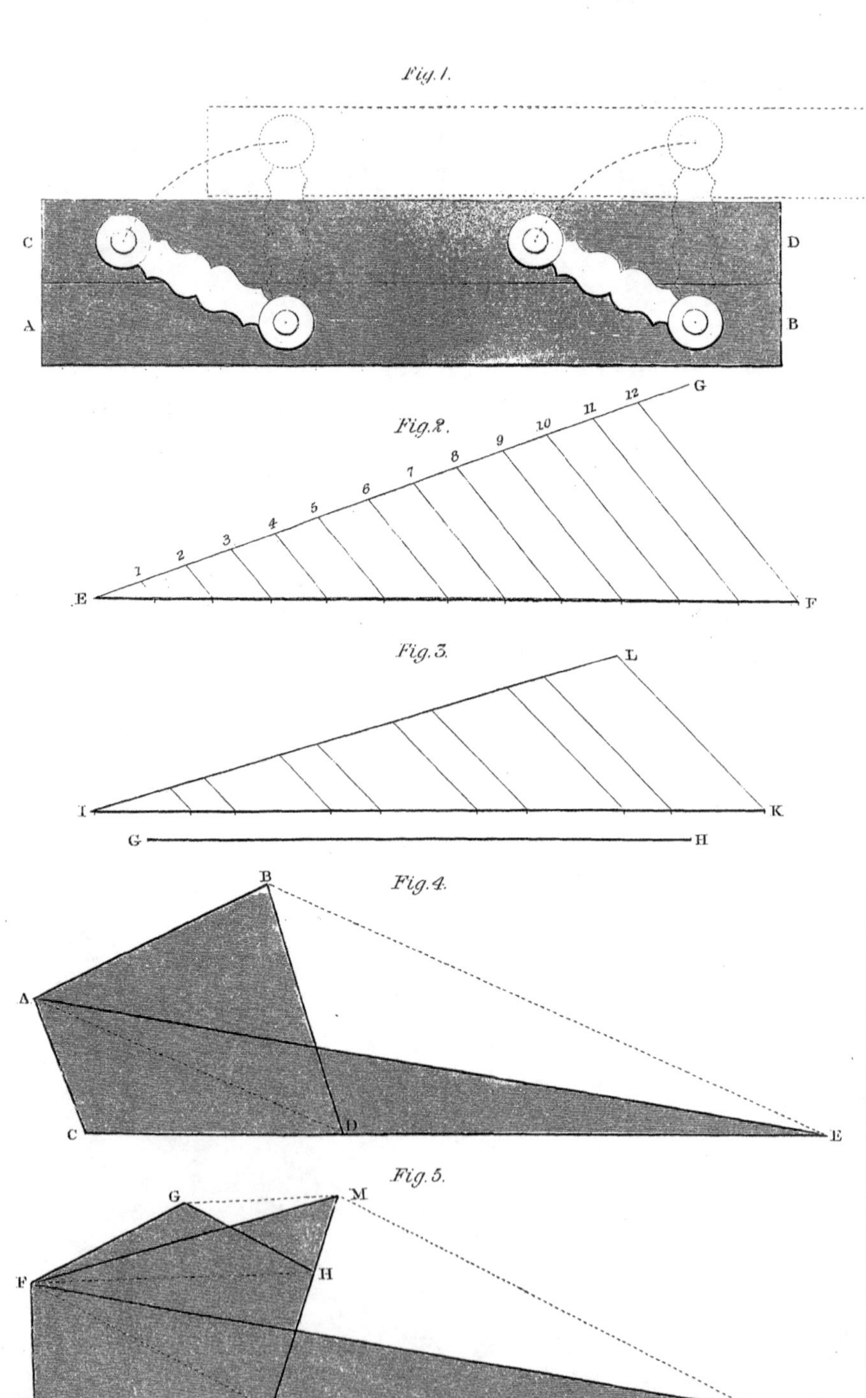

Wm. Minifie

Tilman & Sons

APPLICATION.—PROBLEM 26. FIG. 2.

To divide the Line E. F *into any number of equal parts, say* 12.

1st. From *E* draw *E. G* at any angle to *E. F*, and step off with any opening of the dividers twelve equal spaces on *E. G*.
2nd. Join *F* 12, and with the parallel ruler draw lines through the points of division in *E. G*, parallel to 12 *F*, intersecting *E. F*, and dividing it as required.

PROBLEM 27. FIG. 3.

To divide a Line of the length of G. H *in the same proportion as the Line* I. K *is divided.*

1st. From *I* draw a line at any angle and make *I. L* equal to *G. H.*
2nd. Join the ends *K* and *L* by a right line, and draw lines parallel to it through all the points of division, to intersect *I. L*, then *I. L* will be divided in the same proportion as *I. K*.

PROBLEM 28. FIG. 4.

To reduce the Trapezium A. B. C. D *to a Triangle of equal area.*

1st. Prolong *C. D* indefinitely.
2nd. Draw the diagonal *A. D*, place one edge of the ruler on the line *A. D* and extend the other edge to *B*, then draw *B. E*, cutting *C. D* extended in *E*.
3rd. Join *A. E*, then the area of the triangle *A. E. C* will be equal to the trapezium *A. B. C. D*.

PROBLEM 29. FIG. 5.

To reduce the irregular Pentagon F. G. H. I. K. *to a Tetragon and to a Triangle, each of equal area with the Pentagon.*

1st. Prolong *I. H* indefinitely.
2nd. Draw the diagonal *F. H* and *G. M* parallel to it, cutting *I. H* in *M*, and draw *F. M*.
3rd. Prolong *K. I* indefinitely toward *L*.
4th. Draw the diagonal *F. I* and draw *M. L* parallel to it, cutting *K. L* in *L*.

5th. Draw *F. L,* then the triangle *F. L. K,* and the tetragon *K. F. M. I,* are equal in area to the given pentagon.

PLATE IX.

CONSTRUCTION OF THE SCALE OF CHORDS AND ITS APPLICATION.—PLANE SCALES.

PROBLEM 30. FIG. 1.

To Construct a Scale of Chords.

Let *A. B* be a rule on which to construct the scale.

1st. With any radius, and one foot in *D,* describe a quadrant; then draw the radii *D. C* and *D. E.*

2nd. Divide the arc into three equal parts as follows :—With the radius of the quadrant, and the dividers in *C,* cut the arc in 60; then, with one foot in *E,* cut the arc in 30.

3rd. Divide these spaces each into three equal parts, when the quadrant will be divided into nine equal parts of 10° each.

4th. From *C,* draw chords to each of the divisions, and transfer them, as shewn by the dotted lines, to *A. B.*

5th. Divide each of the spaces on the arc into ten equal parts, and transfer the chords to *A. B,* when we shall have a scale of chords corresponding to the respective degrees.

NOTE 1.—This scale is generally found on the plane scale which accompanies a set of drawing instruments, and marked *C,* or *Ch.*

NOTE 2.—Any scale of chords may be reconstructed by using the chord of 60° as a radius for describing the quadrant.

APPLICATION.—PROBLEM 31. FIG. 2.

To lay down an Angle at F, *of any number of degrees, say 25, the line* G. F *to form one side of the Angle.*

1st. Take the chord of 60° in the dividers, and with one foot in *F,* describe an indefinite arc, cutting *G. F* in *H.*

Plate 9.

SCALE OF CHORDS.

Fig. 1.

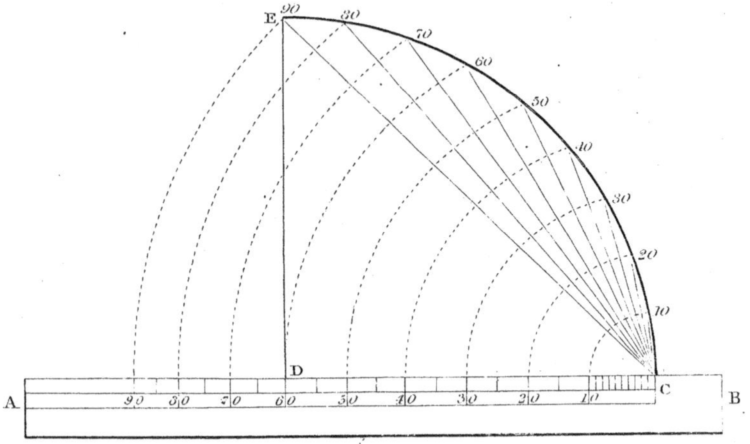

Fig. 2.

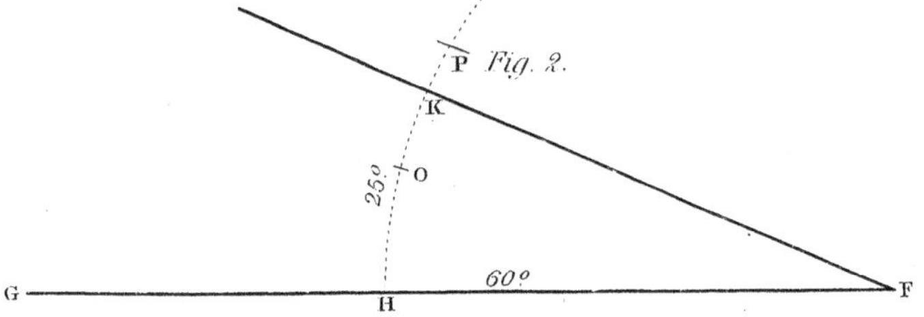

SCALES OF EQUAL PARTS.

Fig. 3.

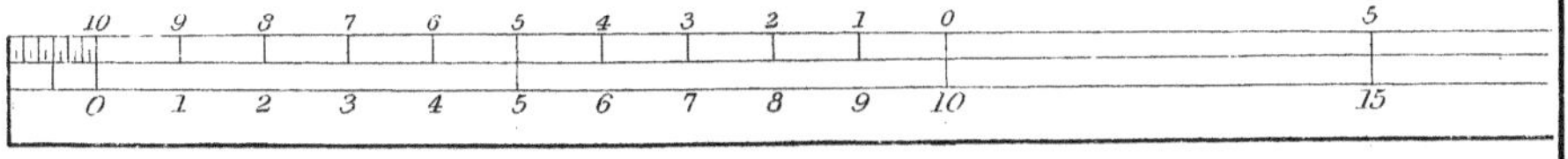

Fig. 4.

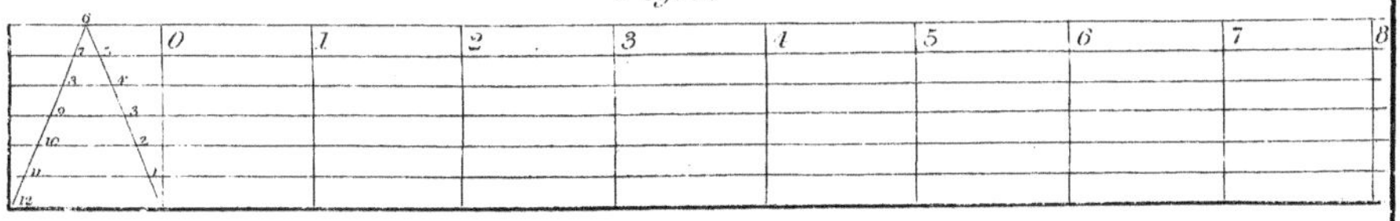

Fig. 5.

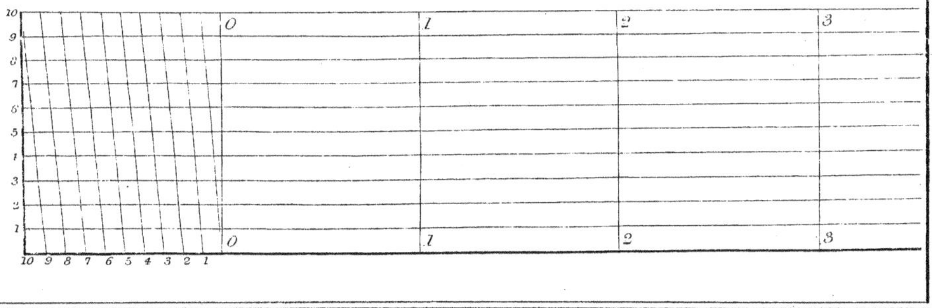

2nd. From the scale take 25° in the dividers, and with one foot in *H*, cut the arc in *K*.
3rd. Through *K*, draw *K. F*, which completes the required angle. If we desire an angle of 15° or 30°, take the required number from the scale, and cut the arc in *O* or *P*, and in the same manner for any other angle.

Problem 32. Fig. 2.

To measure an Angle F, *already laid down.*

1st. With the chord of 60°, and one foot of the dividers in the angular point, cut the sides of the angle in *H* and *K*.
2nd. Take the distance *H. K* in the dividers, and apply it to the scale, which will shew the number of degrees subtended by the angle.

SCALES OF EQUAL PARTS.

1st. Scales of equal parts may be divided into two kinds, viz:— Those which consist of two or three lines, divided by short parallel lines, at right angles to the others, like fig. 3, or those which are composed of several parallel lines, divided by diagonal and vertical lines, like figs. 4 and 5: the first kind are called *simple scales*, the second *diagonal scales*.
2nd. Scales of equal parts may be made of any size, and may be made to represent any unit of measure: thus each part of a scale may be an inch, or the tenth of an inch, or any other space, and may represent an inch, foot, yard, fathom, mile, or degree, or any other quantity.
3rd. The measure which the scale is intended to represent, is called *the unit of measurement*. In architectural or mechanical drawings, the unit of measurement is generally a foot, which is subdivided into inches to correspond with the common foot rule. For working drawings, the scale is generally large. A very common mode of laying down working drawings, is to use a scale of one and a half inches to the foot; this gives one-eighth of an inch to an inch, which is equal to one-eighth of the full size. This is very convenient, as every workman has a scale on

his rule, which he can apply to the drawing with facility. Scales are generally made to suit each particular case, dependant on the size of the object to be represented, and on the size of the paper or board on which the drawing is to be made.

4th. To DRAW A SCALE. If we have a definite size for each part of a required scale, say one-quarter of an inch, we have only to extend the dividers to that measure, step off the parts and number them, reserving the left hand space to be subdivided for inches. Care should be taken to have the scale true. It should be proved by taking two, three, four or five parts in the dividers, and applying it to several parts of the scale; when, if found correct, the drawing may be proceeded with. It is much easier to draw another scale if the first is imperfect, than to correct a drawing made from a false scale.

5th. Fig. 3 requires but little explanation. It is called a quarter of an inch scale, as each unit of the scale is a quarter of an inch; the starting point of a scale marked *O*, is called its ZERO. The term is not very common among practical men, except when applied to the thermometer; and, when we say the thermometer is down to Zero, we mean that it is at the commencement of the scale. It is better to number a scale above and below, as in the figure; for, if we wish to take a measure of any number of feet less than 10, and inches, say 3 feet 6 inches, we place one foot of the dividers at 3, numbered from below, and extend the other out to 6 inches. If, on the other hand, we have to measure a number of feet more than 10, say 13, we should place one foot in the division marked 10, on the top of the scale without the plate, and extend it to 3, when we are enabled to read the quantity at sight, without any mental operation, as we must do if the scale is only numbered as below. For example, to take 13 feet, we must place one foot of the dividers at 20, and extend it to 7. This operation is simple, it is true, but it requires us to subtract 7 from 20 to get 13, instead of reading from the scale as we could do from the upper numbers. In taking a large space in the dividers, it is always better to take the whole numbers first, and add the inches or other fractions afterwards. The space on the left hand in this figure, is divided into twelve parts for inches.

Figure 4.

Is a half inch Diagonal Scale, divided for feet and inches.

To draw a scale of this kind :—

1st. Draw 7 lines parallel to each other, and equidistant.

2nd. Step off spaces of half an inch each, and draw lines through the divisions across the whole of the spaces.

3rd. Divide the top of the first space into two equal parts, draw the diagonal lines, and number them as in the diagram.

To take any measure from this scale, say 2′ 1″, we must place the dividers on the first line above the bottom on the second division on the scale, and extend the other foot to the first diagonal line, numbered 1, which will give the required dimension. If we wish to take 2′ 11″, we must place one leg of the dividers the same as before, and extend the other to the second diagonal line, which gives the dimension. If we wish to take 1′ 3″, we must place the dividers on the middle line in the first vertical division, and extend it to the first diagonal line, numbered 3, and proceed in the same manner for any other dimension.

This is a very useful form of scale. The student should familiarize himself with its construction and application.

Figure 5.

Is an inch Diagonal Scale, divided into tenths and hundredths. It is made by drawing eleven lines parallel to each other, enclosing ten equal spaces, with vertical lines drawn through the points of division across the whole. The left hand vertical space is divided into ten equal parts, and diagonal lines drawn as in the figure.

This scale gives three denominations. Each of the small spaces on the top and bottom lines, is equal to one-tenth of the whole division. The horizontal lines contained between the first diagonal and the vertical line, are divided into tenths of the smaller division, or hundreths of the larger division; for example, the first line from the top contains nine-tenths of the smaller division, the second eight-tenths, the third seven-tenths, and so on as numbered on the end of the scale. To make a diagonal scale of this form, divided into feet, inches, &c., we must draw 13 parallel horizontal lines, and divide the left hand space also into 13.

PLATE X.

CONSTRUCTION OF THE PROTRACTOR.

FIGURE 1.

The protractor is an instrument generally formed of a semicircle and its chord; the semicircle is divided into 180 equal parts or degrees, numbered in both directions from 10° to 180°, as in its application, angles are often required to be measured or laid down on either hand; in portable cases of instruments the protractor is frequently drawn on a flat straight scale as in the diagram. Its mode of construction is sufficiently obvious from the drawing; a small notch or mark in the centre of the straight edge of the instrument denotes the centre from which the semicircle is described, and the angular point in which all the lines meet.

APPLICATION.—PROBLEM 33. FIG. 2.

WITH THE PROTRACTOR, TO PROTRACT OR LAY DOWN ANY ANGLE.

From the point O *let it be required to form a Right Angle to the line* O. P.

1st. Place the straight edge of the protractor to coincide with the line *O. P*, with the centre at *O*, then mark the angle of 90° at *S.*

2nd. From *S* draw *S. O*, which gives the required angle.

While the instrument is in the position described, with its centre at *O*, any other angle may be laid down, thus at *Q* we have 30°, at *R* 60°, at *T* 120°, and at *V* 150°, and so on from the fraction of a degree up to 180.°

The protractor may also be used for constructing any regular polygon in a circle or on a given line; to do so, it is necessary to know the angle formed by said polygon by lines drawn from its corners to the centre of the circle, and also to know the angle formed by any two adjoining faces of the polygon. The table given for this purpose is constructed as follows:

1st. To find the angle formed by any polygon at the centre, divide 360, the number of degrees in the whole circle, by the number of

Plate 10.

PROTRACTOR

Its Construction and Application.

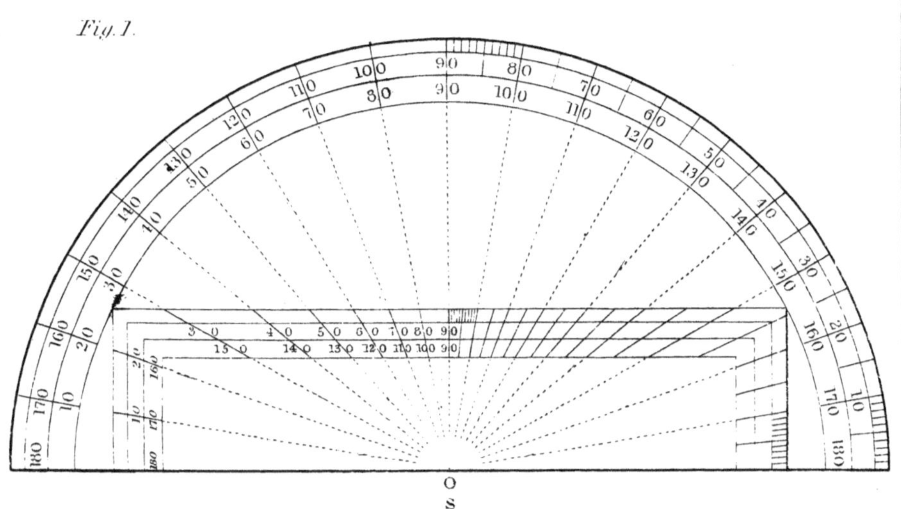

Fig. 2.

S T R V Q O P

Angles of Regular Polygons.

Trigon	120	at the Centre	60	at the Circumference
Tetragon	90	d°	90	d°
Pentagon	72	d°	108	d°
Hexagon	60	d°	120	d°
Octagon	45	d°	135	d°
Enneagon	40	d°	140	d°
Decagon	36	d°	144	d°
Dodecagon	30	d°	150	d°

Wm Minifie. Ilman & Sons.

sides in the required polygon, the quotient will be the *angle at the centre;* for example, let it be required to find the angle at the centre of an octagon:—divide 360 by 8, the number of sides, the quotient will be 45, which is the angle formed by the octagon at the centre.

2nd. To find the angle formed by two adjoining faces of a polygon, we must subtract from 180 the number of degrees in the semicircle, the angle formed by said polygon at the centre, the remainder will be the angle formed at the circumference. For example let us take the octagon; we have found in the last paragraph that the angle formed by that figure in the centre is 45°; then if we subtract 45 from 180 it will leave 135, which is the angle formed by two adjoining faces of the octagon.

PLATE XI.

TO DESCRIBE FLAT SEGMENTS OF CIRCLES AND PARABOLAS.

Very often in practice it would be very inconvenient to find the centre for describing a flat segment of a circle, in consequence of the rise of an arch being so small compared to its span.

PROBLEM 34. FIG. 1.

To describe a Segment with a Triangle.

NOTE.—In all the diagrams in this plate *A. B* is the span of the arch, *A. D* the rise, and *C* the centre of the crown of the arch.

1st. Make a triangle with its longest side equal to the chord or span of the arch and its height equal to one-half the rise.

2nd. Stick a nail at *A* and at *C*, place the triangle as in the diagram and move it round against the nails toward *A*, a pencil kept at the apex of the triangle will describe one-half of the curve.

3rd. Stick another nail at *B*, and with the triangle moving against *C* and *B*, describe the other half of the curve.

PROBLEM 35. FIG. 2.

To describe the same Curve with strips of wood, forming a Triangle.

1st. Drive a nail at *A* and another at *B*, place one strip against *A* and bring it up to the centre of the crown at *C*.

2nd. Place another strip against *B* and crossing the first at *C*, nail them together at the intersection, and nail a brace across to keep them in position.

3rd. With the pencil at *C* and the triangle formed by the strips kept against *A* and *B*, describe the curve from *C* toward *A*, and from *C* toward *B*.

PROBLEM 36. FIG. 3.

To draw a Parabolic Curve by the intersection of lines forming Tangents to the Curve.

1st. Draw *C*. 8 perpendicular to *A*. *B*, and make it equal to *A*. *D*.

2nd. Join *A*. 8 and *B*. 8, and divide both lines into the same number of equal parts, say 8, number them as in the figure, draw 1. 1.—2. 2.—3. 3., &c., then these lines will be tangents to the curve; trace the curve to touch the centre of each of those lines between the points of intersection.

PROBLEM 37. FIG. 4.

To draw the same Curve by another method.

1st. Divide *A*. *D* and *B*. *E*, into any number of equal parts, and *C*. *D* and *C*. *E* into a similar number.

2nd. Draw 1. 1.—2. 2. &c., parallel to *A*. *D*, and from the points of division in *A*. *D* and *B*. *E*, draw lines to *C*. The points of intersection of the respective lines, are points in the curve.

NOTE.—The curves found, as in figs. 3 and 4, are quicker at the crown than a true circular segment; but, where the rise of the arch is not more than one-tenth of the span, the variation cannot be perceived.

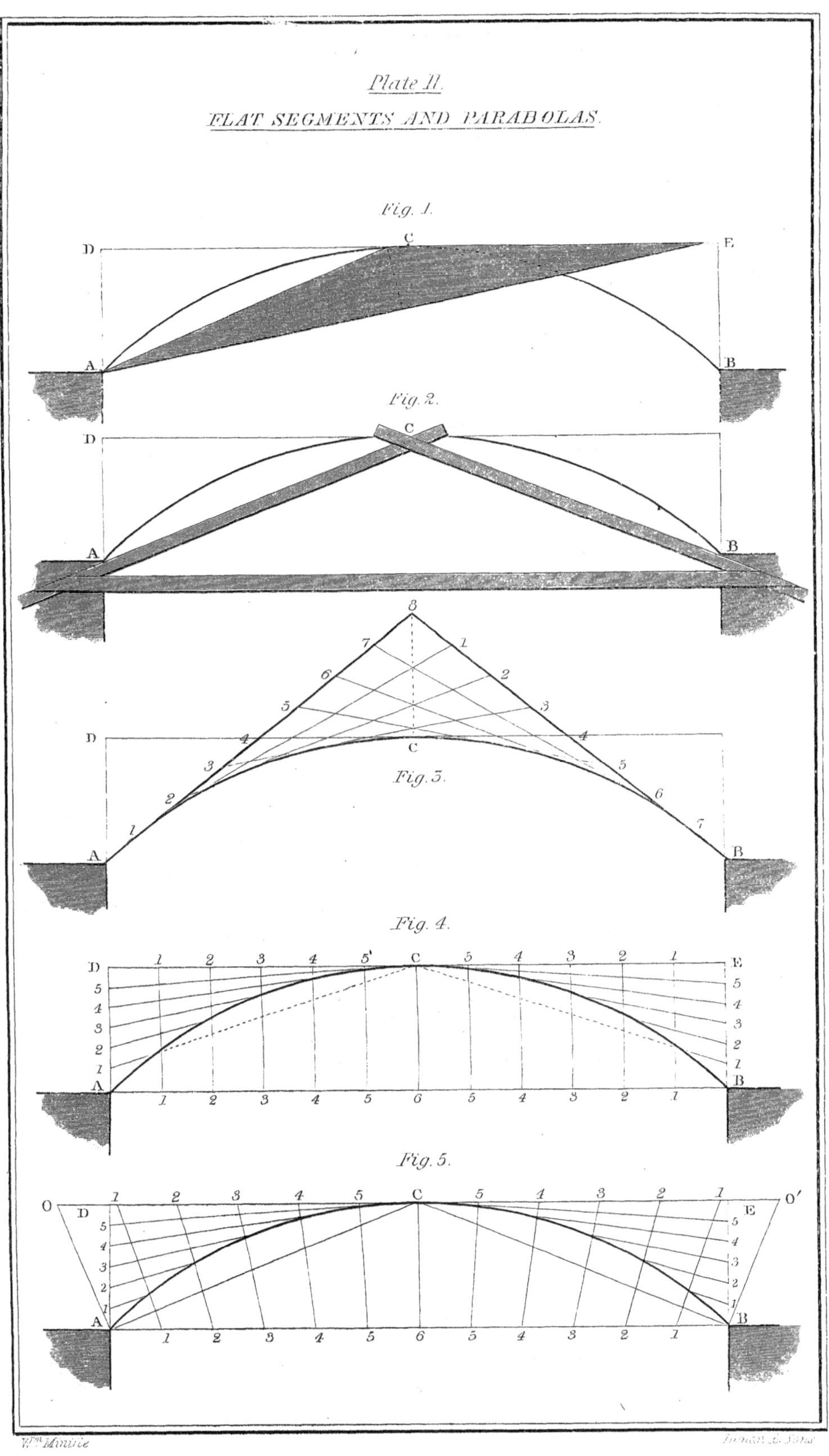

Plate II.
FLAT SEGMENTS AND PARABOLAS.
Fig. 1.
D
C
E
A
B
Fig. 2.
D
C
A
B
Fig. 3.
8
7
6
5
4
3
2
1
D
C
A
B
Fig. 4.
D 1 2 3 4 5 C 5 4 3 2 1 E
A 1 2 3 4 5 6 5 4 3 2 1 B
Fig. 5.
O 1 2 3 4 5 C 5 4 3 2 1 O′
D
E
A 1 2 3 4 5 6 5 4 3 2 1 B

Plate 12.

OVAL FIGURES COMPOSED OF ARCS OF CIRCLES.

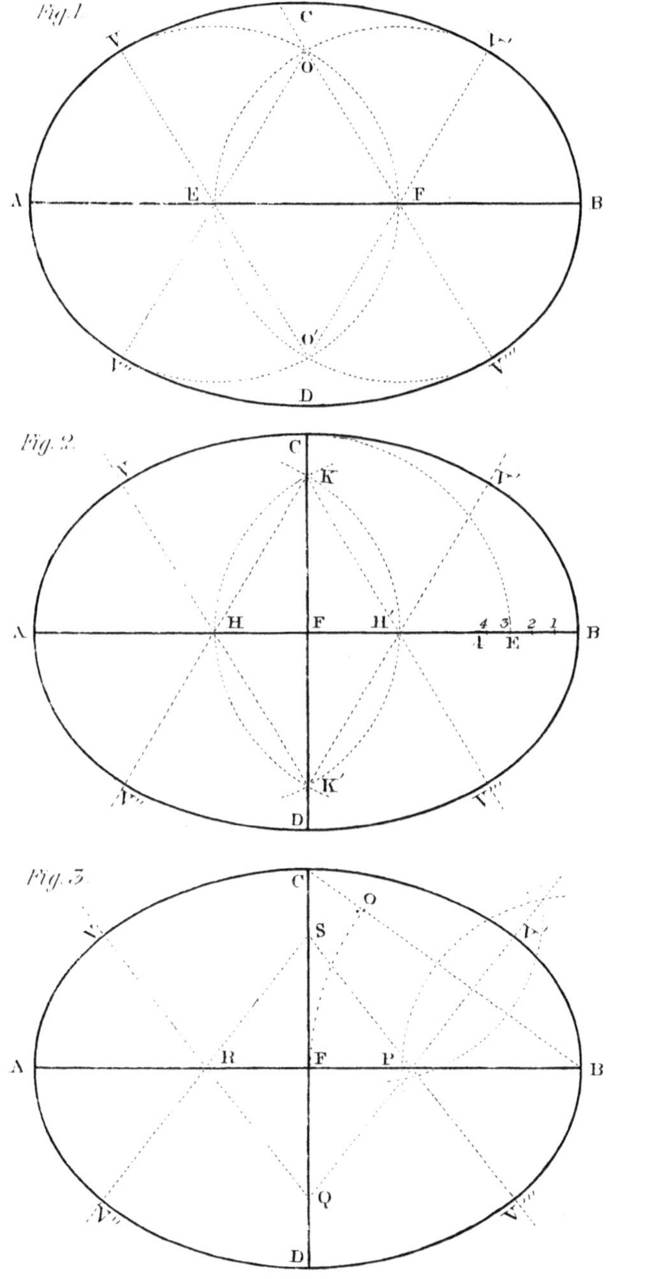

PROBLEM 38. FIG. 5.

To describe a True Segment of a Circle by Intersections.

1st. Draw the chords *A. C* and *B. C*, and *A. O* and *B. O'*, perpendicular to them.

2nd. Prolong *D. E* in each direction to *O. O'*; divide *O. C, C. O', A. D, A.* 6, *B.* 6, and *B. E* into the same number of equal parts.

3rd. Join the points 1. 1.—2. 2. &c., in *A. B* and *O. O'*.

4th. From the divisions in *A. D*, and *B. E*, draw lines to *C*. The points of intersection of these lines with the former, are points in the curve. A semicircle may be described by this method.

PLATE XII.

TO DESCRIBE OVAL FIGURES COMPOSED OF ARCS OF CIRCLES.

PROBLEM 39. FIG. 1.

The length of the Oval A. B. *being given, to describe an Oval upon it.*

1st. Divide *A. B* the given length, into three equal parts, in *E* and *F*.

2nd. With one of those parts for a radius, and the compasses in *E* and *F* successively, describe two circles cutting each other in *O* and *O'*.

3rd. From the points of intersection in *O* and *O'*, draw lines through *E* and *F*, cutting the circles in *V. V,''* and *V.' V.'''*

4th. With one foot of the compasses in *O*, and *O'* successively, and with a radius equal to *O. V,''* or *O.' V*, describe the arcs between *V. V,'* and *V.'' V'''*, to complete the figure.

PROBLEM 40. FIG. 2.

To describe the Oval, the length A. B, *and breadth* C. D, *being given.*

1st. With half the breadth for a radius, and one foot in *F*, describe the arc *C. E*, cutting *A. B* in *E*.

2nd. Divide the difference *E. B* between the semiaxes into three equal parts, and carry one of those divisions toward 4.

3d. Take the distance *B* 4, and set off on each side of the centre *F* at *H* and *H.'*

4th. With the radius *H. H,'* describe from *H* and *H'* as centres, arcs cutting each other in *K* and *K.'*

5th. From *K* and *K,'* through *H* and *H,'* draw indefinite right lines.

6th. With the dividers in *H*, and the radius *H. A*, describe the curve *V. A. V,''* and with the dividers in *H,'* describe the curve *V.' B. V.'''*

7th. From *K* and *K,'* with a radius equal to *K. C*, describe the curves *V. C. V,'* and *V.'' D. V,'''* to complete the figure.

Problem 41. Fig. 3.

Another method for describing the Oval, the length A. B, *and breadth* C. D, *being given.*

1st. Draw *C. B*, and from *B*, with half the transverse axis, *B. F*, cut *B. C* in *O*.

2nd. Bisect *B. O* by a perpendicular, cutting *A. B* in *P*, and *C. D* in *Q*.

3rd. From *F*, set off the distance *F. P* to *R*, and the distance *F. Q* to *S*.

4th. From *S*, through *R* and *P*, and from *Q* through *R*, draw indefinite lines.

5th. From *P* and *R*, and from *S* and *Q*, describe the arcs, completing the figure as in the preceding problem.

Note.—In all these diagrams, the result is nearly the same. Figs 1 and 2 are similar figures, although each is produced by a different process. The proportions of an oval, drawn as figure 1, must always be the same as in the diagram; but, in figs. 2 and 3, the proportions may be varied; but, when the difference in the length of the axes, exceeds one-third of the longer one, the curves have a very unsightly appearance, as the change of curvature is too abrupt. These figures are often improperly called *ellipses*, and sometimes *false ellipses*. Ovals are frequently used for bridges. When the arch is flat, the curve is described from more than two centres, but it is never so graceful as the true ellipsis.

Plate 13.

CYCLOID AND EPICYCLOID.

Fig. 1.

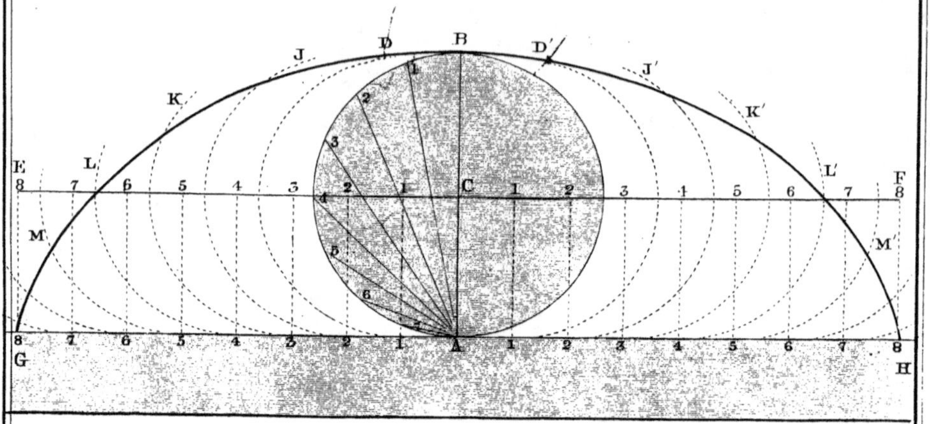

Fig. 2.

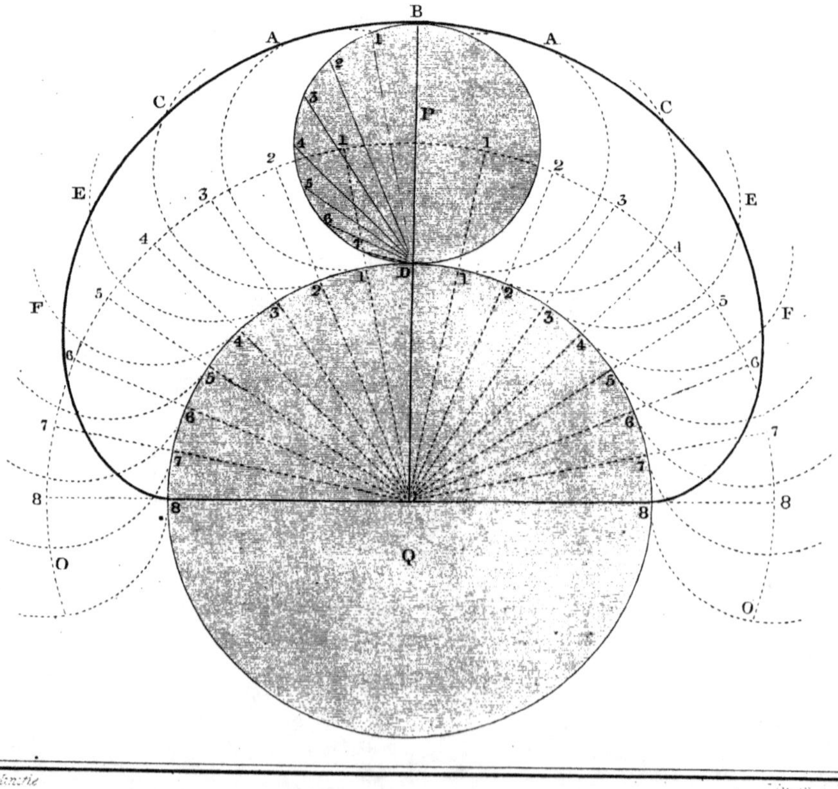

PLATE XIII.

TO DESCRIBE THE CYCLOID AND EPICYCLOID.

The Cycloid is a curve formed by a point in the circumference of a circle, revolving on a level line; this curve is described by any point in the wheel of a carriage when rolling on the ground.

PROBLEM 42. FIG. 1.

To find any number of Points in the Cycloid Curve by the intersection of lines.

1st. Let *G. H* be the edge of a straight ruler, and *C* the centre of the generating circle.

2nd. Through *C* draw the diameter *A. B* perpendicular to *G. H*, and *E. F* parallel to *G. H; then* A. B *is the height of the curve, and* E. F *is the place of the centre of the generating circle at every point of its progress.*

3rd. Divide the semicircumference from *B* to *A* into any number of equal parts, say 8, and from *A* draw chords to the points of division.

4th. From *C*, with a space in the dividers equal to one of the divisions on the circle, step off on each side the same number of spaces as the semicircumference is divided into, and through the points draw perpendiculars to *G. H:* number them as in the diagram.

5th. From the points of division in *E. F*, with the radius of the generating circle, describe indefinite arcs as shewn by the dotted lines.

6th. Take the chord *A* 1 in the dividers, and with the foot at 1 and 1 on the line *G. H*, cut the indefinite arcs described from 1 and 1 respectively at *D* and *D′*, *then* D *and* D′ *are points in the curve.*

7th. With the chord *A* 2, from 2 and 2 in *G. H*, cut the indefinite arcs in *J* and *J′*, with the chord *A* 3, from 3 and 3, cut the arcs in *K* and *K′* and apply the other chords in the same manner, cutting the arcs in *L. M*, &c.

8th. Through the points so found trace the curve.

NOTE.—The indefinite arcs in the diagram represent the circle at that point of its revolution, and the points *D. J. K*, &c., the position of the generating point *B* at each place. This curve is frequently used for the arches of bridges, its proportions are always constant, viz: the span is equal to the circumference of the generating circle and the rise equal to its diameter. *Cycloidal* arches are frequently constructed which are not true cycloids, but approach that curve in a greater or less degree.

FIGURE 2.—THE EPICYCLOID.

This curve is formed by the revolution of a circle around a circle, either within or without its circumference, and described by a point *B* in the circumference of the revolving circle. *P* is the centre of the revolving circle, and *Q* of the stationary circle.

PROBLEM 43.

To find Points in the Curve.

1st. Draw the diameter 8. 8, and from *Q* the centre, draw *Q. B* at right angles to 8. 8.

2nd. With the distance *Q. P* from *Q*, describe an arc *O. O* representing the position of the centre *P* throughout its entire progress.

3rd. Divide the semicircle *B. D* and the quadrants *D.* 8 into the same number of equal parts, draw chords from *D* to 1, 2, 3, &c., and from *Q* draw lines through the divisions in *D.* 8 to intersect the curve *O. O* in 1, 2, 3, &c.

4th. With the radius of *P* from 1, 2, 3, &c., in *O. O* describe indefinite arcs, apply the chords *D* 1, *D* 2, &c., from 1, 2, 3, &c., in the circumference of *Q*, cutting the indefinite arcs in *A. C. E. F*, &c., which are points in the curve.

PLATE XIV.

DEFINITIONS OF SOLIDS

On referring back to our definitions, we find that a *point* has position without magnitude.

A *Line* has length, without breadth or thickness, consequently has but one dimension.

Plate II.

THE CUBE.

its Sections and Surface.

Fig. 1.

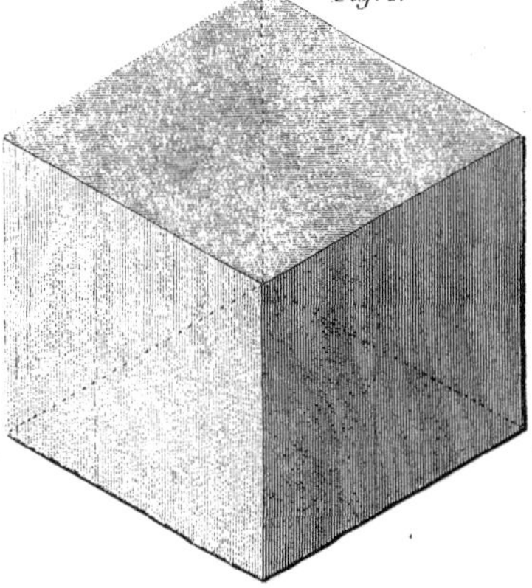

Fig. 2.

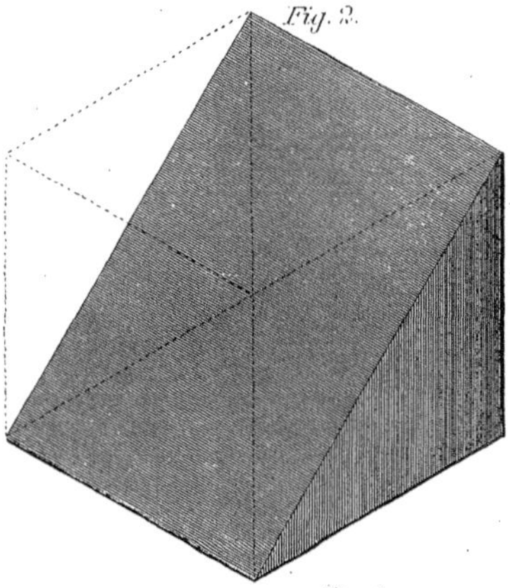

Fig. 3.

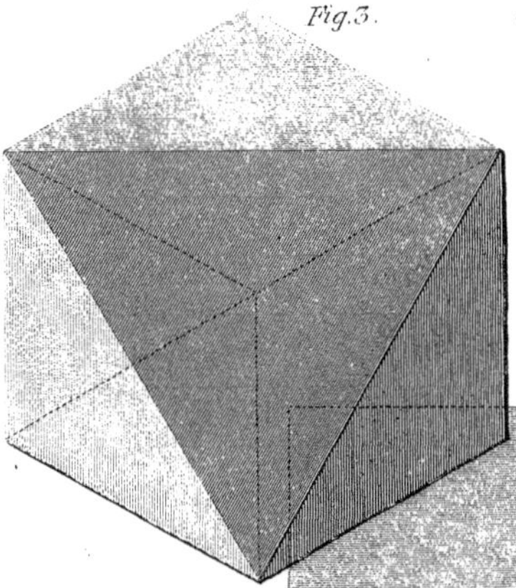

Fig. 4.

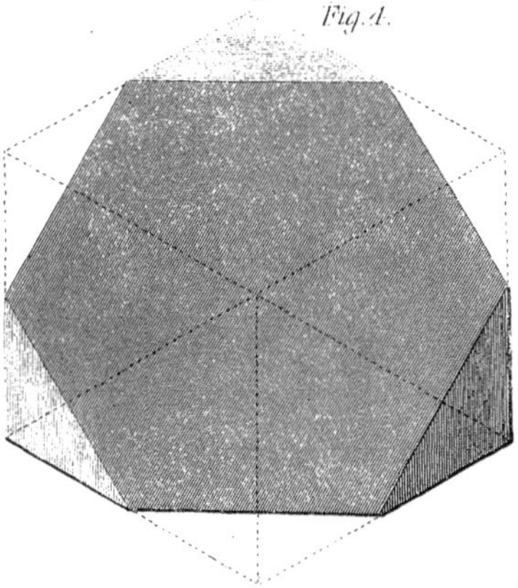

Fig. 5.

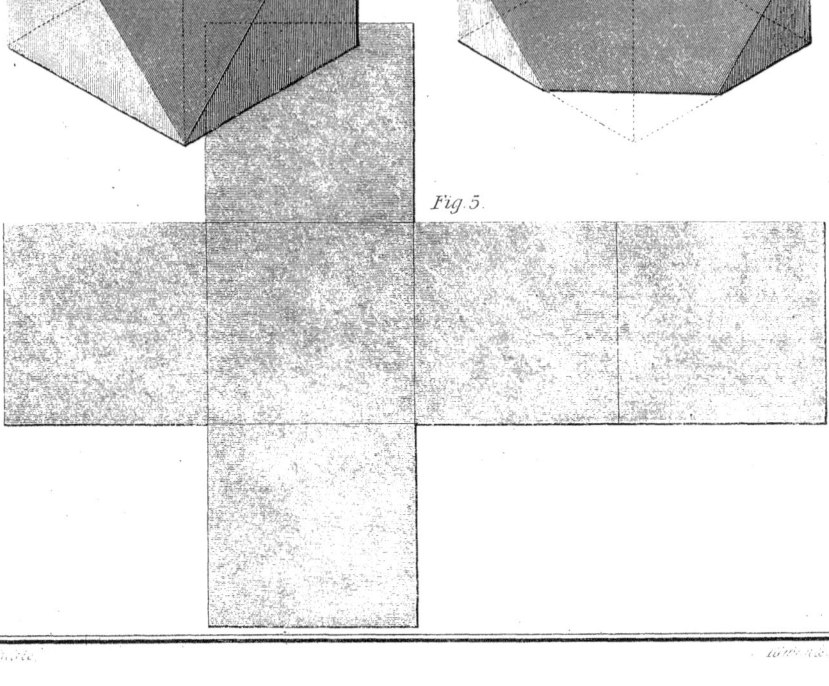

A *Surface* has length and breadth, without thickness, consequently has two dimensions, which, multiplied together, give the content of its surface.

A *Solid* has length, breadth and thickness. These three dimensions multiplied together, give its solid content.

Lineal Measure, is the measure of lines.

Superficial or *Square Measure*, the measure of surfaces.

Cubic Measure, is the measure of solids.

For Example.—If we take a cube whose edge measures two feet, then two feet is the lineal dimension of that line. If the edge is two feet long, the adjoining edge is also two feet long; then, two feet multiplied by two, gives four feet, which is the superficial content of a face of the cube.

Then, if we multiply the square or superficial content, by two feet, which is the thickness of the cube, it will give eight feet, which is its solid content.

Then, two *lineal* feet is the length of the edge.
" four *square* " the surface of one side.
And eight *cubic* " the solid content of the cube.

THE CUBE OR HEXAHEDRON, ITS SECTIONS AND SURFACE.

FIGURE 1.

1st. The cube is one of the regular polyhedrons, composed of six regular square faces, and bounded by twelve lines of equal length; the opposite sides are all parallel to each other.

2nd. If a cube be cut through two of its opposite edges, and the diagonals of the faces connecting them, the section will be an oblong rectangular parallelogram, as fig. 2.

3rd. If a cube be cut through the diagonals of three adjoining faces, as in fig 3, the section will be an equilăteral triangle, whose side is equal to the diagonal of a face of the cube. Two such sections may be made in a cube by cutting it again through the other three diagonals, and the second section will be parallel to the first.

4th. If a cube be cut by a plane passing through all its sides, the line of section, in each face, to be parallel with the diagonal, and midway between the diagonal and the corner of the face, as in fig. 4, the section will be a *regular hexagon*, and will be parallel with, and exactly midway between the triangular sections defined in the last paragraph.

5th. If a cube be cut by any other plane passing through all its sides, the section will be an irregular hexagon.

6th. The surface of the cube fig. 1, is shewn at fig. 5, and if a piece of pasteboard be cut out, of that form, and cut half through in the lines crossing the figure, then folded together, it will form the regular solid. All the other solids may be made of pasteboard, in the same manner, if cut in the shape shewn in the coverings of the diagrams in the following plates.

7th. The *measure* of the *surface* of a cube is six times the square of one of its sides. Thus, if the side of a cube be one foot, the surface of one side will be one square foot, and its whole surface would be six square feet.

Its *solidity* would be one cubic foot.

NOTE.—The cube may also, in general, be called a *prism*, and a *parallelopipedon*, as it answers the description given of those bodies, but the terms are seldom applied to it.

PLATE XV.

SOLIDS AND THEIR COVERINGS.

FIG. 1. Is a solid, bounded by six rectangular faces, each opposite pair being parallel, and equal to each other; the sides are oblong parallelograms, and the ends are squares. It is called a right SQUARE PRISM, PARALLELOPIPED, or PARALLELOPIPEDON.

FIG. 2. Is its covering stretched out.

FIG. 3. Is a *triangular prism;* its sides are rectangles, and its ends equal triangles.

FIG. 4. Is its covering.

PRISMS derive their names from the shape of their ends, and the angles of their faces, thus: Fig. 1 is a *square prism*, and fig. 2 a *triangular prism*. If the ends were pentagons, the prism would be *pentagonal;* if the ends were hexagons, the prism

Plate 15.

SOLIDS AND THEIR COVERINGS.

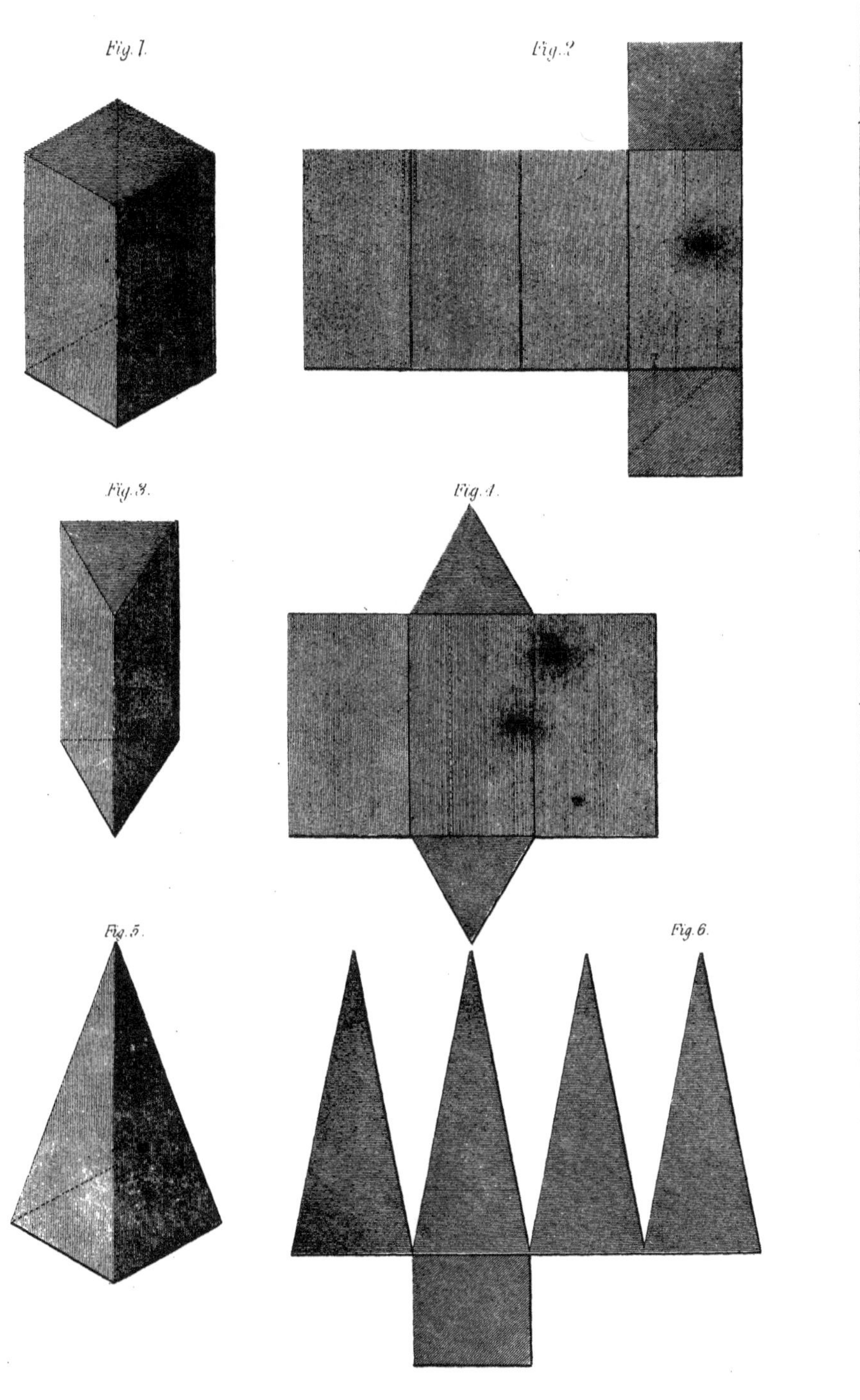

would be *hexagonal, &c.* The sides of all regular prisms are equal rectangular parallelograms.

FIG. 5. Is a SQUARE PYRAMID, bounded by a square at its base, and four regular triangles, as shewn at fig. 6.

Pyramids, like prisms, derive their names from the shape of their bases; thus we may have a square pyramid, as in fig. 5, or a triangular, pentagonal, or hexagonal pyramid, &c., as the base is a triangle, pentagon, hexagon, or any other figure.

The sides of a pyramid incline together, forming a point at the top. This point is called its *vertex*, *apex*, or *summit*.

The *axis* of a pyramid, is a line drawn from its summit, to the centre of its base. *The length of the axis, is the *altitude* of the pyramid. When the base of a pyramid is perpendicular to its axis, it is called a *right pyramid;* if they are not perpendicular to each other, the pyramid is *oblique*. If the top of a pyramid be cut off, the lower portion is said to be *truncated;* it is also called a *frustrum* of a pyramid, and the upper portion is still a pyramid, although only a segment of the original pyramid.

A pyramid may be divided into several *truncated pyramids*, or *frustrums*, and the upper portion remain a pyramid, as the name does not convey any idea of size, but a definite idea of form, viz:* a solid, bounded by an indefinite number of equal triangles, with their edges touching each other, forming a point at the top.

A pyramid is said to be acute, right angled or obtuse, dependant on the form of its summit.

An OBELISK is a pyramid whose height is very great compared to the breadth of the base. The top of an obelisk is generally truncated and cut off, so as to form a small pyramid, resting on the frustrum, which forms the lower part of the obelisk.

When the polygon, forming the base of a pyramid, is irregular, the sides of the figure will be unequal, and the pyramid is called an *irregular pyramid.*

* These definitions are applied to pyramids that are right and regular: it is not necessary to say, "*a right, regular pyramid,*" as when a pyramid is named, it is always supposed to be right and regular, unless otherwise expressed.

Plate 16.

SOLIDS AND THE DEVELOPEMENT OF THEIR SURFACES.

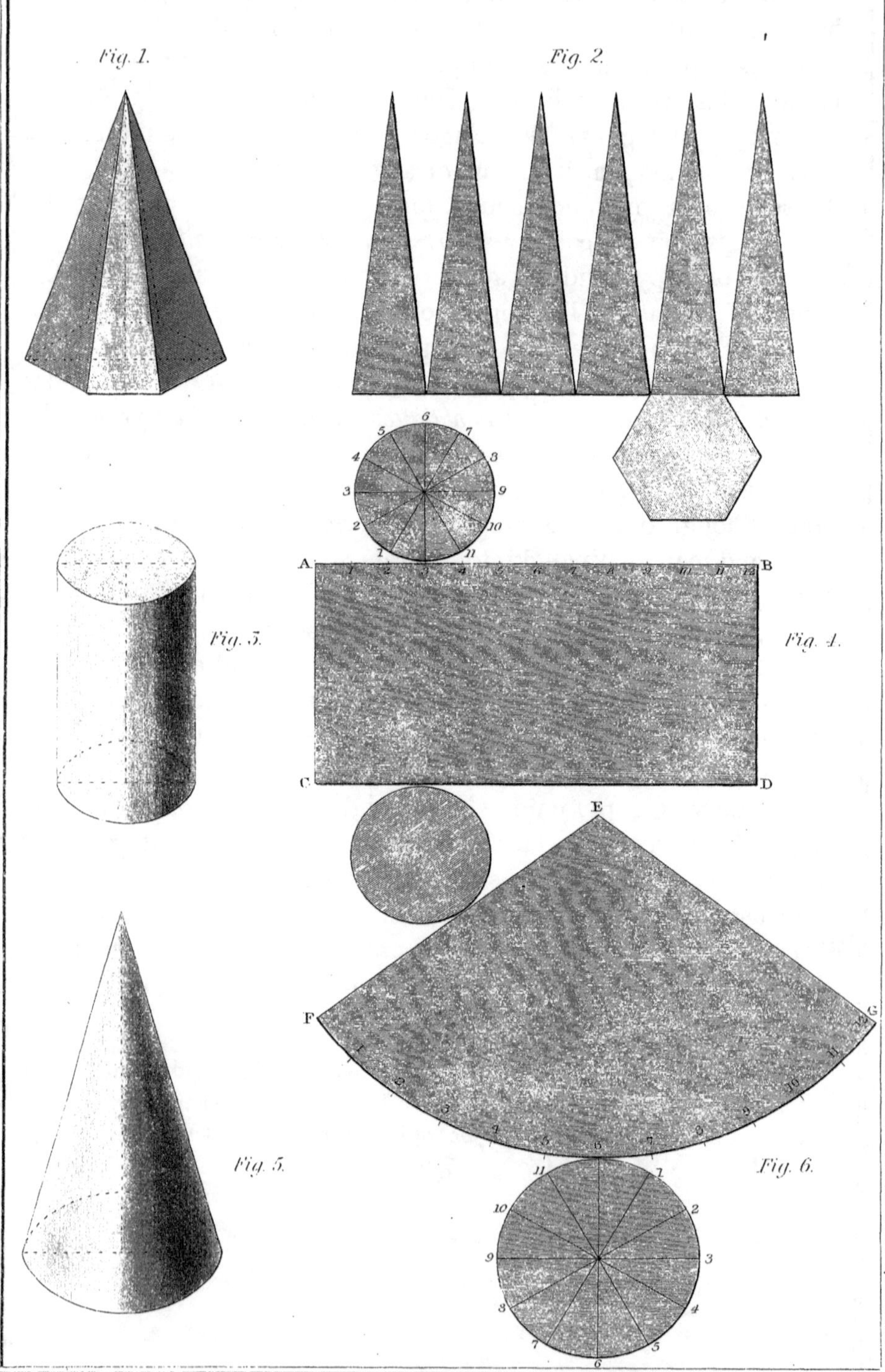

Wm. Minifie. Illman & Sons

Plate 17.

SURFACES OF SOLIDS.

Fig. 1.

Fig. 2.

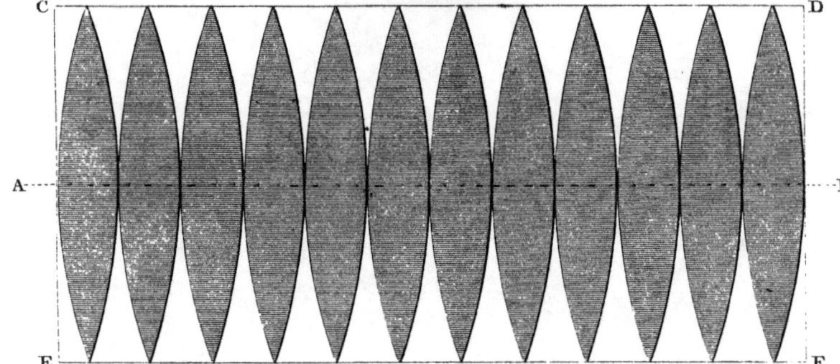

Fig. 3.

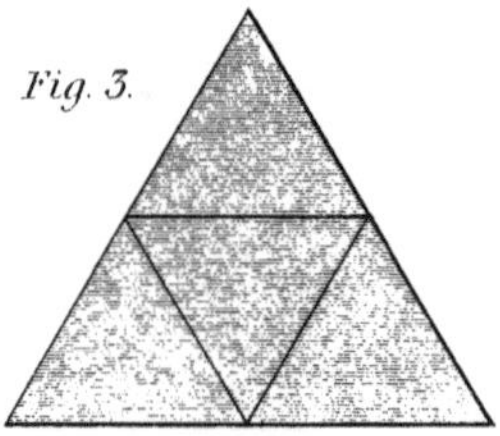

Fig. 4.

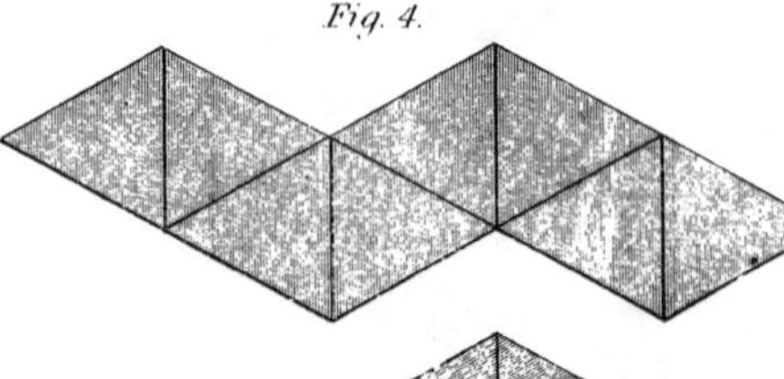

Fig. 5.

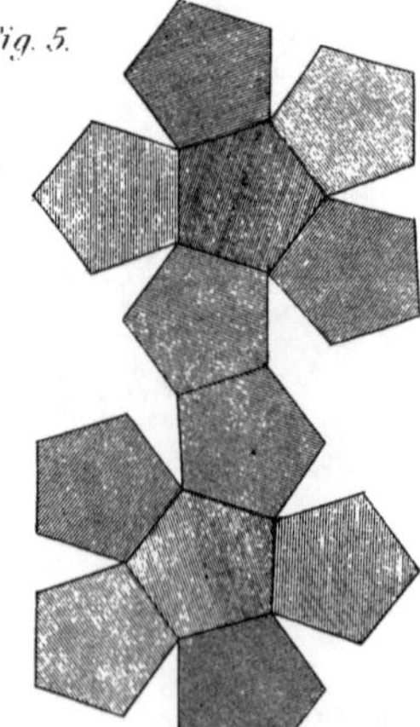

Fig. 6.

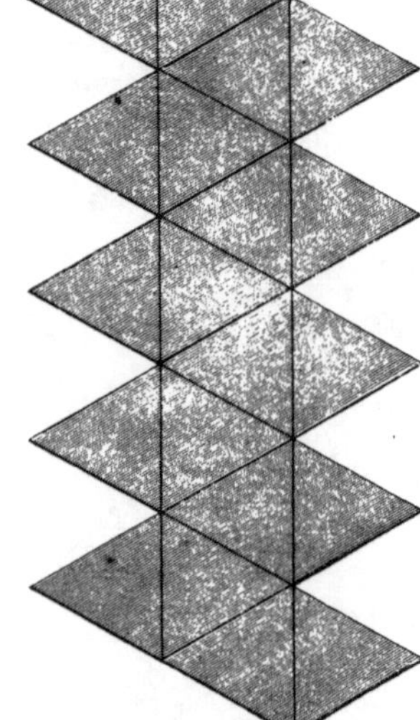

Wm. Mini[illegible]. Ulman & [illegible]

PLATE XVII.

COVERINGS OF SOLIDS.

Fig. 1. The Sphere

Is a solid figure presenting a circular appearance when viewed in any direction; its surface is every where equidistant from a point within, called its centre.

1st. It may be formed by the revolution of a semicircle around its chord.

2nd. The chord around which it revolves is called the *axis*, the ends of the axis are called *poles*.

3rd. Any line passing through the centre of a sphere to opposite points, is called a *diameter*.

4th. Every section of a sphere cut by a plane must be a circle, if the section pass through the centre, its section will be a *great circle* of the sphere; any other section gives a *lesser circle*.

5th. When a sphere is cut into two equal parts by a plane passing through its centre, each part is called a *hemisphere;* any part of a sphere less than a hemisphere is called a segment; this term may be applied to the larger portion as well as to the smaller.

Problem 46. Fig. 2.

To draw the Covering of the Sphere.

1st. Divide the circumference into twelve equal parts.

2nd. Step off on the line *A. B* the same number of equal parts, and with a radius of nine of those parts, describe arcs through the points in each direction; these arcs will intersect each other in the lines *C. D* and *E. F*, and form the covering of the sphere.

Figure 3.

Is the surface of a regular Tetrahedron, it is bounded by four equal equilateral triangles.

Figure 4.

The regular **Octahedron** is bounded by eight equal equilateral triangles.

Figure 5.

The **Dodecahedron** is bounded by twelve equal pentagons.

Figure 6.

The **Icosahedron** is bounded by twenty equal equilateral triangles.

The four last figures, together with the hexahedron delineated on Plate 14, are all the regular polyhedrons. All the faces and all the solid angles of each figure are respectively equal. These solids are called platonic figures.

PLATE XVIII.

THE CYLINDER AND ITS SECTIONS.

1st. If we suppose the right angled parallelogram *A. B. C. D*, fig. 1, to revolve around the side *A. B*, it would describe a solid figure; the sides *A. D* and *B. C* would describe two circles whose diameters would be equal to twice the length of the revolving sides; the side *C. D* would describe a uniform surface connecting the opposite circles together throughout their whole circumference. The solid so described would be a **right cylinder.**

2nd. The line *A. B*, around which the parallelogram revolved, is called the **axis** of the cylinder, and as it connects the centres of the circles forming the ends of the cylinder, it is every where equidistant from its sides.

3rd. If the ends of a cylinder be not at right angles to its axis, it is called an **oblique cylinder.**

4th. If a cylinder be cut by any plane parallel to its axis, the section will be a parallelogram, as *E. F. G. H*, fig. 1.

PLATE XVI.

SOLIDS AND THEIR COVERINGS.

Fig. 1. Is an HEXAGONAL PYRAMID; and fig. 2 its covering.

Fig. 3. A RIGHT CYLINDER, is bounded by two uniform circles, parallel to each other. The line connecting their centres, is called the axis. The sides of the cylinder is one uniform surface, connecting the circumferences of the circle, and everywhere equidistant from its axis.

Problem 44. Fig. 4.

To find the Length of the Parallelogram A. B. C. D, *to form the Side of the Cylinder.*

1st. Draw the ends, and divide one of them into any number of equal parts, say twelve.

2nd. With the space of one of those parts, step off the same number on *A. B*, which will give the breadth of the covering to bend around the circles.

Fig. 5. Is A RIGHT CONE; its base is a circle, its sides sloping equally from the base to its summit. A line drawn from its summit to the centre of the base, is called its *axis*. If the axis and base are not perpendicular to each other, it forms an *oblique*, or *scalene* cone.

Problem 45. Fig. 6.

To draw the Covering.

1st. With a radius equal to the sloping height of the cone, from *E*, describe an indefinite arc, and draw the radius *E. F*.

2nd. Draw the circle of the base, and divide its circumference into any number of equal parts, say twelve.

3rd. With one of those parts in the dividers, step off from *F* the same number of times to *G*, then draw the radius *E. G*, to complete the figure.

Plate 18.

THE CYLINDER AND SECTIONS.

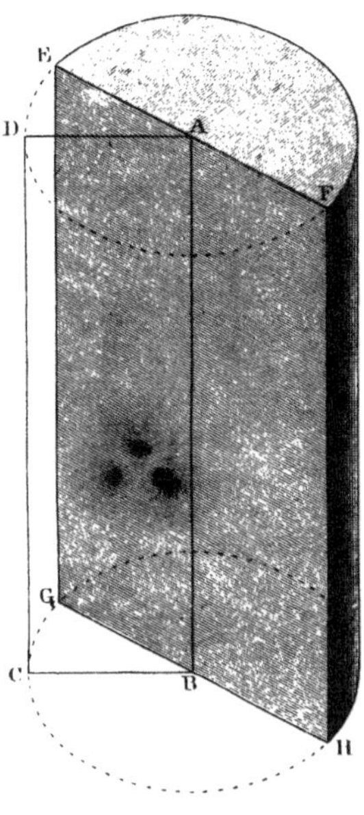

Fig. 1.

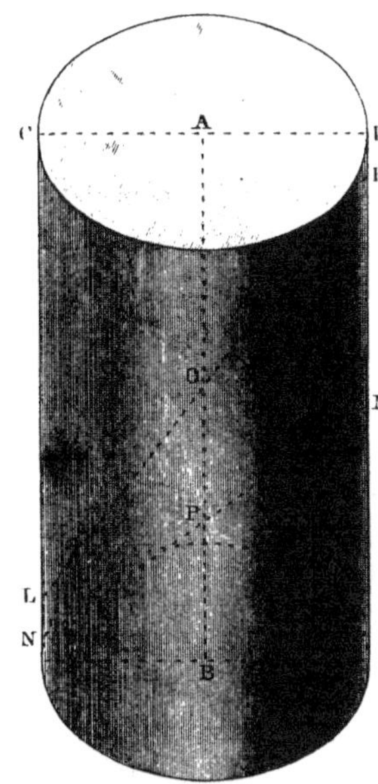

Fig. 2.

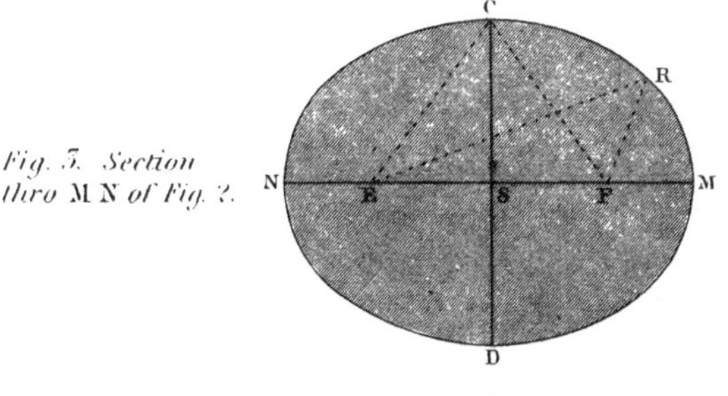

Fig. 3. Section thro M N of Fig. 2.

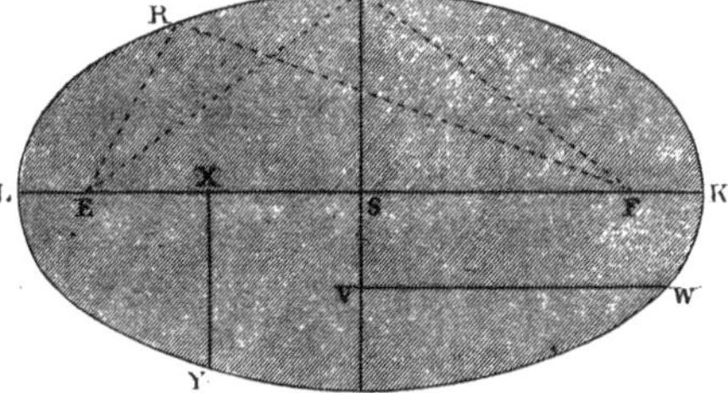

Fig 4. Section thro L K Fig. 2.

Wm. Minifie. Ilman & Sons

5th. If a cylinder be cut by any plane at right angles to its axis, the section will be a circle.

6th. If a cylinder be cut by any plane not at right angles to its axis, passing through its opposite sides, as at *K. L* or *M. N*, fig. 2, the section will be an ELLIPSIS, of which the line of section *K. L* or *M. N* would be the longest diameter, called the TRANSVERSE OR MAJOR DIAMETER, and the diameter of the cylinder *C. D* would be the shortest diameter, called the CONJUGATE or MINOR DIAMETER.

PROBLEM 47. FIG. 3

To describe an Ellipsis from the Cylinder with a string and two pins.

1st. Draw the right lines *N. M* and *C. D* at right angles to each other, cutting each other in *S.*

2nd. Take in your dividers the distance *P. M* or *P. N*, fig. 2, and set it off from *S* to *M* and *N*, fig. 3, which will make *M. N* equal to *M. N*, fig. 2.

3d. From *A*, fig. 2, take *A. D* or *A. C*, and set it off from *S* to *C* and *D*, making *C. D* equal to the diameter of the cylinder.

4th. With a distance equal to *S. M* or *S. N* from the points *D* and *C*, cut the transverse diameter in *E* and *F;* then *E* and *F* are the FOCI for drawing the ellipsis.

NOTE.—*E* is a FOCUS, and *F* is a FOCUS. *E* and *F* are FOCI.

5th. In the foci, stick two pins, then pass a string around them, and tie the ends together at *C.*

6th. Place the point of a pencil at *C*, and keeping the string tight, pass it around and describe the curve.

NOTE.—The sum of all lines drawn from the foci, to any point in the curve, is always constant and equal to the major axis: thus, the length of the lines *E. R*, and *F. R*, added together, is equal to the length of *E. C*, and *F. C*, added together, or to two lines drawn from *E* and *F*, to any other point in the curve.

7th. Fig. 4 is the section of the cylinder, through *L. K*, fig. 2, and is described in the same way as fig. 3. The letters of reference are the same in both diagrams, except that the transverse diameter *L. K*, is made equal to the line of section *L. K*, in fig. 2.

8th. The line *N. M*, fig. 3, or *L. K*, fig. 4, is called the TRANSVERSE, or MAJOR AXIS, (plural AXES,) and the line *C. D*, its CONJUGATE, or MINOR AXIS. They are also called the transverse and conjugate diameters, as above defined. The transverse axis is the longest line that can be drawn in an ellipsis.

9th. Any line passing through the centre *S*, of an ellipsis, and meeting the curve at both extremities, is called a DIAMETER: every diameter divides the ellipsis into two equal parts. The CONJUGATE of any diameter, is a line drawn through the centre, terminated by the curve, parallel to a tangent of the curve at the vertex of the said diameter. The point where the diameter meets the curve, is the *vertex* of that diameter.

10th. An ORDINATE to any diameter, is a line drawn parallel to its conjugate, and terminated by the curve and the said diameter. An ABSCISSA is that portion of a diameter intercepted between its vertex and ordinate. Unless otherwise expressed, ordinates are in general, referred to the axis, and taken as perpendicular to it. Thus, in fig. 4, *X. Y* is the ordinate to, and *L. X* and *K. X*, the abscissæ of the axis *K. L.*—*V. W* is the ordinate to, and *C. V*, and *D. V*, the abscissæ of the axis *C. D*.

PLATE XIX.

THE CONE AND ITS SECTIONS.

DEFINITIONS.

1st. A CONE is a solid, generated by the revolution of a right angled triangle about one of its sides.

2nd. If both legs of the triangle are equal, as *S. N* and *N. O*, fig. 2, it would generate a RIGHT ANGLED CONE; the angle *S* being a right angle.

3rd. If the stationary side of the triangle be longest, as *M. N*, the cone will be ACUTE, and if shortest, as *T. N*, it will be OBTUSE angled.

4th. The BASE of a cone is a circle, from which the sides slope regularly to a point, which is called its VERTEX, APEX, or SUMMIT.

Plate 19.

THE CONE AND ITS SECTIONS.

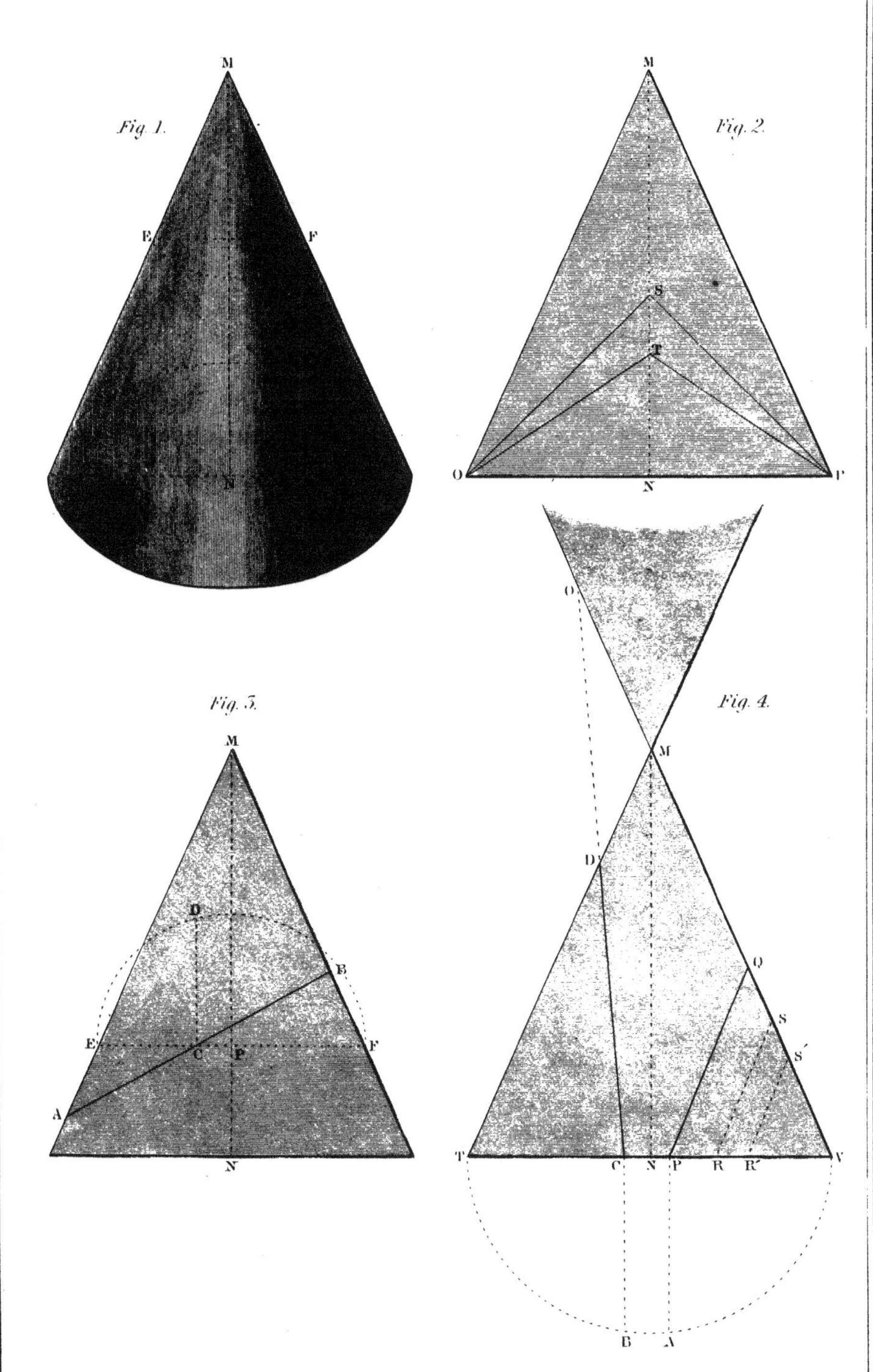

Wm Minifie.

5th. The **AXIS** of a cone, is a line passing from the vertex to the centre of the base, as *M. N*, figs. 1, 2, 3 and 4, and represents the line about which the triangle is supposed to rotate.

6th. A **RIGHT CONE**. When the axis of a cone is perpendicular to its base, it is called a right cone; if they are not perpendicular to each other, it is called an **OBLIQUE CONE**.

7th. If a cone be cut by a plane passing through its vertex to the centre of its base, the section will be a **TRIANGLE**.

8th. If cut by a plane, parallel to its base, the section will be a **CIRCLE**, as at *E. F*, fig. 1.

9th. If the upper part of fig. 1 should be taken away, as at *E. F*, the lower part would be a **TRUNCATED CONE**, or **FRUSTRUM**, the part above *E. F*, would still be a cone; and, if another portion of the top were cut off from it, another truncated cone would be formed: thus a cone may be divided into several truncated cones, and the portion taken from the summit, would still remain a cone. Similar remarks have already been applied to the pyramid.

10th. If a cone be cut by any plane passing through its opposite sides, as at *A. B*, fig. 3, the section will be an *ellipsis*.

11th. If a cone be cut by a plane, parallel with one of its sides, as at *P. Q.*, *R. S*, or *R′. S′*, fig. 4, the section will be a **PARABOLA**.

12th. If a cone be cut by a plane, which, if continued, would meet the opposite cone, as through *C. D*, fig. 4, meeting the opposite cone at *O*, the section will be an **HYPERBOLA**.

PROBLEM 48. FIG. 3.

To describe the Ellipsis from the Cone.

1st. Let fig. 3 represent the elevation of a right cone, and *A. B* the line of section.

2nd. Bisect *A. B* in *C*.

3rd. Through *C*, draw *E. F* perpendicular to the axis *M. N*, cutting the axis in *P*.

4th. With one foot of the dividers in *P*, and a radius equal to *P. E*, or *P. F*, describe the arc *E. D. F*.

5th. From *C*, the centre of the line of section *A. B*, draw *C. D* parallel to the axis, cutting the arc *E. D. F* in *D*.

6th. Then *A. B is the transverse axis,* and *C. D its semiconjugate of an ellipsis,* which may be described with a string, as explained for the section of the cylinder, or by any of the other methods to be hereafter described.

NOTE.—A section of the cylinder, as well as of a cone, passing through its opposite sides, is always an ellipsis. In the cone, the length of both axes vary with every section, but in the cylinder, the conjugate axis is always equal to the diameter of the cylinder, whatever may be the inclination of the line of section.

PROBLEM 49. FIG. 4.

To find the length of the base line for describing the other sections.

1st. With one foot of the dividers in *N,* and a radius equal to *N. T,* or *N. V,* describe a semicircle, equal to half the base of the cone.

2nd. From *C* and *P,* the points where the sections intersect the base, draw *P. A,* and *C. B,* cutting the semicircle in *A* and *B.* Then *A. P* is one-half the base of the *parabola,* and *C. B* is one-half the base of the *hyperbola.* The methods for describing these curves, are shewn in Plates 20 and 21.

PLATE XX.

TO DESCRIBE THE ELLIPSIS AND HYPERBOLA.

PROBLEM 50. FIG. 1.

To find Points in the Curve of an Ellipsis by Intersecting Lines.

Let *A. B,* be the given transverse axis, and *C. D,* the conjugate.

1st. Describe the parallelogram *L. M. N. O,* the boundaries passing through the ends of the axes.

2nd. Divide *A. L,—A. N,—B. M,* and *B. O,* into any number of equal parts, say 4, and number them as in the diagram.

3rd. Divide *A. S,* and *B. S,* also into 4 equal parts, and number them from the ends toward the centre.

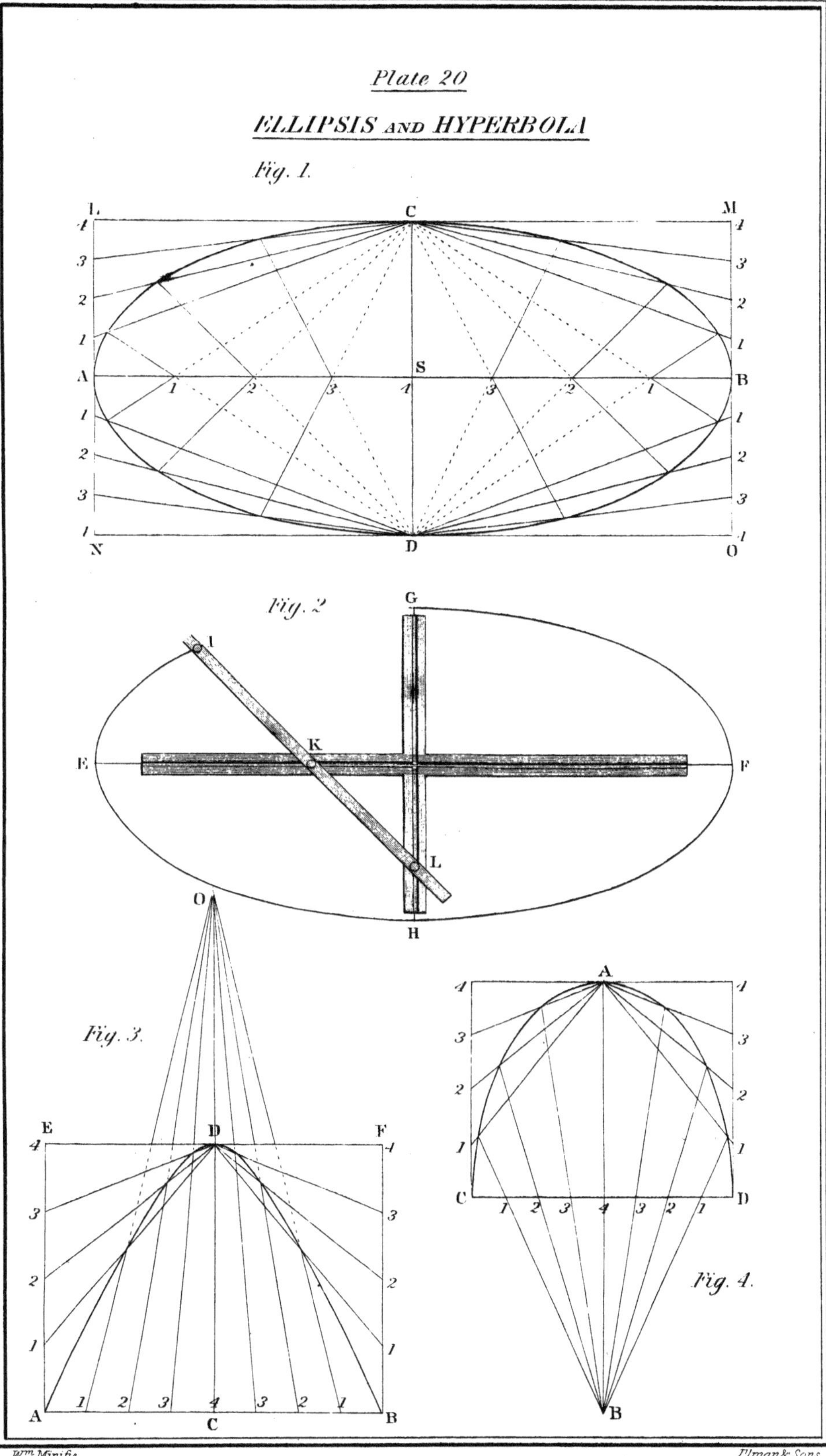
Plate 20
ELLIPSIS AND HYPERBOLA
Fig. 1.
L
C
M
A
S
B
N
D
O
Fig. 2
G
I
K
E
F
L
H
O
Fig. 3.
E
D
F
A
C
B
A
C
D
B
Fig. 4.
Wm Minifie
Ellman & Sons

4th. From the divisions in *A. L* and *B. M*, draw lines to one end of the conjugate axis at *C;* and, from the divisions in *B. O* and *A. N*, draw lines to the other end at *D*.

5th. From *D*, through the points 1, 2, 3, in *A. S*, draw lines to intersect the lines 1, 2, 3 drawn from the divisions on *A. L*, and in like manner through *B. S*, to intersect the lines from *B. M.* These points of intersection are points in the curve.

6th. From *C*, through the divisions 1, 2, 3, on *S. A* and *S. B*, draw lines to intersect the lines 1, 2, 3 drawn from *A. N* and *B. O*, which will give the points for drawing the other half of the curve.

7th. Through the points of intersection, trace the curve.

NOTE.—If required on a small scale, the curve can be drawn by hand; but, if required on a large scale, for practical purposes, it is best to drive sprigs at the points of intersection, and bend a thin flexible strip of pine around them, for the purpose of tracing the curve. Any number of points may be found by dividing the lines into the requisite number of parts.

FIGURE 4.

Is a semi-ellipsis, drawn on the conjugate axis by the same method, in which *A. B* is the transverse, and *C. D* the conjugate axis.

NOTE.—This method will apply to an ellipsis of any length or breadth.

PROBLEM 51. FIG. 2.

To draw an Ellipsis with a Trammel.

The TRAMMEL shewn in the diagram is composed of two pieces of wood halfened together at right angles to each other, with a groove running through the centre of each, the groove being wider at the bottom than at the top. *I. K. L* is another strip of wood with a point at *I*, or with a hole for inserting a pencil at *I*, and two sliding buttons at *K* and *L;* the buttons are generally attached to small morticed blocks sliding over the strip, with wedges or screws for securing them in the proper place; (the pins are only shewn in the diagram,) the buttons attached to the pins are made to slide freely in the grooves.

Mode of Setting the Trammel.

1st. Make the distance *I. K* equal to the semi-conjugate axis, and the distance from *I* to *L* equal to the semi-transverse axis.

2nd. Set the grooved strips to coincide with the axes of the ellipsis, and secure them there.

3rd. Move the point *I* around and it will trace the curve correctly.

NOTE.—This is a very useful instrument, and was formerly used very frequently by carpenters to lay off their work, and also by plasterers to run their mouldings around elliptical arches, &c., the mould occupying the position of the point *I.* It was rare then to find a carpenter's shop without a trammel or to find a good workman who was not skilled in the use of it; but since Grecian architecture with its horizontal lintels has taken the place of the arch, it is seldom a trammel is required, and when required, much more rare to find one to use; but as it is sometimes wanted, and few of our young mechanics know how to apply it, at the risk of being thought tedious, we have been thus minute in its description.

PROBLEM 52. FIG. 3.

To describe the Hyperbola from the Cone.

1st. Draw the line *A. C. B* and make *C. B* and *C. A* each equal to *C. B,* fig. 4, plate xix, then *A. B* will be equal to the base of the hyperbola.

2nd. Perpendicular to *A. B,* draw *A. E* and *B. F,* and make them equal to *C. D,* fig. 4, plate xix.

3rd. Join *E. F,* from *C* erect a perpendicular *C. D. O,* and make *C. O* equal to *C. O,* fig. 4, plate xix.

4th. Divide *A. E* and *B. F* each into any number of equal parts, say 4, and divide *B. C* and *C. A* into the same number, and number them as in the diagram.

5th. From the points of division on *A. E* and *B. F,* draw lines to *D.*

6th. From the points of division in *A. B,* draw lines toward *O,* and the points where they intersect the other lines with the same numbers will be points in the curve. The curve *A. D. B* is the section of the cone through the line *C. D,* fig. 4, plate xix.

PLATE XXI.

PARABOLA AND ITS APPLICATION.

PROBLEM 53. FIG. 1.

To describe the Parabola by Tangents.

1st. Draw *A. P. B*, make *A. P* and *P. B* each equal to *A. P*, fig. 4, plate xix.

2nd. From *P* draw *P. Q. R* perpendicular to *A. B*, and make *P. R* equal to twice the height of *P. Q*, fig. 4, plate xix.

3rd. Draw *A. R* and *B. R*, and divide them each into the same number of equal parts, say eight; number one side from *A* to *R*, and the other side from *R* to *B*.

4th. Join the points 1. 1.—2. 2.—3. 3, &c.; the lines so drawn will be tangents to the curve, which should be traced to touch midway between the points of intersection.

The curve *A. Q. B* is a section of the cone through *P. Q*, fig. 4, plate xix.

PROBLEM 54. FIG. 2.

To describe the Parabola by another method.

Let *A. B* be the width of the base and *P. Q* the height of the curve.

1st. Construct the parallelogram *A. B. C. D.*

2nd. Divide *A. C* and *A. P*—*P. B* and *B. D* respectively into a similar number of equal parts; number them as in the diagram.

3rd. From the points of division in *A. C* and *B. D*, draw lines to *Q*.

4th. From the points of division on *A. B* erect perpendiculars to intersect the other lines; the points of intersection are points in the curve.

Problem 55. Fig. 3.

To describe a Parabola by continued motion, with a Ruler, String and Square.

Let *C. D* be the width of the curve and *H. J* the height.

1st. Bisect *H. D* in *K*, draw *J. K* and *K. E* perpendicular to *J. K*, cutting *J. H* extended in *E*. Then take the distance *H. E* and set it off from *J* to *F*, then *F* is the focus.

2nd. At any convenient distance above *J*, fasten a ruler *A. B*, parallel to the base of the parabola *C. D*.

3rd. Place a square *S*, with one side against the edge of the ruler, *A. B*, the edge *O. N* of the square to coincide with the line *E. J*.

4th. Tie one end of a string to a pin stuck in the focus at *F*, place your pencil at *J*, pass the string around it, and bring it down to *N*, the end of the square, and fasten it there.

5th. With the pencil at *J*, against the side of the square, and the string kept tight, slide the square along the edge of the ruler towards *A;* the pencil being kept against the edge of the square, with the string stretched, will describe one half of the parabola, *J. C*.

6th. Turn the square over, and draw the other half in the same manner.

Definitions.

1st. The FOCUS of a parabola is the point *F*, about which the string revolves. The edge of the ruler *A. B*, is the *directrix* of the parabola.

2nd. The AXIS is the line *J. H*, passing through the focus, and perpendicular to the base *C. D*.

3rd. The principal VERTEX, is the point *J*, where the top of the axis meets the curve.

4th. The PARAMETER, is a line passing through the focus, parallel to the base, terminated at each end by the curve.

5th. Any line, parallel to the axis, and terminating in the curve, is called a DIAMETER, and the point where it meets the curve, is called the *vertex* of that diameter.

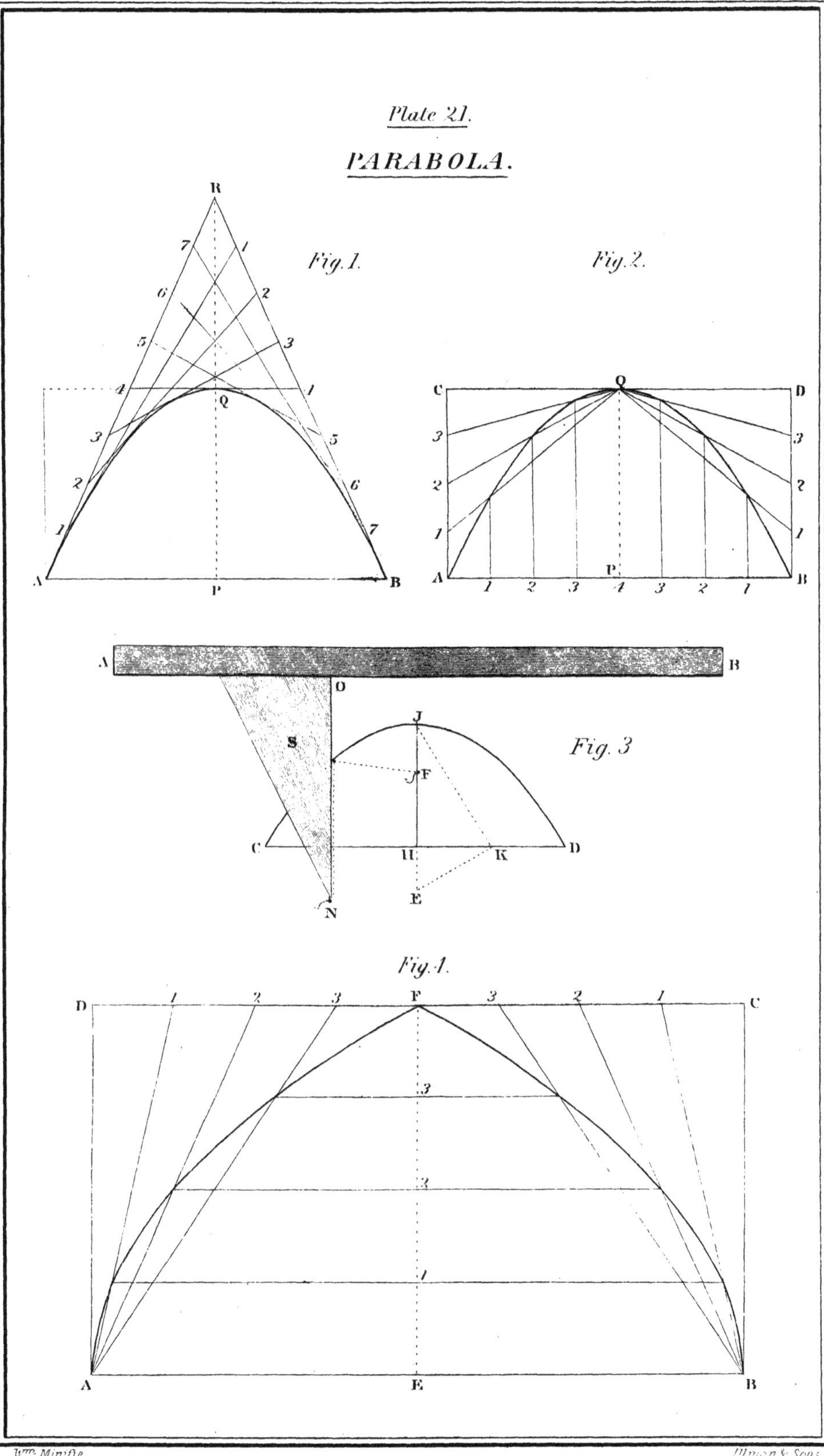
Plate 21.
PARABOLA.
Fig. 1.
Fig. 2.
Fig. 3
Fig. 1.
Wm Minifie.

Problem 56. Fig. 4.

To apply the Parabola to the construction of Gothic Arches.

1st. Draw *A. B,* and make it equal to the width of the arch at the base.

2nd. Bisect *A. B* in *E,* draw *E. F* perpendicular to *A. B,* and make *E. F* equal to the height of the arch.

3rd. Construct the parallelogram *A. B. C. D.*

4th. Divide *E. F* into any number of equal parts, and *D. F* and *F. C* each into a similar number, and number them as in the diagram.

5th. From the divisions on *F. D,* draw lines to *A,* and from the divisions on *F. C,* draw lines to *B.*

6th. Through the divisions on *E. F,* draw lines parallel to the base, to intersect the other lines drawn from the same numbers on *D. C.* The points of intersection are points in the curve through which it may be traced.

Note.—If we suppose this diagram to be cut through the line *E. F,* and turned around until *E. A* and *E. B* coincide, it will form a parabola, drawn by the same method as fig. 2; and, if we were to cut fig. 2 by the line *P. Q,* and turn it around until *P. A* and *P. B* coincide, it would form a gothic arch, described by the same method as fig. 4; and, if the proportions of the two figures were the same, the curves would exactly coincide.

PLATE XXII.

Problem 57.

Given the position of three points in the circumference of a Cylinder, and their respective heights from the base, to find the section of the segment of the Cylinder through these three points.

1st. Let *A. B. C* be three points in the circumference of the base of the cylinder, immediately under the three given points, and *A′. D′,—C′. F′,* and *B′.—E′,*—the height of the given points, respectively, above the base.

2nd. Join the points *A* and *B,* and draw *A. D,—C. F,* and *B. E,* perpendicular to *A. B.*

3rd. Make *A. D* equal to *A′. D′*, the height of the given point above the base at *A*,—make *B. E* equal to *B′. E′*, and *C. F* equal to *C′. F′*.

4th. Produce *B. A* and *E. D*, to meet each other in *H.*

5th. Draw *C. G* parallel to *B. H*, and *F. G* parallel to *E. H.*

6th. Join *G. H.*

7th. In *G. H*, take any point as *G*, and draw *G. K* perpendicular to *G. C*, cutting *B. H* in *K.*

8th. From the point *K*, draw *K. I* perpendicular to *E. H*, cutting *E. H* in *L.*

9th. From *H*, with the radius *H. G*, describe the arc *G. I*, cutting *K. L* in *I*, and join *H. I.*

10th. Divide the circumference of the segment *A. C. B* into any number of equal parts, and from the points of division, draw lines to *A. B*, parallel to *G. H*, cutting *A. B* in 1, 2, 3, &c.

11th. From the points 1, 2, 3, &c. in *A B*, draw lines parallel to *B. E*, cutting the line *D. E* in 1, 2, 3, &c.

12th. From the points 1, 2, 3, &c. in *D. E*, draw lines parallel to *H. I*, and make 1. 0 equal to 1. 1 on the base of the cylinder, make 2. 0 equal to 2. 2, 3. 0 equal to 3. 3, &c.

13th. Through the points 0, 0, 0, &c., trace the curve, which will be the contour of the section required.

NOTE.—It will be perceived that the line 2. 2 intersects *A. B* in *A*, and that the line *A. D* obviates the necessity of drawing the perpendicular from 2, as required by the 11th step in the problem.

PLATE XXIII.

PROBLEM 58. FIG 1.

To draw the Boards for covering Circular Domes.

To lay the boards vertically. Let *A. D. C* be half the plan of the dome; let *D. C* represent one of the ribs, and *E. F* the width of one of the boards.

1st. Draw *D. O*, and continue the line indefinitely toward *H.*

2nd. Divide the rib *D. C* into any number of equal parts, and

Plate 22

TO FIND THE SECTION OF THE SEGMENT OF A CYLINDER THROUGH THREE GIVEN POINTS.

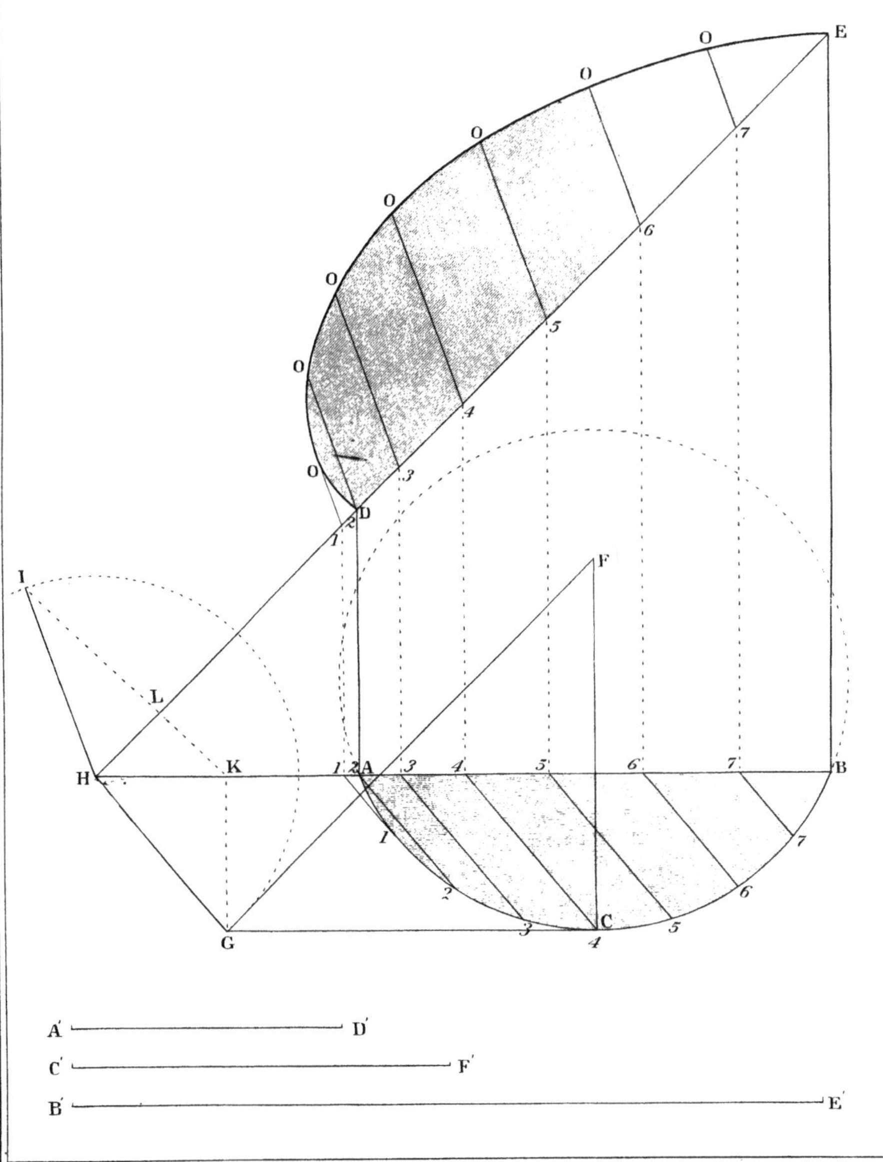

Wm. Minifie

Illman & Sons

Plate 23

TO DRAW THE BOARDS FOR COVERING HEMISPHERICAL DOMES.

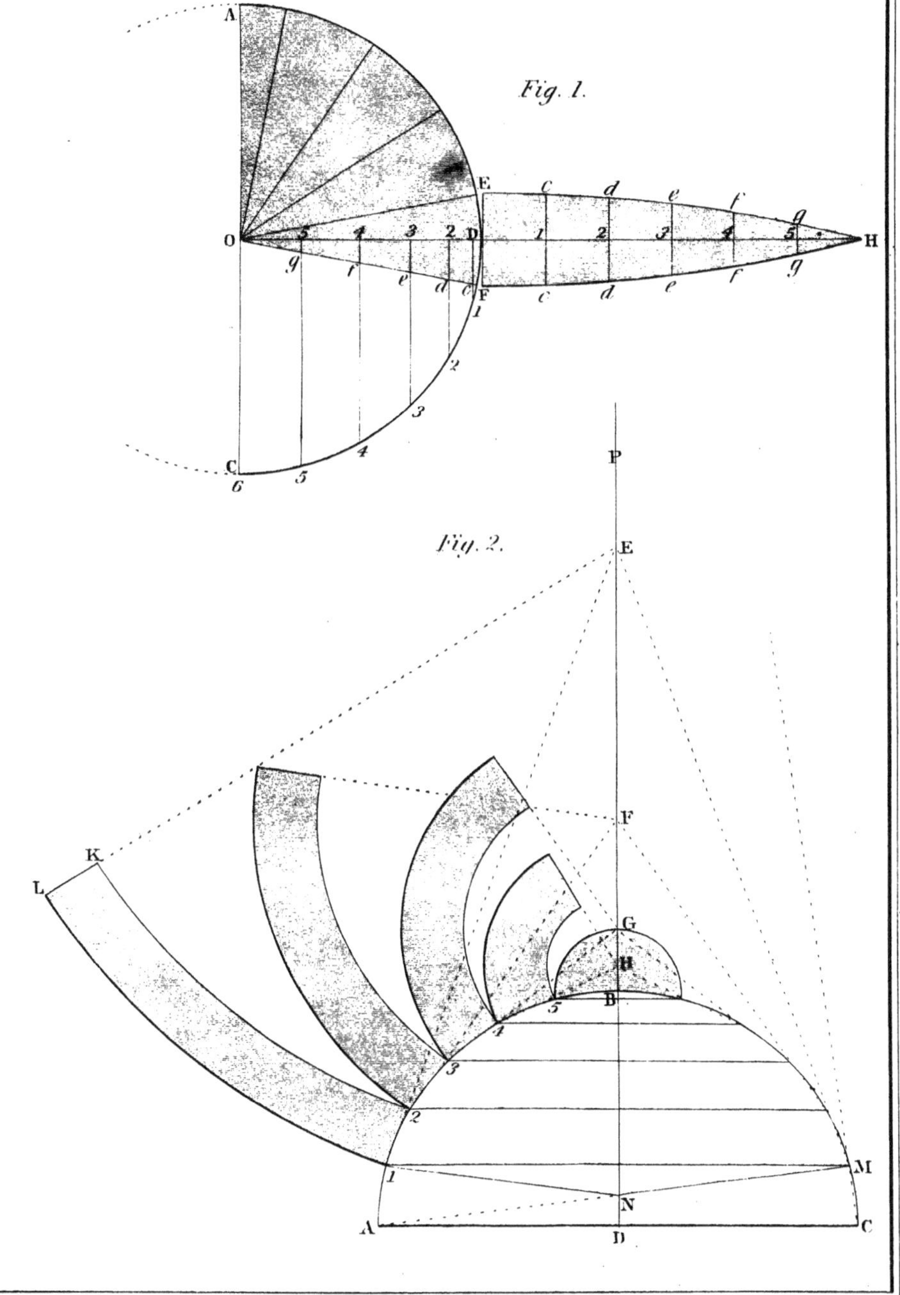

Wm Minifie

Illman & Sons

from the points of division, draw lines parallel to *A. C,* meeting *D. O* in 1, 2, 3, &c.

3rd. With an opening of the dividers equal to one of the divisions on *D. C,* step off from *D* toward *H,* the same number of parts as *D. C* is divided into, making the right line *D. H,* nearly equal to the curve *D. C.*

4th. Join *E. O* and *F. O.*

5th. Make 1. *c*—2. *d*—3. *e*—4. *f* and 5 *g,* on each side of *D. H,* equal to 1. *c*—2. *d*—3. *e,* &c. on *D. O.*

6th. Through the points *c. d. e. f. g,* trace the curve, which will be an arc of a circle; and if a series of boards made in the same manner, be laid on the dome, the edges will coincide.

NOTE.—In practice, where much accuracy is required, the rib should be divided into at least twelve parts.

PROBLEM 59. FIG. 2.

To lay the boards Horizontally.

Let *A. B. C* be the vertical section of a dome through its axis.

1st. Bisect *A. C* in *D,* and draw *D. P* perpendicular to *A. C.*

2nd. Divide the arc *A. B* into such a number of equal parts, that each division may be less than the breadth of a board. (If we suppose the boards to be used to be of a given length, each division should be made so that the curves struck on the hollow side should touch the ends, and the curves on the convex side should touch the centre.)

3rd. From the points of division, draw lines parallel to *A. C* to meet the opposite side of the section. Then if we suppose the curves intercepted by these lines to be straight lines, (and the difference will be small,) each space would be the frustrum of a cone, whose vertex would be in the line *D. P,* and the vertex of each frustrum would be the centre from which to describe the curvature of the edges of the board to fit it.

4th. From 1 draw a line through the point 2, to meet the line *D P* in *E;* then from *E,* with a radius equal to *E.* 1, describe the curve 1. *L,* which will give the lower edge of the board, and with a radius equal to *E.* 2, describe the arc 2. *K,* which will give the upper edge. The line *L. K* drawn to *E,* will give the cut for the end of a board which will fit the end of any other board cut to the same angle.

5th. From 2 draw a line through 3, meeting *D. P* in *F.* From 3, draw a line through 4, meeting *D. P* in *G,* and proceed for each board, as in paragraph 4.

6th. If from *C* we draw a line through *M,* and continue it upward, it would require to be drawn a very great distance before it would meet *D. P;* the centre would consequently be inconveniently distant.

For the bottom board, proceed as follows:

1st. Join *A. M,* cutting *D. P* in *N,* and join *N.* 1.

2nd. Describe a curve, by the methods in Problems 34 or 35, Plate 11, through 1. *N. M,* which will give the centre of the board,from which the width on either side may be traced.

PLATE XXIV.

CONSTRUCTION OF ARCHES.

Arches in architecture are composed of a number of stones arranged symmetrically over an opening intended for a door, window, &c., for the purpose of supporting a superincumbent weight. The depth of the stones are made to vary to suit each particular case, being made deeper in proportion as the width of an opening becomes larger, or as the load to be supported is increased; the size of the stones also depends much on the quality of the material of which they are composed: if formed of soft sandstone they will require to be much deeper than if formed of granite or some other hard strong stone.

DEFINITIONS. FIG. 2.

1st. The SPAN of an arch is the distance between the points of support, which is generally the width of the opening to be covered, as *A. B.* These points are called the springing points; the mass against which the arch rests is called the ABUTMENT.

3rd. The RISE, HEIGHT or VERSED SINE of an arch, is the distance from *C* to *D.*

2nd. The SPRINGING LINE of an arch is the line *A. B,* being a horizontal line drawn across the tops of the support where the arch commences.

4th. The **crown** of an arch is the highest point, as *D.*

5th. **Voussoirs** is the name given to the stones forming the arch.

6th. The **keystone** is the centre or uppermost voussoir D, so called, because it is the last stone set, and wedges or keys the whole together. Keystones are frequently allowed to project from the face of the wall, and in some buildings are very elaborately sculptured.

7th. The **intrados** or **soffit** of an arch is the under side of the voussoirs forming the curve.

8th. The **extrados** or **back** is the upper side of the voussoirs.

9th. The **thrust** of an arch is the tendency which all arches have to descend in the middle, and to overturn or *thrust* asunder the points of support.

Note.—The amount of the thrust of an arch depends on the proportions between the rise and the span, that is to say, the *span* and *weight* to be supported being *definite;* the thrust will be diminished in proportion as the rise of the arch is increased, and the thrust will be increased in proportion as the crown of the arch is lowered.

10th. The **joints** of an arch are the lines formed by the adjoining faces of the voussoirs; these should generally radiate to some definite point, and each should be perpendicular to a tangent to the curve at each joint. In all curves composed of arcs of circles, a tangent to the curve at any point would be perpendicular to a radius drawn from the centre of the circle through that point, consequently the joints in all such arches should radiate to the centre of the circle of which the curve forms a part.

11th. The **bed** of an arch is the top of the abutment; the shape of the bed depends on the quality of the curve, and will be explained in the diagrams.

12th. A **rampant arch** is one in which the springing points are not in the same level.

13th. A **straight arch**, or as it is more properly called, a **plat band**, is formed of a row of wedge-shaped stones of equal depth placed in a horizontal line, the upper ends of the stones being broader than the lower, prevents them from falling into the void below.

14th. Arches are named from the shape of the curve of the under side, and are either *simple* or *complex.* I would define simple curves to be those that are struck from one centre, as any segment of a circle, or by continued motion, as the *ellipsis, parabola, hyperbola, cycloid* and *epicycloid;* and **complex arches** to be those described from two or more fixed centres, as many of the Gothic or pointed arches. The simple curves have all been described in our problems of practical Geometry; we shall however repeat some of them for the purpose of showing the method of drawing the joints.

PROBLEM 60. FIG. 1.

To describe a Segment or Scheme Arch, and to draw the Joints.

1st. Let *E* and *F* be the abutments, and *O* the centre for describing the curve.

2nd. With one foot of the dividers in *O*, and the distance *O. F*, describe the line of the intrados.

3rd. Set off the depth of the voussoirs, and with the dividers at *O*, describe the line of the extrados.

4th. From *E* and *F* draw lines radiating to *O*, which gives the line of the *beds* of the arch. This line is often called by masons a *skew-back*.

5th. Divide the intrados or extrados, into as many parts as you design to have stones in the arch, and radiate all the lines to *O*, which will give the proper direction of the *joints*.

6th. If the point *O* should be at too great a distance to strike the curve conveniently, it may be struck by Problem 34 or 35, Plate 11; and the joints may be found as follows: Let it be desired to draw a joint at 2, on the line of the extrados; from 2 set off any distance on either side, as at 1 and 3; and from 1 and 3, with any radius, draw two arcs intersecting each other at 4—then from 4 through 2 draw the joint which will be perpendicular to a tangent, touching the curve at 2. This process must be repeated for each joint. The *keystone* projects a little above and below the lines of the arch.

PROB. 61. FIG. 2.—THE SEMICIRCULAR ARCH.

This requires but little explanation. *A. B* is the span and *C* the centre, from which the curves are struck, and to which the lines of all the joints radiate. The centre *C* being in the springing line of the arch the beds are horizontal.

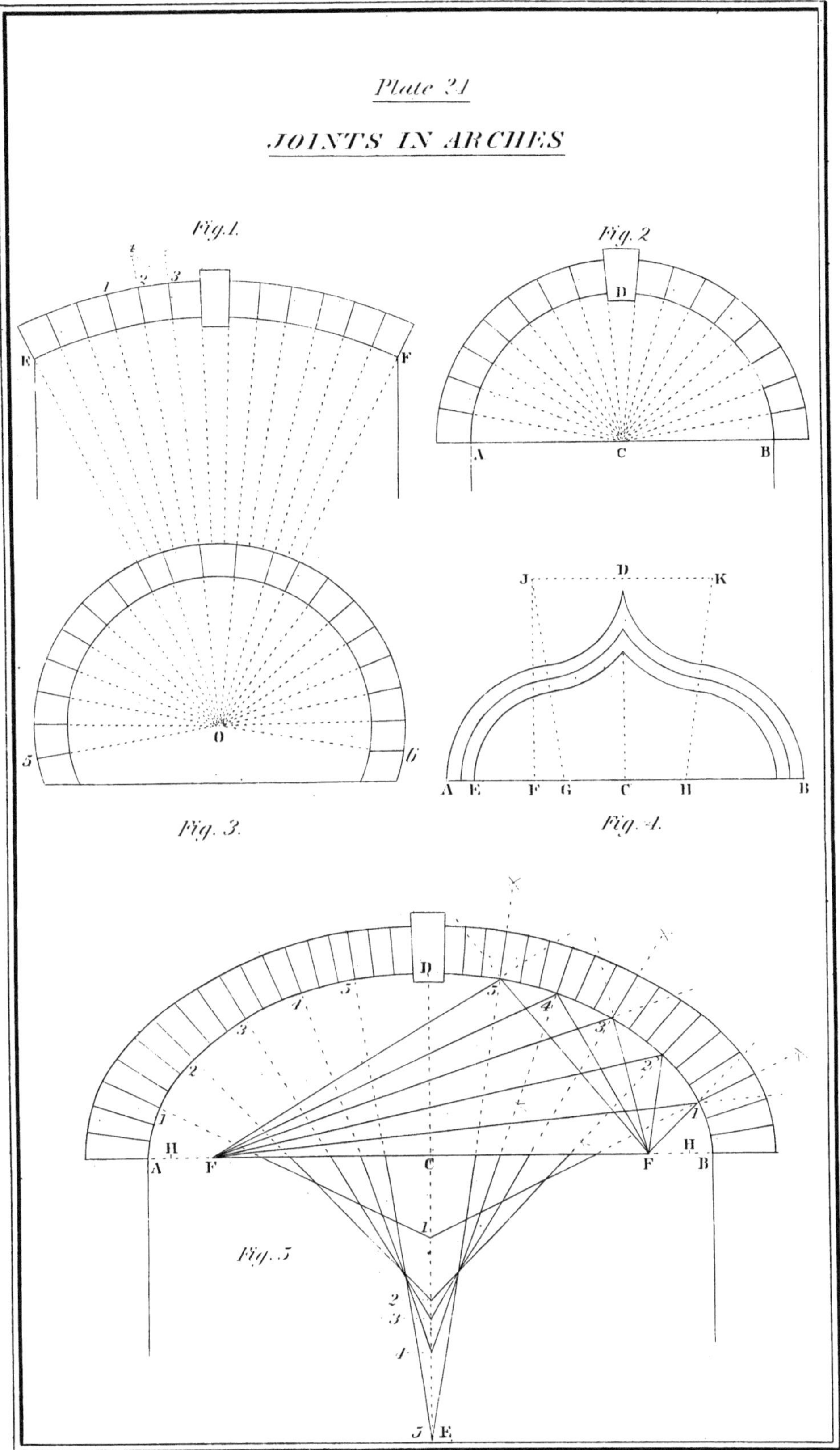
Plate 21
JOINTS IN ARCHES
Fig. 1.
1 2 3 4
E F
Fig. 2
D
A C B
O
5 6
Fig. 3.
J D K
A E F G C H B
Fig. 4.
D
1 2 3 4 5
A H F C F H B
1 2 3 4 5
Fig. 5
5 E

PROB. 62. FIG. 3.—THE HORSE SHOE ARCH.

Is an arc of a circle greater than a semicircle, the centre *O* being above the springing line.

This arch is also called the SARACENIC or MORESCO arch, because of its frequent use in these styles of architecture. The joints radiate to the centre, as in fig. 2. The joint at 5, below the horizontal line, also radiates to *O*. This may do very well for a mere ornamental arch, that has no weight to sustain; but if, as in the diagram, the first stone rests on a horizontal bed, it would be larger on the inside than on the outside, and would be liable to be forced out of its position by a slight pressure, much more so than if the joint were made horizontal, as at 6. These remarks will also apply to fig. 4, Plate 25.

PROBLEM 63. FIG. 4.

To describe an Ogee Arch, or an Arch of Contrary Flexure.

NOTE.—This arch is seldom used over a large opening, but occurs frequently in *canopies* and *tracery* in Gothic architecture, the rib of the arch being moulded.

1st. Let *A. B* be the outside width of the arch, and *C. D* the height, and let *A. E* be the breadth of the rib.

2nd. Bisect *A. B* in *C*, and erect the perpendicular *C. D;* bisect *A. C* in *F*, and draw *F. J* parallel to *C. D*.

3rd. Through *D* draw *J. K* parallel to *A. B*, and make *D. K* equal to *D. J*.

4th. From *F* set off *F. G*, equal to *A. E* the breadth of the rib, and make *C. H* equal to *C. G*.

5th. Join *G. J* and *H. K;* then *G* and *H* will be the centres for drawing the lower portion of the arch, and *J* and *K* will be the centres for describing the upper portion, and the contrary curves will meet in the lines *G. J* and *H. K*.

PROBLEM 64. FIG. 5.

To draw the Joints in an Elliptic Arch.

Let *A. B* be the span of the arch, *C. D* the rise, and *F. F* the foci, from which the line of the intrados may be described.

The voussoirs near the spring of the arch are increased in depth, as they have to bear more strain than those nearer the crown; the outer curve is also an ellipsis, of which *H* and *H* are the foci.

To draw a joint in any part of the curve, say at 5.

1st. From *F* and *F* the foci, draw lines cutting each other in the given point 5, and continue them out indefinitely.

2nd. Bisect the angle 5 by Problem 11, Page 18, the line of bisection will be the line of the joint.

The joints are found at the points 1 and 3 in the same manner.

3d. If we bisect the internal angle, as for the joints 2 and 4, the result will be the same.

4th. To draw the corresponding joints on the opposite side of the arch, proceed as follows:

5th. Prolong the line *C. D* indefinitely toward *E,* and prolong the lines of bisection 1, 2, 3, 4 and 5, to intersect *C. E* in 1, 2, 3, &c., and from those points draw the corresponding joints between *A* and *D.*

PLATE XXV.

TO DESCRIBE GOTHIC ARCHES AND TO DRAW THE JOINTS.

The most simple form of Pointed or Gothic arches are those composed of two arcs of circles, whose centres are in the springing line.

Figure 1.—The Lancet Arch.

When the length of the span *A. B* is much less than the length of the chord *A. C,* as in the diagram, the centres for striking the curves will be some distance beyond the base, as shewn by the rods; the joints all radiate to the opposite centres.

Fig. 2.—The Equilateral Arch.

When the span *D. E,* and the chords *D. F* and *E. F* form an equilateral triangle, the arch is said to be equilateral, and the

Plate 25

POINTED ARCHES

Fig. 1.

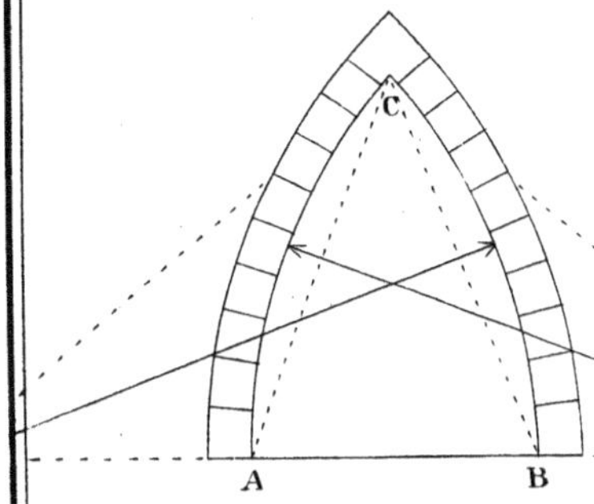

C
A B

Fig. 2

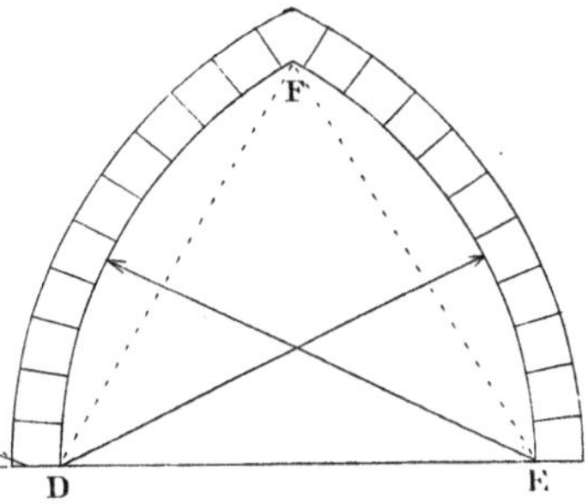

F
D E

Fig. 3

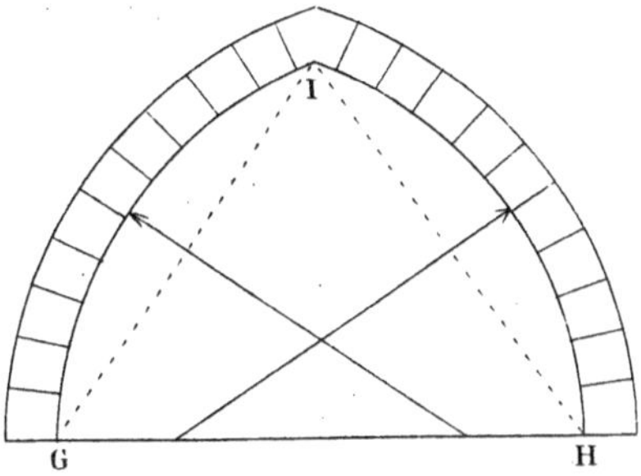

I
G H

Fig. 4.

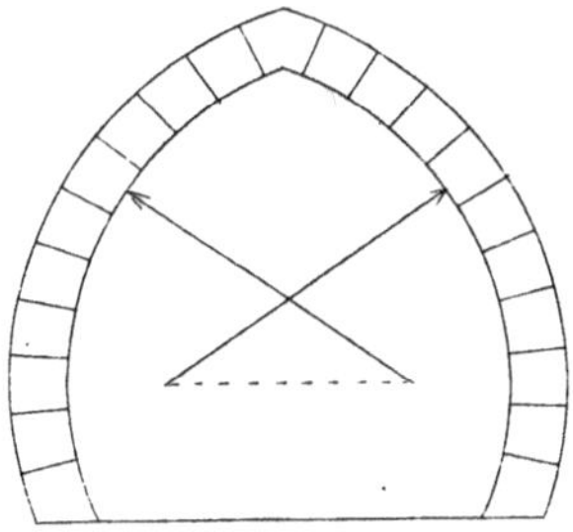

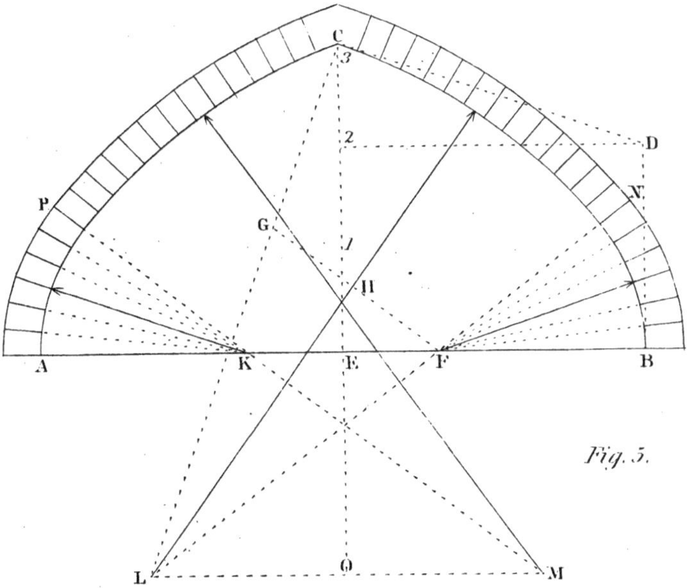

C
3
2 D
P N
G 1
H
A K E F B
L O M

Fig. 5.

centres are the points *D* and *E* in the base of the arch, to which all the joints radiate.

Fig. 3.—The Depressed Arch

Has its centres within the base of the arch, the chords being shorter than the span; the joints radiate to the centres respectively.

Note.—There are no definite proportions for Gothic arches, except for the equilateral; they vary from the most acute to those whose centres nearly touch, and which deviate but little from a semicircle.

Fig. 4.—The Pointed Horseshoe Arch.

This diagram requires no explanation; the centres are above the springing line. See fig. 3, plate xxiv, page 57.

Figure 5.

To describe the Four Centred Pointed Arch.

1st. Let *A. B* be the springing line, and *E. C* the height of the arch.

2nd. Draw *B. D* parallel to *E. C*, and make it equal to two-thirds of the height of *E. C.*

3rd. Join *D. C*, and from *C* draw *C. L* perpendicular to *C. D.*

4th. Make *C. G* and *B. F* both equal to *B. D.*

5th. Join *G. F*, and bisect it in *H*, then through *H* draw *H. L* perpendicular to *G. F* meeting *C. L* in *L.*

6th. Join *L. F*, and continue the line to *N.* Then *L* and *F* are the centres for describing one-half of the arch, and the curves will meet in the line *L. F. N.*

7th. Draw *L. M* parallel to *A. B*, make *O. M* equal to *O. L*, and *E. K* equal to *E. F.* Then *K* and *M* are the centres for completing the arch, and the curves will meet in the line *M. K. P.*

8th. The joints from *P* to *C* will radiate to *M;* from *C* to *N* they will radiate to *L;* from *N* to *B* they will radiate to *F*, and from *P* to *A* they will radiate to *K.*

Note 1.—As the joint at *P* radiates to both the centres *K* and *M*, and the joint at *N* radiates both to *F* and *L*, the change of direction of the lower joints is easy and pleasing to the eye, so much so that we should be unconscious of the change, if the constructive lines were removed.

NOTE 2.—When the centres for striking the two centred arch are in the springing line, as in diagrams 1, 2 and 3, the vertical side of the opening joins the curve, without forming an unpleasant angle, as it would do if the vertical lines were continued up above the line of the centres; it is true that examples of this character may be cited in Gothic buildings, but its ungraceful appearance should lead us to avoid it.

PLATES XXVI AND XXVII.

DESIGN FOR A COTTAGE.

Fig. 1. Is the elevation of the south-east front.

Fig. 2. Plan of the ground floor.

Fig. 3. Section through the line *E. F* on the plan fig. 2, the front part of the house supposed to be taken away.

Fig. 4. Plan of the chamber floor.

This simple design is given for the purpose of shewing the method of drawing the *plans*, *section*, *elevation* and *details* of a building; it is not offered as a "model cottage," although it would make a very comfortable residence for a small family.

The PLAN of a building is a horizontal section; if we suppose the house cut off just above the sills of the windows of the second floor and the upper portion taken away, it would expose to view the whole interior arrangement, shewing the thickness of the walls, the situation and thickness of the partitions and the position of doors, windows, &c.; all these interior arrangements are intended to be represented by fig. 4.

If we perform the same operation above the sills of the first floor windows, the arrangements of that floor, including the stairs and piazzas, would appear as in fig. 2.

A SECTION of a building is a *vertical plan* in which the thicknesses of the walls, sections of the fire-places and flues, sizes and direction of the timbers for the floors and roof, depth of the foundations and heights of the stories are shewn, all drawn to a uniform scale.

If the front of the building is supposed to be removed, as in fig. 3, the whole of the inside of the back wall will be seen in elevation, shewing the size and finish of the *doors* and *windows*, the height of the *washboards*, and the *stucco cornice* in the parlor. In looking through the door at *K*, the first flight of *stairs* in the back building is seen in elevation.

If we suppose the spectator to be looking in the opposite direction, the back part of the house removed, he would see the inside of the front windows &c. instead of the back.

An ELEVATION of a building is a drawing of the front, side or back, in which every part is laid down to a scale, and from which the size of every object may be measured.

A PERSPECTIVE VIEW of a building, is a drawing representing it as it would appear to a spectator from some definite point of view, and in which, all objects are diminished as they recede from the eye.

The PLANS, SECTIONS and ELEVATIONS, give the true size and arrangements of the building drawn to a scale, and shew the whole construction.

The PERSPECTIVE VIEW should shew the building complete, in connection with the surrounding objects, which would enable the proprietor to judge of the *effect* of his intended improvement.

The whole constitutes the DESIGN, which for a country house cannot be considered complete without a perspective view.

To make a design for a dwelling house, or other building, it is necessary before we commence the drawing, that we should know the site on which it is to be erected, and the amount of accommodation required.

In choosing a site for a country residence many subjects should be taken into consideration; for example, it should be easy of access, have a good supply of pure water, be on elevated ground to allow the rain and other water to flow freely from it, but not so high as to be exposed to the full blasts of the winter storms; it should have a good prospect of the surrounding country, and above all, it should be in a salubrious locality, free from the malaria arising from the vicinity of low or marshy grounds, with free scope to allow the house to front toward the most eligible point of the compass.

The ASPECT of a country house is of much importance; for if the site commands an extensive view, or pleasant prospect in any direction, the windows of the sitting and principal sleeping rooms, should front in that direction: provided it does not also face the point from which blow the prevailing storms of the climate, this should be particularly considered in choosing the site. Rooms to be cheerful and pleasant, should front south of due east or west; at the same time it is desirable that the view of disagreeable or unsightly objects should be excluded, and as many as possible of the agreeable and beautiful objects of the neighborhood brought into view. The design before us, is made to front the south-east, all the openings except two are excluded from the north easterly storms, which are the most disagreeable in the Atlantic States; the sun at noon would be opposite the angle *A*, and would shine equally on the front and side, consequently the front would have the sun until the middle of the afternoon, and the side of the front house and front of the back building would have the evening sun, rendering the whole dry and pleasant.

The end of the back building, containing the kitchen and stairs, is placed against the middle of the back wall of the front building, to allow the back windows in the parlor, &c., to be placed in the middle of each room. These windows may be closed in stormy weather with substantial shutters; but in warm weather they will add much to the coolness of the rooms, by allowing a thorough ventilation.

The broad projecting cornice of the house, and the continuous piazza, are the most important features in the elevation; besides the advantage of keeping the walls dry, and throwing the rain-water away from the foundation, they give an air of comfort, which would be entirely wanting without them; for if we were to take away the piazza, and reduce the eave cornice to a slight projection, the appearance would be bald and meagre in the extreme.

The projection of the piazza is increased on the front and rear, to give more room to the entrances.

The front building is 36 feet wide from *A* to *B*, fig. 2, and 20 feet deep from *A* to *D*. The back building is 16 feet wide, by 20 feet deep. The scale at the bottom of each plate must be used to get the sizes of all the minor parts. The height of the first story is 10 feet in the clear, and of the second story 8′ 6″; these heights are laid off on a rod *R*, to the right of fig. 1; so are also the heights of the windows, which shews at a glance, their position with regard to the floors and ceilings. This method should always be resorted to in drawing an elevation, as it will the better enable the draughtsman to make room for the interior finish of the windows and for the cornice of the room.

In laying down a plan, the whole of the outer walls should be first drawn, and in setting off openings and party walls, the measurements should be taken from both corners, to prove that you are correct. For example, in setting off the front door, take the width 5. 0 from the whole width of the front, which will leave 31. 0; then lay off 15′. 6″ from *A*, and also from *B*, then if the width of 5. 0 is left between the points so measured, you are sure the front door is laid off correctly; as the windows *C* and *H* are midway between the front door and the corner of the building, the same plan should be followed, and as a general rule that will save trouble by preventing errors, *you should never depend on the measurements from one end or corner, if you have the means of proving them by measuring from the opposite end also.*

The winding steps in the stairs may be dispensed with by adding 3 steps to the bottom flight bringing it out to the kitchen door, and by adding 1 step to the top flight; or a still better arrangement might be made by adding 3 steps to the bottom flight, and retaining two of the winders: this would give 17 risers instead of 16, the present number, which would reduce the height of each to 7 3-4 inches.

To ascertain the number of steps required to a story, proceed as follows: Add to the clear height of the story the breadth of the joists and floor, which will give the full height from the top of one floor to the top of the next. In constructing the stairs this height is laid off on a rod, and then divided into the requisite number of risers; but in drawing the plan, as in the case before us, set down the height in feet, inches and parts, and divide by the height you propose for your rise: this will give you the number of risers. If there is any remainder, it may be divided and added to your proposed rise, or another step may be added, and the height of the rise reduced; or the height of the story may be divided by the number of risers, which will give the exact height of the riser in inches and parts. For example:

The clear height of the story in the design is 10′. 0.″ } =11′. 0″
The breadth of the joist and thickness of the floor 1. 0. }

this multiplied by 12 would give 132 inches, and 132 inches divided by 16, the number of risers on fig. 1, will give 8 1-4 inches; or divided by 17 would give 7 3-4 inches and a fraction. As the floor of the upper story forms one step, there will be always one tread less than there are risers. The vertical front of each step is called the *rise* or *riser*, and the horizontal part is called the *tread* or *step*. When the eaves of the house are continued around the building in the same horizontal line as in this design, the roof is said to be *hipped,* and the rafter running from the corner of the roof diagonally to the ridge is called the *hip rafter.*

REFERENCES TO THE DRAWINGS.

Similar letters in the plans and sections refer to the same parts: thus *T* the fire-place of the parlor in *fig.* 2, is shewn in section at *T, fig.* 3, and *M* the plan of the back parlor window in fig. 2, is shewn in elevation at *M,* fig. 3.

A. B, fig. 2, is the plan, and *A. B,* fig. 1, the elevation of the front wall.

E. F, fig. 2, the line of the section.

G, fig. 2, the front door.

K, fig. 2, the plan, and *K,* fig. 3, the elevation of the door leading to the back building.

L, fig. 2, the plan, and *L,* fig. 3, the elevation of the first flight of stairs.

M and *N,* fig. 2, the plans, and *M* and *N,* fig. 3, elevation of the back first floor windows.

O and *P,* fig. 4, the plans, and *O* and *P,* fig. 3, elevation of chamber windows.

Q, fig. 2, the plan, and *Q,* fig. 3, section of the parlor side window.

R, fig. 4, the plan, and *R,* fig. 3, section of chamber side window.

S, fig. 4, the plan, and *S,* fig. 3, elevation of railing on the landing.

T, fig. 2, the plan, and *T,* fig. 3, section of parlor fire-place.

U, fig. 2, the plan, and *U,* fig. 3, section of breakfast room fire-place.

V and *W,* fig. 4, the plans, and *V* and *W,* fig. 3, sections of chamber fire-place.

X and *Y,* fig. 2, the plans, and *X* and *Y,* fig. 3, elevations of side posts on piazza.

Z. Z. Z, fig. 4, plans of closets.

a. a. a., fig. 4, flues from fire-places of ground floor.

b. b, fig. 3, section of eave cornice.

c. c, fig. 3, rafters of building.

d. d, fig. 3, rafters of piazza.

e. e. e. e. e. e. e. e. e, joists of the different stories; the ends of the short joists framed around the fire-places and flues are shewn in dark sections; the projection around the outside walls of fig. 4, shews the roof of the piazza.

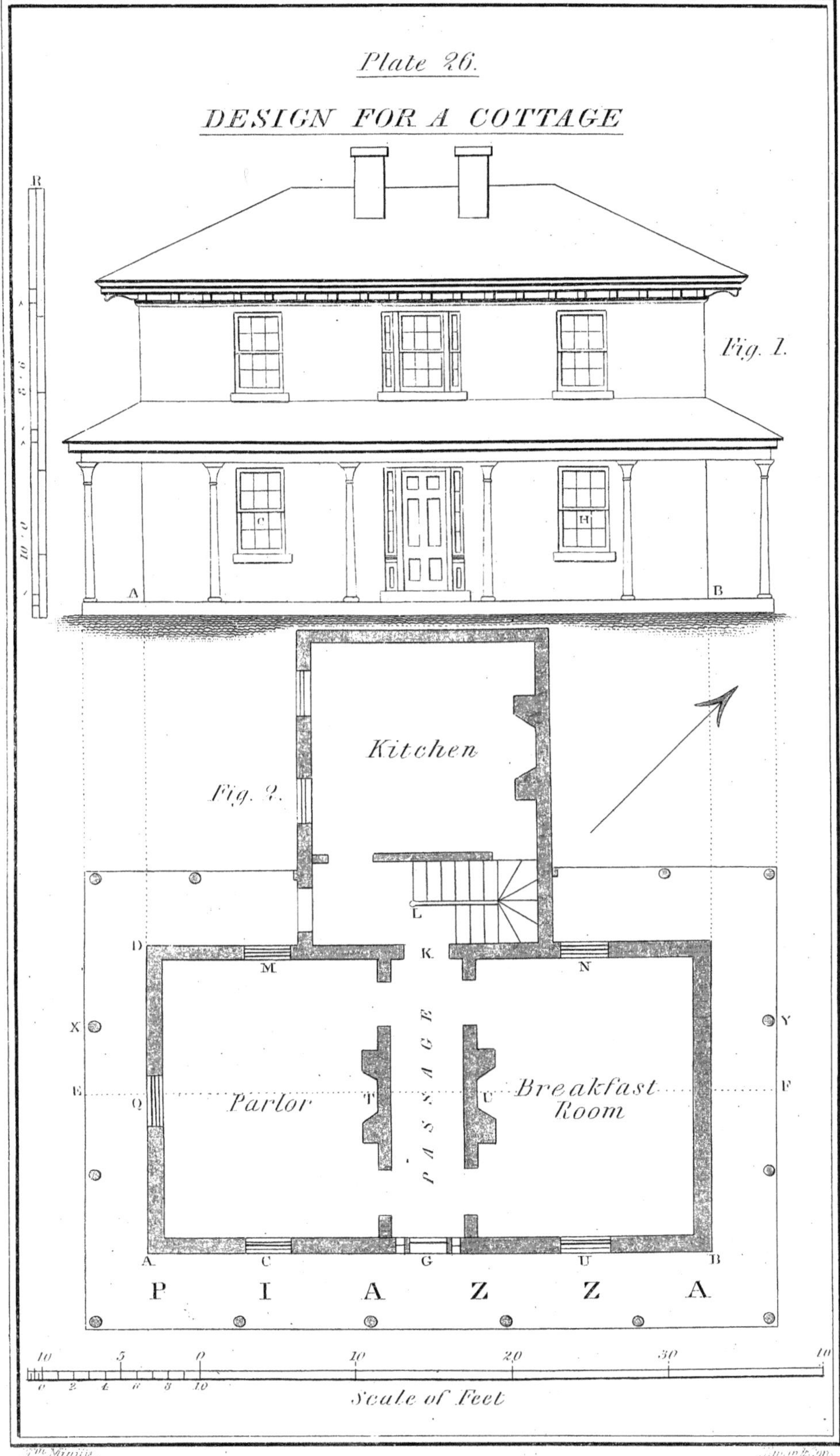
Plate 26.
DESIGN FOR A COTTAGE
Fig. 1.
Fig. 2.
Kitchen
Parlor
Breakfast Room
PASSAGE
P I A Z Z A
Scale of Feet

Plate 27.
DESIGN FOR A COTTAGE
Fig. 3.
Fig. 4.
Chamber
Landing
Chamber
Dressing Room
Chamber
Scale of Feet
X V Q X XX
Wm Minifie.

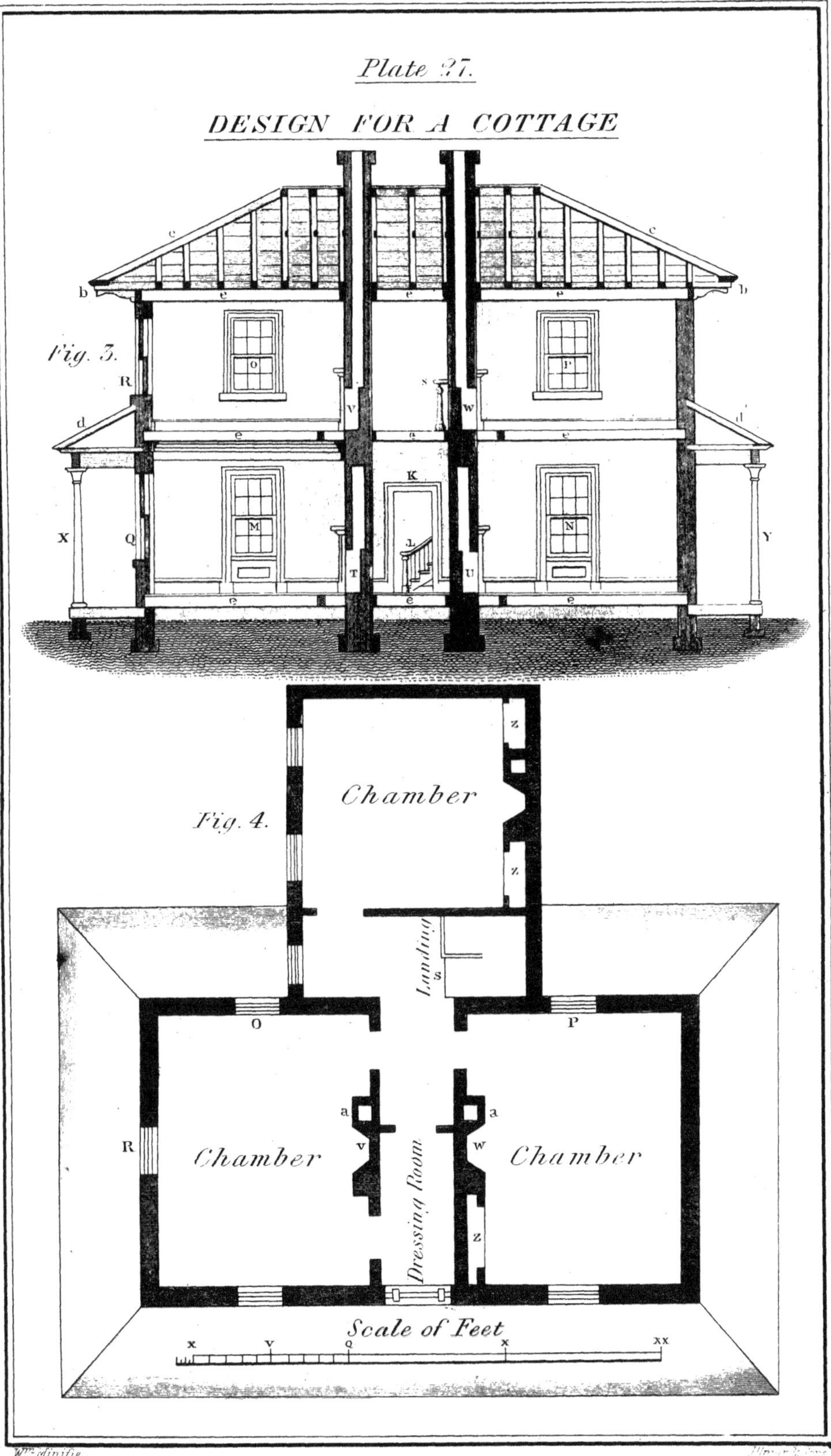

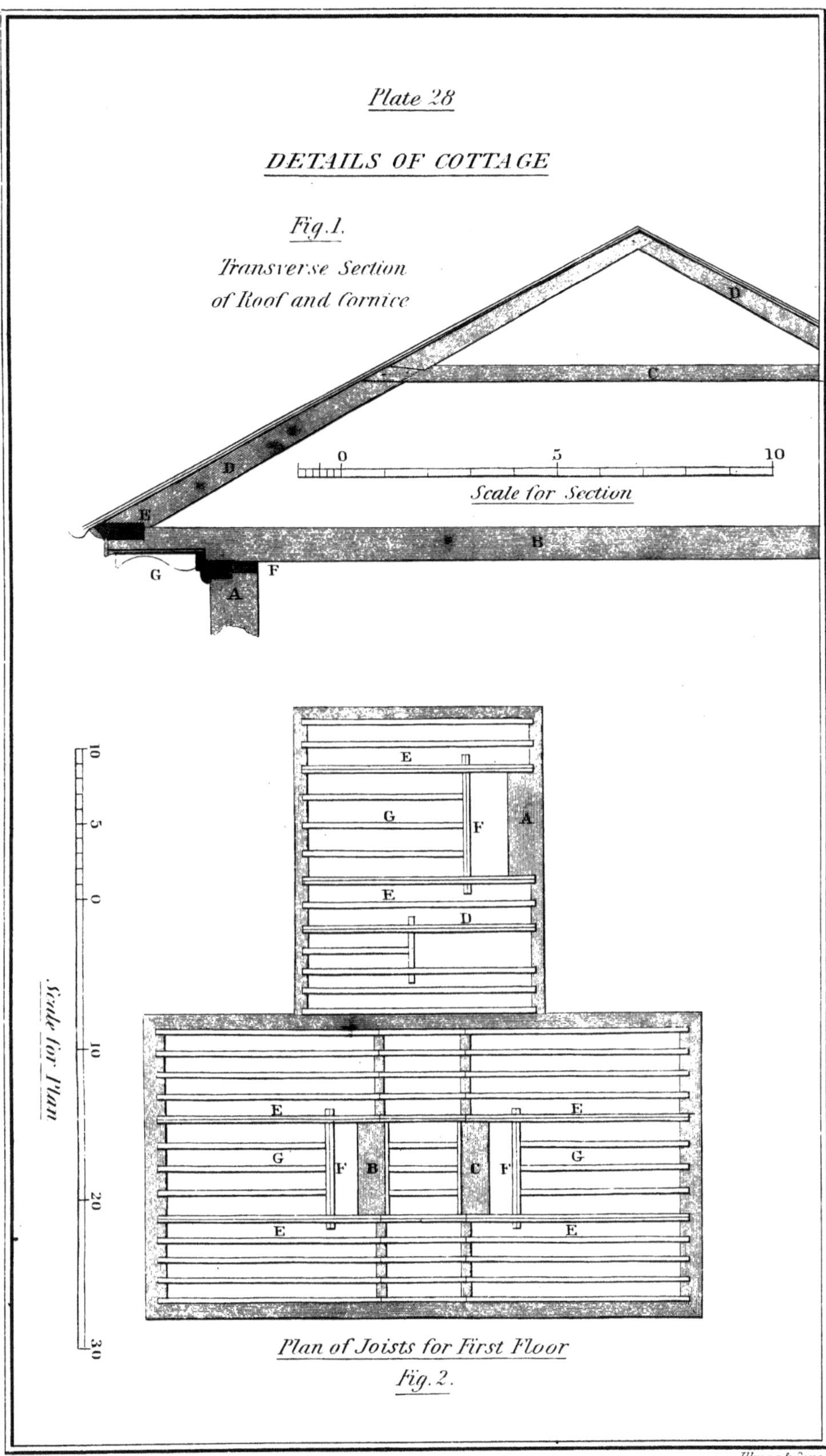

Wm Minifie. Illman & Sons

PLATE XXVIII.

Details.

Fig. 1 is an elevation of one pair of rafters, shewing also a section through the cornice and top of the wall.
A, section of the top of the wall.
B, ceiling joist, the outside end notched to receive the cornice.
C, collar beam. *D. D*, rafters.
E, raising plate. *F*, wall plate.
G, cantilever and section of cornice.

Figure 2.

Plan of First Floor Joists.

A, foundation of kitchen chimney.
B, foundation of parlor chimney; *C*, of breakfast room do.
D, double joist to receive the partition dividing the stairway from the kitchen.
E. E, &c. double joists resting on the walls and supporting the short joists *F. F. F*, forming the framing around the fire-places.
The joists *E. E. E* and *D*, are called *trimming* joists.
The short joists *F. F. F* are called *trimmers*, and the joists *G. G. G*, framed into the trimmers with one end resting on the wall are called *tail joists.*

PLATE XXIX.

Details.

Fig. 1, horizontal section through the parlor window.
A, is the outside of the wall. *B* the inside of wall.

C, the hanging stile of sash frame.
D, the inside lining. *E* the outside lining.
F, the back lining. *G*. *G* the weights.
H, the stile* of the outside or top sash.
I, the stile of the inside or bottom sash.
K, inside stop bead. *L*, jamb lining.
M, ground.† *N*, plastering.
O, architrave. *P*, (dotted line) the projection of the plinth.

* The *stiles* of a sash, door, or any other piece of framing, are the vertical outside pieces; the horizontal pieces are called rails.

† Grounds are strips of wood nailed against the wall to regulate the thickness of the plastering, and to receive the casings or plinth.

Figure 2.

Vertical Section through the Sills.

A, outside of the wall.
Q, stone sill of the window.
R, wooden sub-sill.
S, bottom rail of sash. *T*, bondtimber
U, framing under window, called the back.
V, cap of the back. *K*, the inside stop bead.

Figure 3.

Plinth of Parlor.

M. *M*, grounds. *N*, plastering.
V, plinth or washboard. *W*, the base moulding.
X, the floor.

Many more detail drawings might be made of this design, and where a contract is to be entered into, many more should be made. Enough is here given to explain the method of drawing them; their use is to shew the construction of each part, and when drawn to a large scale, as in plate xxix, a workman of any intelligence would be able to get out any part of the work required.

Plate 29.

DETAILS OF COTTAGE

One fourth of full size.

Horizontal section through Parlor window.

Fig. 1.

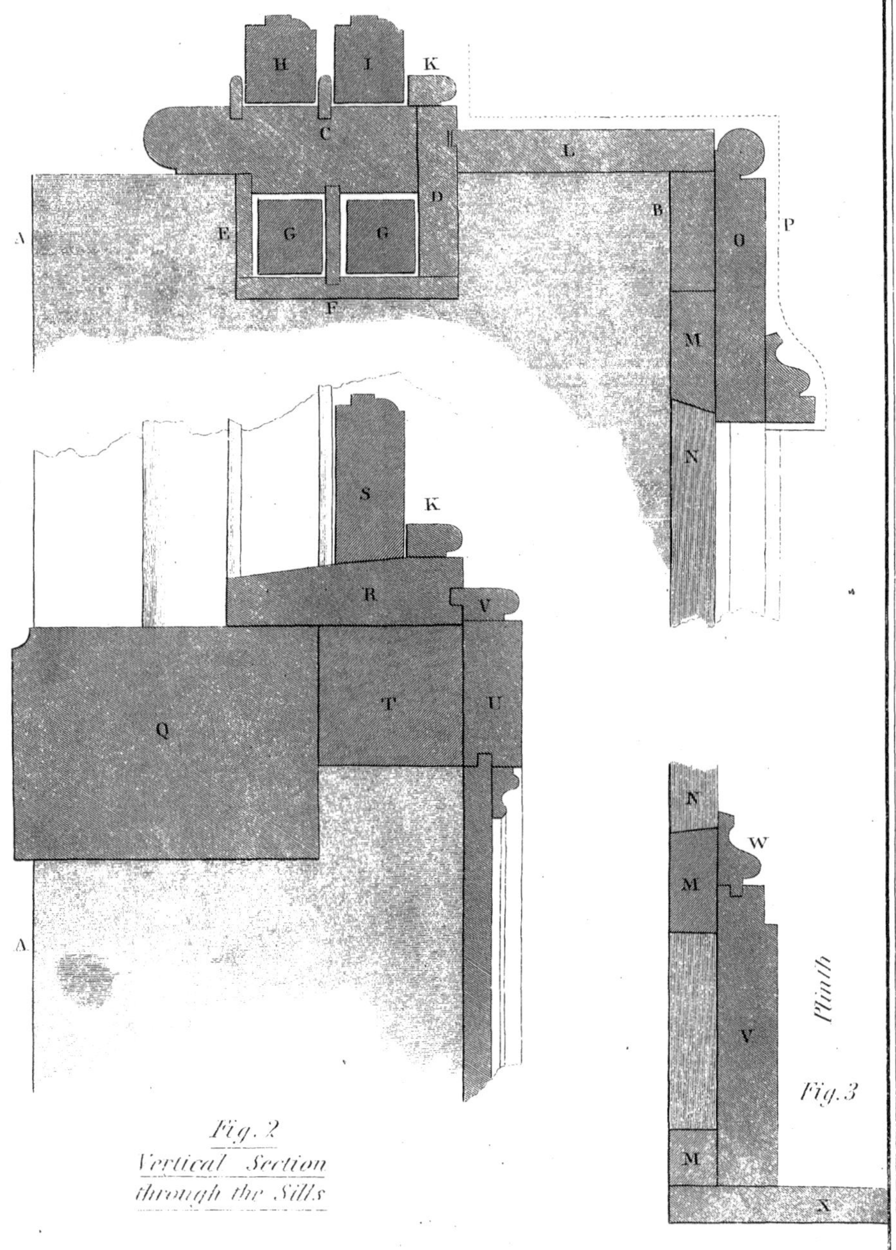

Fig. 2
Vertical Section through the Sills

Plate 30

OCTAGONAL PLAN AND ELEVATION.

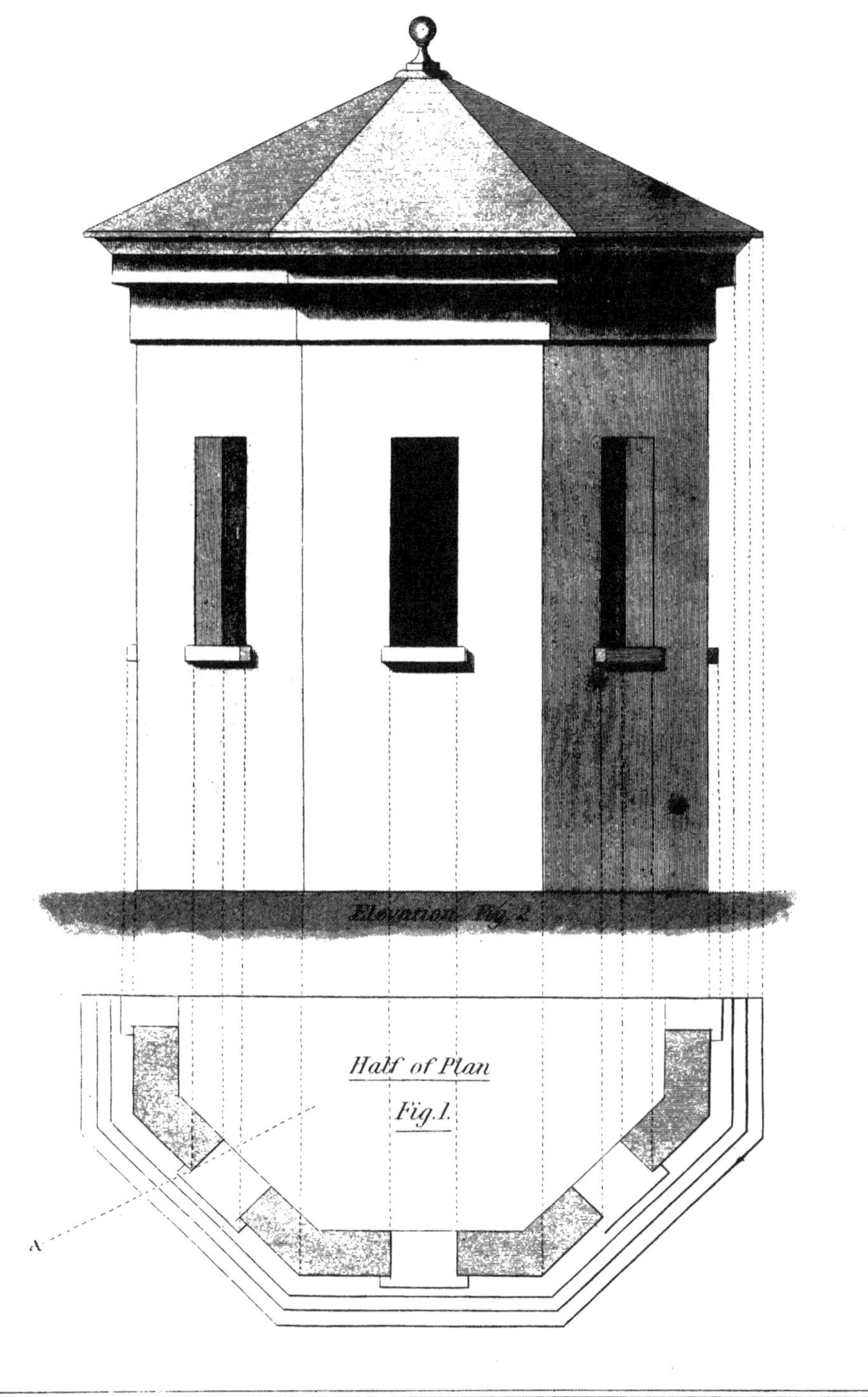

Plate 31

CIRCULAR PLAN AND ELEVATION

Wm Minifie.

PLATE XXX.

OCTAGONAL PLAN AND ELEVATION.

Fig. 1.—Half the Plan. Fig. 2.—Elevation.

This plate requires but little explanation, as the dotted lines from the different points of the plan, perfectly elucidate the mode of drawing the elevation.

The dotted line *A*, shews the direction of the rays of light by which the shadows are projected; the mode of their projection will be explained in Plates 55 and 56.

PLATE XXXI.

CIRCULAR PLAN AND ELEVATION.

This plate shews the mode of putting circular objects in elevation. The dotted lines from the different points of the plan, determine the widths of the *jambs* (sides) of the door and windows, and the projections of the sills and cornice. One window is farther from the door than the other, for the purpose of shewing the different apparent widths of openings, as they are more or less inclined from the front of the picture.

This, as well as Plate 30, should be drawn to a much larger size by the learner; he should also vary the position and width of the openings. As these designs are not intended for a particular purpose, any *scale of equal parts* may be used in drawing them.

PLATE XXXII.

ROMAN MOULDINGS.

Roman mouldings are composed of straight lines and arcs of circles.

NOTE.—Each separate part of a moulding, and each moulding in an assemblage of mouldings, is called a *member*.

FIG. 1.—A FILLET, BAND OR LISTEL

Is a raised square member, with its face parallel to the surface on which it is placed.

FIG. 2.—BEAD.

A moulding whose surface is a semicircle struck from the centre *K*.

FIG. 3.—TORUS.

Composed of a semicircle and a fillet. The projection of the circle beyond the fillet, is equal to the radius of the circle, which is shewn by the dotted line passing through the centre *L*. The curved dotted line above the fillet, and the square dotted line below the circle, shew the position of those members when used as the base of a Doric column.

FIG. 4.—THE SCOTIA

Is composed of two quadrants of circles between two fillets. *B* is the centre for describing the large quadrant; *A* the centre for describing the small quadrant. The upper portion may be made larger or smaller than in the diagram, but the centre *A* must always be in the line *B. A.* The scotia is rarely, if ever used alone; but it forms an important member in the bases of columns.

Plate 32.

ROMAN MOULDINGS.

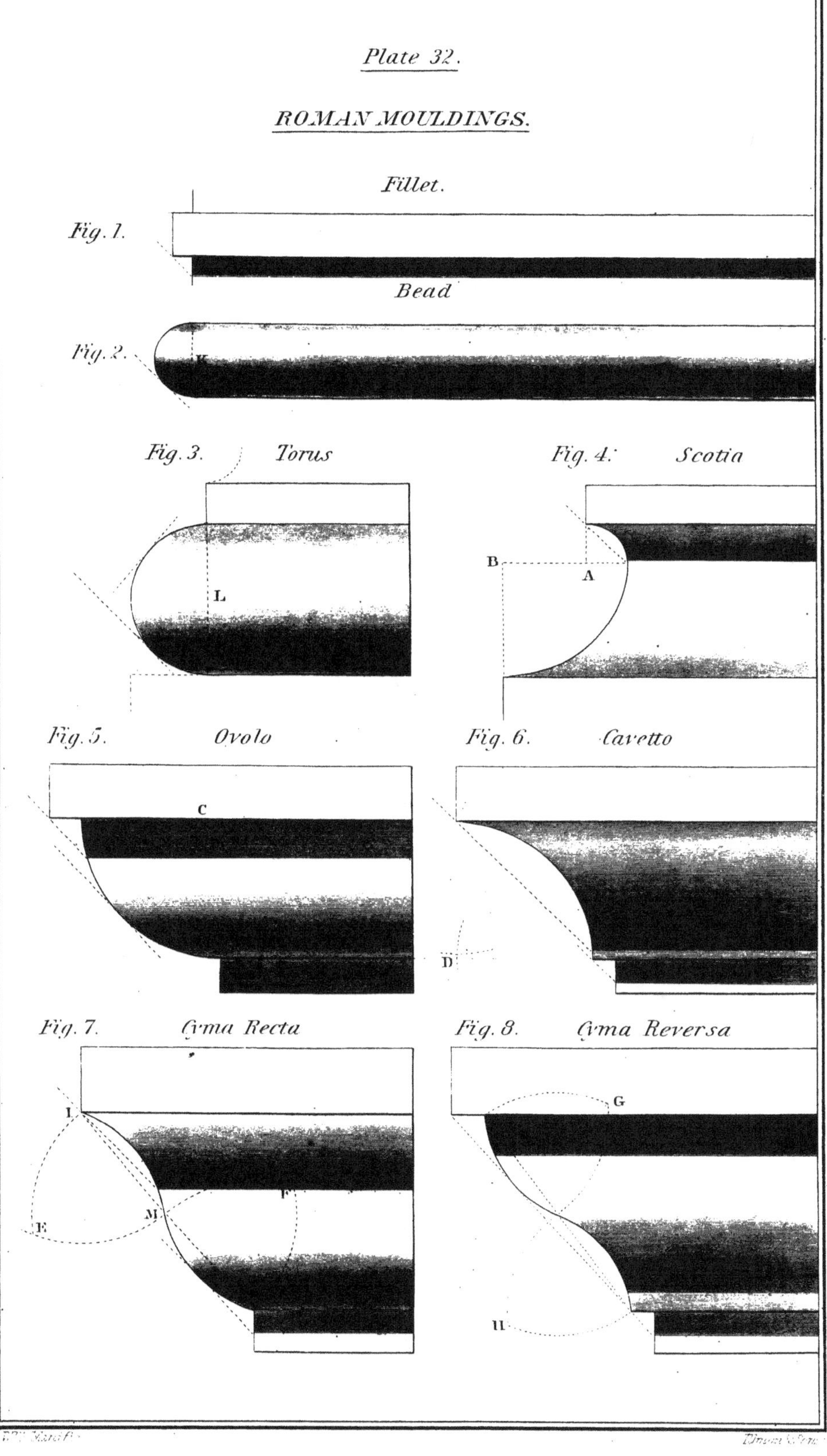

FIG. 5.—THE OVOLO

Is composed of a quadrant between two fillets. *C* is the centre for describing the quadrant. The upper fillet projects beyond the curve, and by its broad shadow adds much to the effect of the moulding. The ovolo is generally used as a bed moulding, or in some other position where it supports another member.

FIG 6.—THE CAVETTO,

Like the ovolo, is composed of a quadrant and two fillets. The concave quadrant is used for the cavetto described from *D*; it is consequently the reverse of the ovolo. The cavetto is frequently used in connection with the ovolo, from which it is separated by a fillet. It is also used sometimes as a crown moulding of a cornice; the crown moulding is the uppermost member.

FIG. 7.—THE CYMA RECTA

Is composed of two arcs of circles forming a waved line, and two fillets.

To describe the cyma, let *I* be the upper fillet and *N* the lower fillet.

1st. Bisect *I. N.* in *M.*

2nd. With the radius *M. N* or *M. I*, and the foot of the dividers in *N* and *M*, successively describe two arcs cutting each other in *F*, and from *M* and *I* with the same radius, describe two arcs, cutting each other in *E*.

3rd. With the same radius from *E* and *F*, describe two arcs meeting each other in *M*.

The proportions of this moulding may be varied at pleasure, by varying the projection of the upper fillet.

FIG. 8.—THE CYMA REVERSA, TALON OR OGEE.

Like the cyma recta, it is composed of two circular arcs and two fillets; the upper fillet projects beyond the curve, and the lower fillet recedes within it.

The curves are described from *G* and *H*.

The CYMA, or CYMA RECTA has the concave curve uppermost.

The CYMA REVERSA has the concave curve below.

The CYMA RECTA is used as the upper member of an assemblage of mouldings, for which it is well fitted from its light appearance.

The CYMA REVERSA from its strong form, is like the ovolo, used to sustain other members.

The dotted lines drawn at an angle of 45° to each moulding, shew the direction of the rays of light, from which the shadows are projected.

NOTE.—When the surface of a moulding is carved or sculptured, it is said to be ENRICHED.

PLATE XXXIII.

GRECIAN MOULDINGS

Are composed of some of the curves formed by the sections of a cone, and are said to be elliptic, parabolic, or hyperbolic, taking their names from the curves of which they are formed.

FIGURES 1 AND 2

To draw the Grecian ECHINUS *or* OVOLO, *the fillets* A *and* B, *the tangent* C. B, *and the point of greatest projection at* D *being given.*

1st. Draw *B. H,* a continuation of the upper edge of the under fillet.

2nd. Through *D,* draw *D. H* perpendicular to *B. H,* cutting the tangent *B. C* in *C.*

3rd. Through *B,* draw *B. G* parallel to *D. H,* and through *D,* draw *D. E* parallel to *H. B,* cutting *G. B* in *E.*

4th. Make *E. G* equal to *E. B,* and *E. F* equal to *H. C,* join *D. F.*

5th. Divide the lines *D. F* and *D. C* each into the same number of equal parts

6th. From the point *B,* draw lines to the divisions 1, 2, 3, &c. in *D. C.*

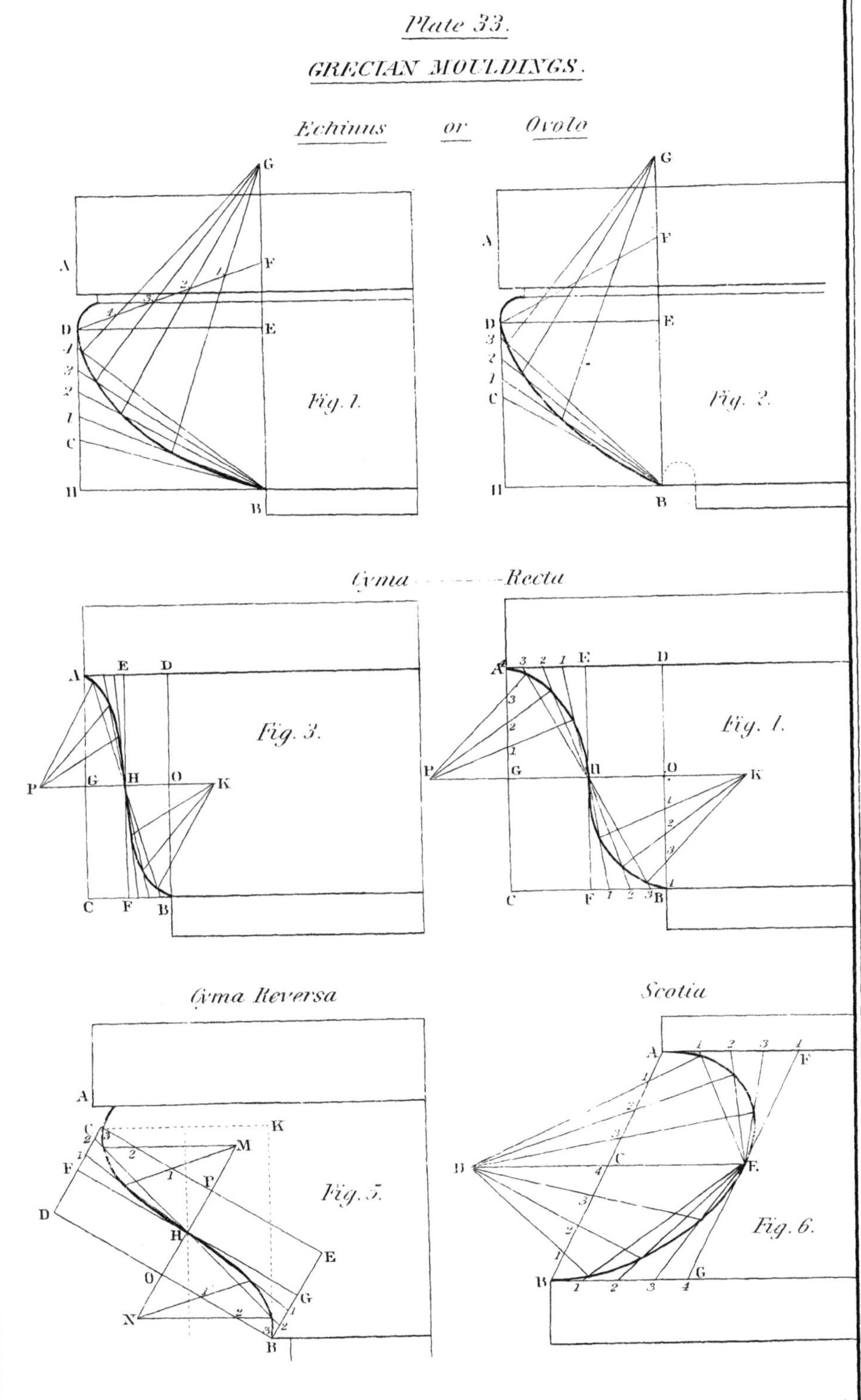

Wm. Minifie.

Illman & Sons

7th. From the point *G*, draw lines through the divisions in *D. F*, to intersect the lines drawn from *B*.

8th. Through the points of intersection trace the curve.

NOTE.—A great variety of form may be given to the echinus, by varying the projections and the inclination of the tangent *B. C.*

NOTE 2.—If *H. C* is less than *C. D*, as in fig. 1, the curve will be *elliptic;* if *H. C* and *C. D* are equal, as in fig. 2, the curve is *parabolic;* if *H. C* be made greater than *D., C*, the curve will be *hyperbolic.*

NOTE 3.—The echinus, when enriched with carving, is generally cut into figures resembling eggs, with a dart or tongue between them.

FIGS. 3 AND 4.—THE GRECIAN CYMA.

To describe the Cyma Recta, the perpendicular height B. D *and the projection* A. D *being given.*

1st. Draw *A. C* and *B. D* perpendicular to *A. D* and *C. B* parallel to *A. D*.

2nd. Bisect *A. D* in *E*, and *A. C* in *G;* draw *E. F* and *G. O*, which will divide the rectangle *A. C. B. D* into four equal rectangles.

3rd. Make *G. P* and *O. K* each equal to *O. H*.

4th. Divide *A. G—O. B—A. E* and *B. F* into a similar number of equal parts.

5th. From the divisions in *A. E* and *F. B*, draw lines to *H;* from *P* draw lines through the divisions on *A. G* to intersect the lines drawn from *A. E*, and from *K* through the divisions in *O. B*, draw lines to intersect the lines drawn from *F. B*.

6th. Through the points of intersection draw the curve.

NOTE.—The curve is formed of two equal converse arcs of an ellipsis, of which *E. F* is the transverse axis, and *P. H* or *H. K* the conjugate. The points in the curve are found in the same manner as in fig. 1, plate 20.

FIG. 5.—THE GRECIAN CYMA REVERSA, TALON OR OGEE.

To draw the Cyma Reversa, the fillet A, *the point* C, *the end of the curve* B, *and the line* B. D *being given.*

1st. From *C*, draw *C. D*, and from *B*, draw *B. E* perpendicular to *B. D*, then draw *C. E* parallel to *B. D*, which completes the rectangle.

2nd. Divide the rectangle *B. E. C. D* into four equal parts, by drawing *F. G* and *O. P*.

3rd. Find the points in the curve as in figs. 3 and 4.

Note 1.—If we turn the figure over so as to bring the line *F. G* vertical, *G* being at the top, the point *B* of fig. 5, to coincide with the point *A* of fig. 3, it will be perceived that the curves are similar, *F. G.* being the transverse axis, and *N. H* or *M. H* the conjugate axis of the ellipsis.

Note 2.—The nearer the line *B. D* approaches to a horizontal position, the greater will be the degree of curvature, the conjugate axis of the ellipsis will be lengthened, and the curve become more like the Roman ogee.

Figure 6.—The Grecian Scotia.

To describe the Grecian Scotia, the position of the fillets A *and* B *being given.*

1st. Join *A. B*, bisect it in *C*, and through *C* draw *D. E* parallel to *B. G*.

2nd. Make *C. D* and *C. E* each equal to the depth intended to be given to the scotia; then *A. B* will be a diameter of an ellipsis, and *D. E* its conjugate.

3rd. Through *E*, draw *F. G* parallel to *A. B*.

4th. Divide *A. F* and *B. G* into the same number of equal parts, and from the points of division draw lines to *E*.

5th. Divide *A. C* and *B. C* into the same number of equal parts, as *A. F*, then from *D* through the points of division in *A. B*, draw lines to intersect the others, which will give points in the curve.

PLATE XXXIV.

PLAN, SECTION AND ELEVATION OF A WHEEL AND PINION.

The cross lines on *Q. R*, fig. 2, shewing the teeth of the wheel and pinion, are drawn from the elevation as described in Plate 31, which explains the method of drawing an elevation from a circular plan.

This plate is introduced to give the learner an example for drawing machinery; it requires but little explanation, as the relative

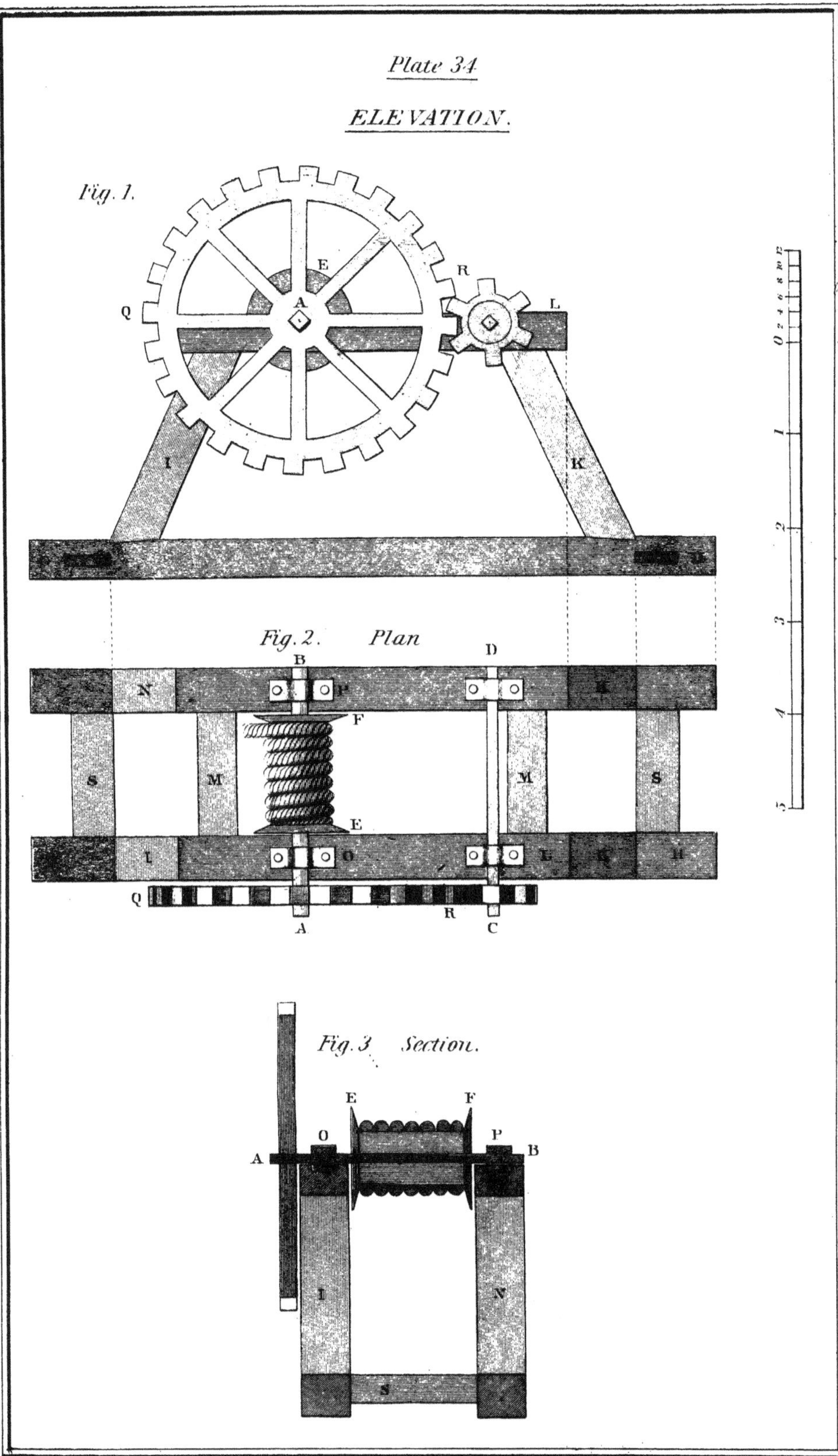

Wm. Minifie. Illman & Sons

parts are plain and simple; the same letters refer to the same parts in each figure.

Thus *A*, fig. 1, is the end of the axle of the wheel.
A. *B*, fig. 2, the top of the axle of the wheel.
A. *B*, fig. 3, section through the centre of the wheel.
C. *D*, the axle of the pinion.
E. *F*, flanges of the barrel, with the rope coiled between them.
G. *H*, bottom piece of frame.
I. *K*. *K*. *N*, inclined uprights of frame.
L, top of frame. *M*. *M*, top cross pieces of frame.
O. *P*, bearings of the wheel.
Q. *R*, plan and elevation of wheel.
R, intersection of wheel and pinion.
S. *S*, bottom cross pieces of frame.

When two wheels engage each other, the smallest is called a pinion.

PLATE XXXV.

TO DRAW THE TEETH OF WHEELS.

1st. The LINE of CENTRES is the line *A*. *B*. *D*, fig. 1, passing through *K* and *C*, the centres of the wheel and pinion.

2nd. The PROPORTIONAL or primitive diameter of the wheel, is the line *A*. *B*; the proportional radius *A*. *K* or *K*. *B*. The true radii are the distances from the centres to the extremities of the teeth.

3rd. The PROPORTIONAL DIAMETER of the pinion is the line *B*. *D*; the proportional radius *C*. *B*.

4th. The PROPORTIONAL CIRCLES OR PITCH LINES are circles described with the proportional radii touching each other in *B*.

5th. The PITCH of a wheel is the distance on the pitch circle including a tooth and a space, as *E*. *F* or *G*. *H*, or *O*. *D*, fig. 2.

6th. The DEPTH of a tooth is the distance from the pitch circle to the bottom, as *L*. *K*, fig. 1, and the height of a tooth is the distance from the pitch circle to the top of the tooth, as *L*. *M*.

To draw the Pitch Line of a Pinion to contain a definite number of Teeth of the same size as in the given wheel K.

1st. Divide the proportional diameter *A. B* of the given wheel into as many equal parts as the wheel has teeth, viz. 16.

2nd. With a distance equal to one of these parts, step off on the line *B. D* as many steps as the pinion is to contain teeth, which will give the proportional diameter of the pinion; the diagram contains 8.

3rd. Draw the pitch circle, and on it with the distance *E. F*, the pitch, lay off the teeth.

4th. Sub-divide the pitch for the tooth and space, draw the sides of the teeth below the pitch line toward the centre, and on the tops of the teeth describe epicycloids.

NOTE.—The circumferences of circles are directly as their diameters; if the diameter of one circle be four times greater than another, the circumference will also be four times greater.

Fig. 2 is another method for drawing the teeth; *A. B* is the pitch circle on which the width of the teeth and spaces must be laid down. Then with a radius *D. E* or *D. F*, equal to a pitch and a fourth, from the middle of each tooth on the pitch circle as at *D*, describe the tops of the teeth *E* and *F*, from *O* describe the tops of the teeth *G* and *D*, and so on for the others. The sides of the teeth within the pitch circle may be drawn toward the centre, as at *F* and *H*, or from the centre *O*, with a radius equal to *O. Q* or *O. P*, describe the lower part of the teeth *G* and *D*.

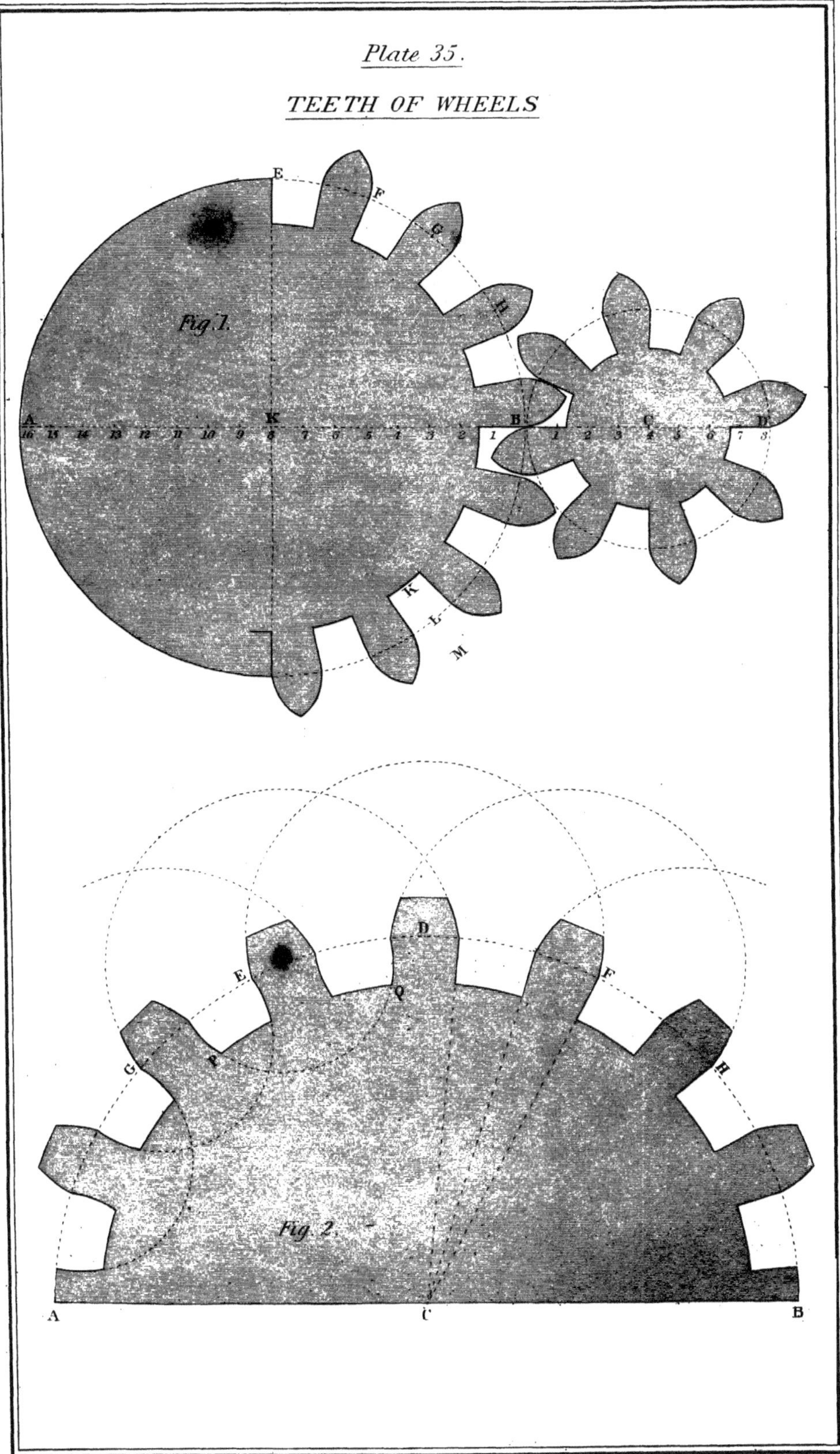
Plate 35.
TEETH OF WHEELS
Fig. 1.
Fig. 2.
Wm. Minifie.
Illman & Sons

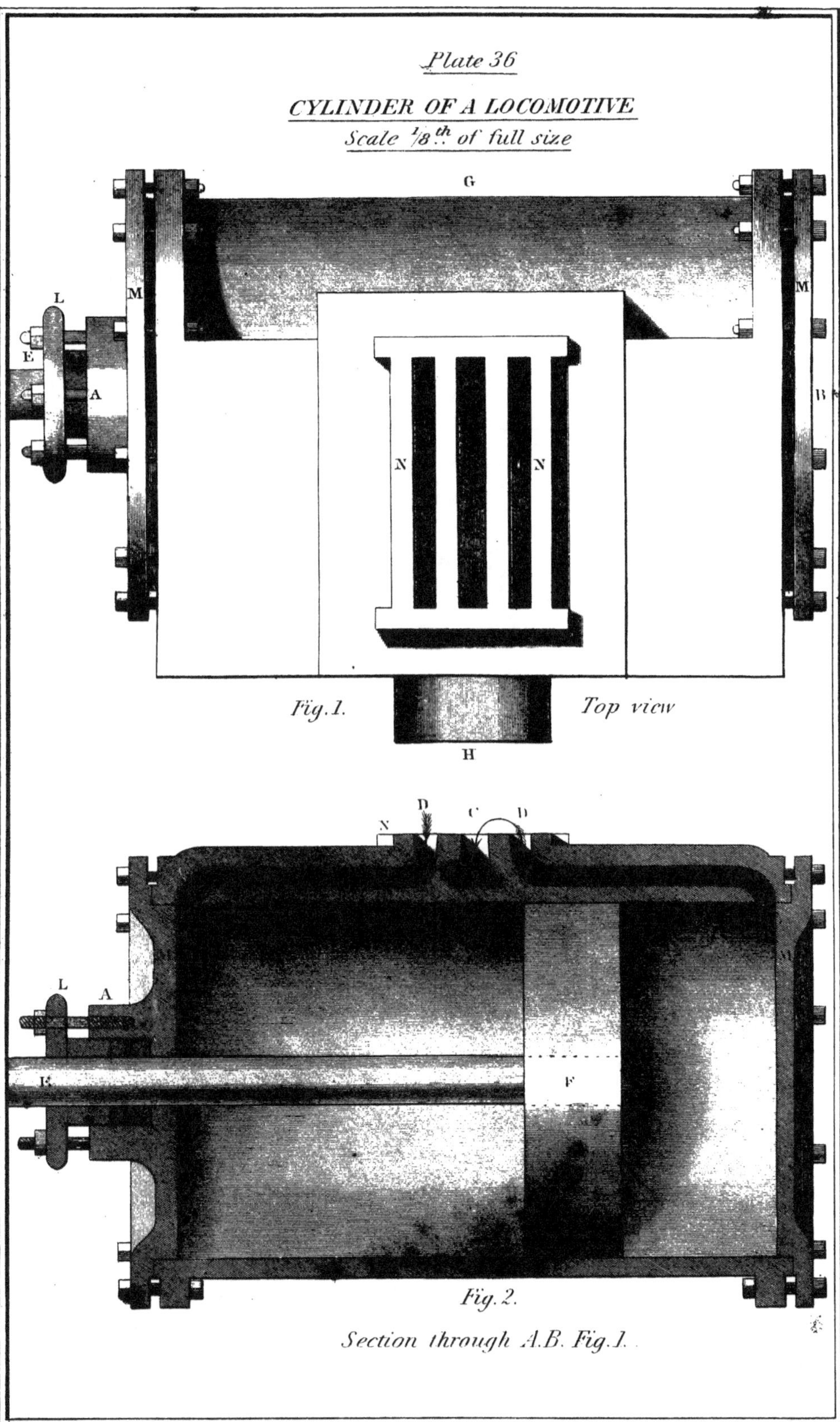
Plate 36
CYLINDER OF A LOCOMOTIVE
Scale 1/8th of full size
G
M
M
L
E
A
B
N
N
H
Fig. 1.
Top view
D
C
D
N
L
A
E
F
Fig. 2.
Section through A.B. Fig. 1.
Wm Minitie.
Illman & Sons

Plate 37

CYLINDER OF A LOCOMOTIVE

Scale 1/8th of full size

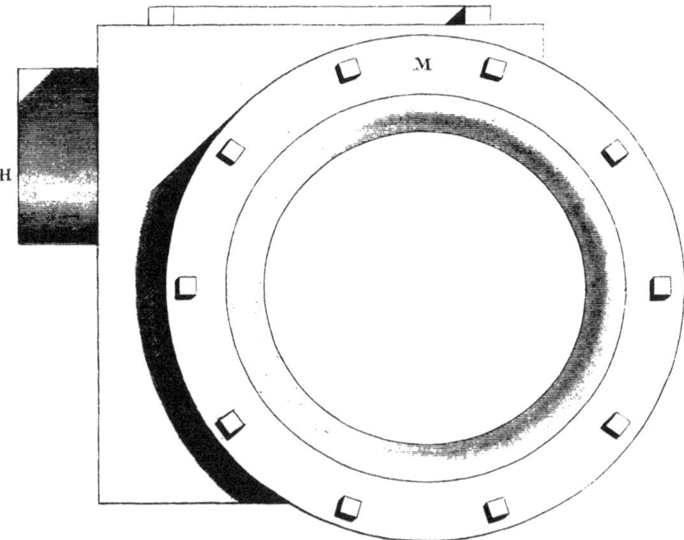

Fig. 3. End view

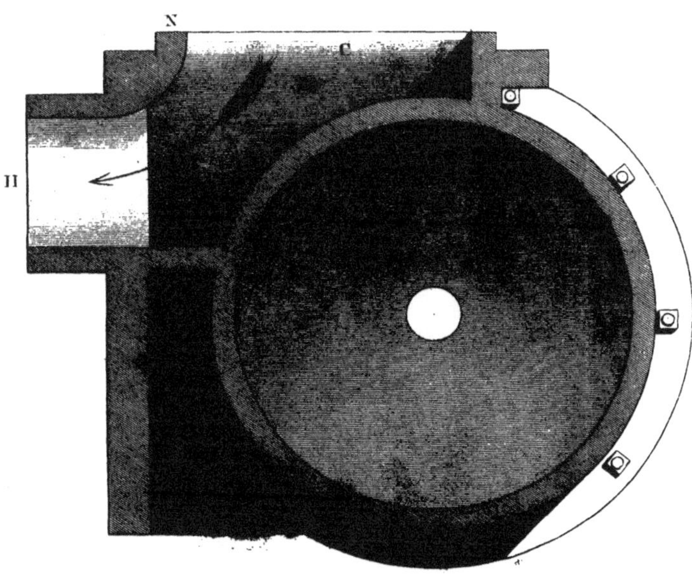

Fig. 4. Section through G.H. Fig. 1. Plate 36.

Wm. Minifie

Dinon & Sons

PLATES XXXVI AND XXXVII.

PLAN, SECTIONS AND END ELEVATION OF A CYLINDER FOR A LOCOMOTIVE ENGINE.

Fig. 1. Top view or Plan.
Fig. 2. Longitudinal Section through *A. B*, fig. 1.
Fig. 3. Elevation of the end *B*, fig. 1.
Fig. 4. Transverse Section through *G. H*, fig. 1.

REFERENCES.

A. Stuffing box.
A. B. Line of longitudinal section.
C. Steam exhaust port, or Exhaust.
D. D. Steam ports or Side openings.
E. Piston rod.
F. Piston shewn in elevation.
G. H. Line of transverse section.
H. Exhaust pipe.
K. Packing.
L. Gland or Follower.
M. M. Heads of cylinder.
N. Valve face.

The piston is represented in the drawing as descending to the bottom of the cylinder; the bent arrows from *D* to *C*, fig. 2, and from *C* to *H*, fig. 4, shew the course of the steam escaping from the cylinder through the steam port and exhaust port to the exhaust pipe; the other arrow at *D*, fig. 2, the direction of the steam entering the cylinder.

PLATE XXXVIII.

ISOMETRICAL DRAWING.

FIGURE 1.

To draw the Isometrical Cube.

Let *A* be the centre of the proposed drawing.

1st. With one foot of the dividers in *A*, and any radius, describe a circle.

2nd. Through the centre *A*, draw a diameter *B. C* parallel to the sides of the paper.

3rd. With the radius from the points *B* and *C* lay off the other corners of a hexagon, *D. E. F. G.*

4th. Join the points and complete the hexagon

5th. From the centre *A*, draw lines to the alternate corners of the hexagon, which will complete the figure.

The isometrical cube is a hexahedron supposed to be viewed at an infinite distance, and in the direction of the diagonal of the cube; in the diagram, the eye is supposed to be placed opposite the point *A*: if a wire be run through the point *A* to the opposite corner of the cube, the eye being in the same line, could only see the end of the wire, and this would be the case no matter how large the cube, consequently the front top corner of the cube and the bottom back corner must be represented by a dot, as at the point *A*. As the cube is a solid, the eye from that direction will see three of its sides and nine of its twelve edges, and as the distance is infinite, all these edges will be of equal length, the edges seen are those shewn in fig. 1 by continuous lines; three of the edges and three of the sides could not be seen, these edges are shewn by dotted lines in fig. 1, but if the cube were transparent all the edges and sides could be seen. The apparent opposite angles in each side are equal, two of them being 120°, and the other two 60°; all the opposite boundary lines are parallel to each other, and as they are all of equal length may be measured by one *common scale*, and all lines parallel to any of the edges of the cube may be measured by the same scale. The lines *F. G*, *A. C* and *E. D* represent the vertical *edges* of the cube, the par-

Plate 38

CONSTRUCTION OF THE ISOMETRICAL CUBE

Fig. 1.

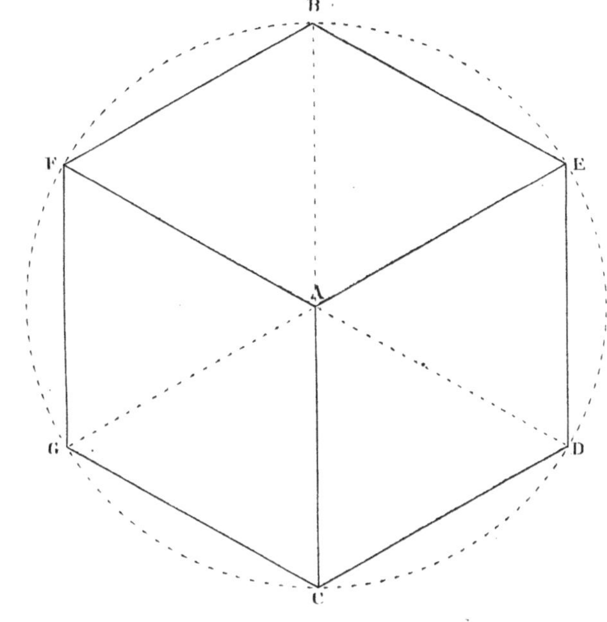

Fig. 2.

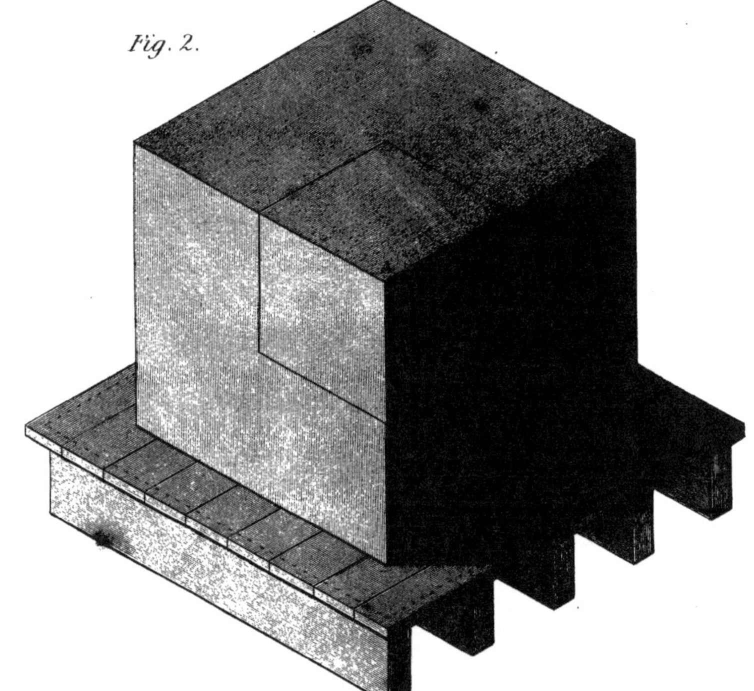

Wm. Minifie. Ilman & Sons

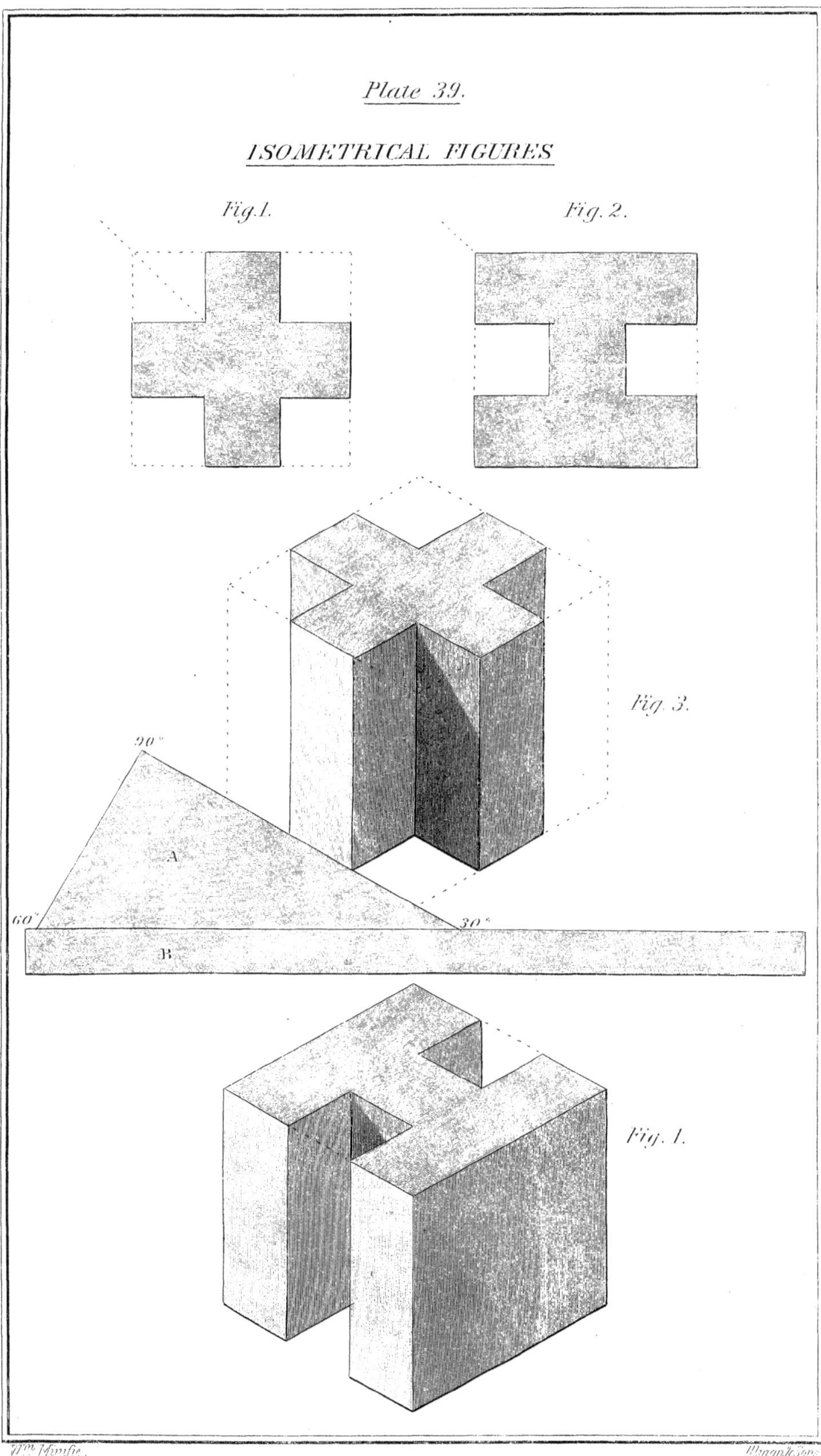

Wm. Minifie. Illman & Sons

allelograms *A. C. D. E* and *A. C. F. G*, represent the vertical *faces* of the cube, and the parallelogram *A. B. E. F* represents the horizontal face of the cube; consequently, vertical as well as horizontal lines and surfaces may be delineated by this method and measured by the same scale, for this reason the term ISOMETRICAL *(equally measurable)* has been applied to this style of drawing.

Figure 2

Is a cube of the same size as fig. 1, shaded to make the representation more obvious; the sides of the small cube *A*, and the boundary of the square platform on which the cube rests, as well as of the joists which support the floor of the platform, are all drawn parallel to some of the edges of the cube, and forms a good illustration for the learner to practice on a larger scale.

NOTE.—A singular optical illusion may be witnessed while looking at this diagram, if we keep the eye fixed on the point *A*, and imagine the drawing to represent the interior of a room, the point *A* will appear to recede; then if we again imagine it to be a cube the point will appear to advance, and this rising and falling may be continued, as you imagine the angle *A* to represent a projecting corner, or an internal angle.

PLATE XXXIX.

EXAMPLES IN ISOMETRICAL DRAWING.

Figs. 1 and 2 are plans of cubes with portions cut away. Figs. 3 and 4 are isometrical representations of them.

To draw a part of a regular figure, as in these diagrams, it is better to draw the *whole outline* in pencil, as shewn by the dotted lines, and from the corners lay off the indentations.

The circumscribing cube may be drawn as in fig. 1, Plate 38, with a radius equal to the side of the plan, or with a triangle having one right angle, one angle of 60°, and the other angle 30°, as shewn at *A*. Proceed as follows:—

Let *B* be the tongue of a square or a straight edge applied horizontally across the paper, apply the hypothenuse of the triangle to the tongue or straight edge, as in the diagram, and draw the left hand inclined lines; then reverse the triangle and draw the right hand inclined lines; turn the short side of the triangle against the tongue of the square, and the vertical lines may be drawn.

This instrument so simplifies isometrical drawing, that its application is but little more difficult than the drawing of flat geometrical plans or elevations.

PLATE XL.

EXAMPLES IN ISOMETRICAL DRAWING—CONTINUED.

Fig 1 is the side, and fig. 2 the end elevation of a block pierced through as shewn in fig 1, and with the top chamfered off, as shewn in figs. 1 and 2.

FIGURE 3.

To draw the figure Isometrically.

1st. Draw the isometrical lines *A. B* and *C. D;* make *A. B* equal to *A. B* fig. 1, and *C. D* equal to *C. D* fig. 2.

2nd. From *A. B* and *D*, draw the vertical lines, and make them equal to *B. G*, fig. 1.

3rd. Draw *K. H* and *L. I* parallel to *A. B*, and *H. I* and *K. L* parallel to *C. D*.

4th. Draw the diagonals *H. D* and *I. C*, and through their intersection draw a vertical line *M. G. F*. Make *G. F* equal to *G. F*, fig. 1.

5th. Through *G*, draw *G. N*, intersecting *L. K* in *N*, and from *N* draw a vertical line *N. E*.

6th. Through F, draw *F. E*, intersecting *N. E* in *E;* then *E. F* represents the line *E. F* in fig. 1.

7th. From *E* and *F*, lay off the distances *O* and *P*, and from *O* and *P* draw the edges of the chamfer *O. K—O. L—P. H* and *P. I*, which complete the outline.

8th. On *A. B* lay off the opening shewn in fig. 1, and from *R*, draw a line parallel to *C. D*.

Plate 40

ISOMETRICAL FIGURES.

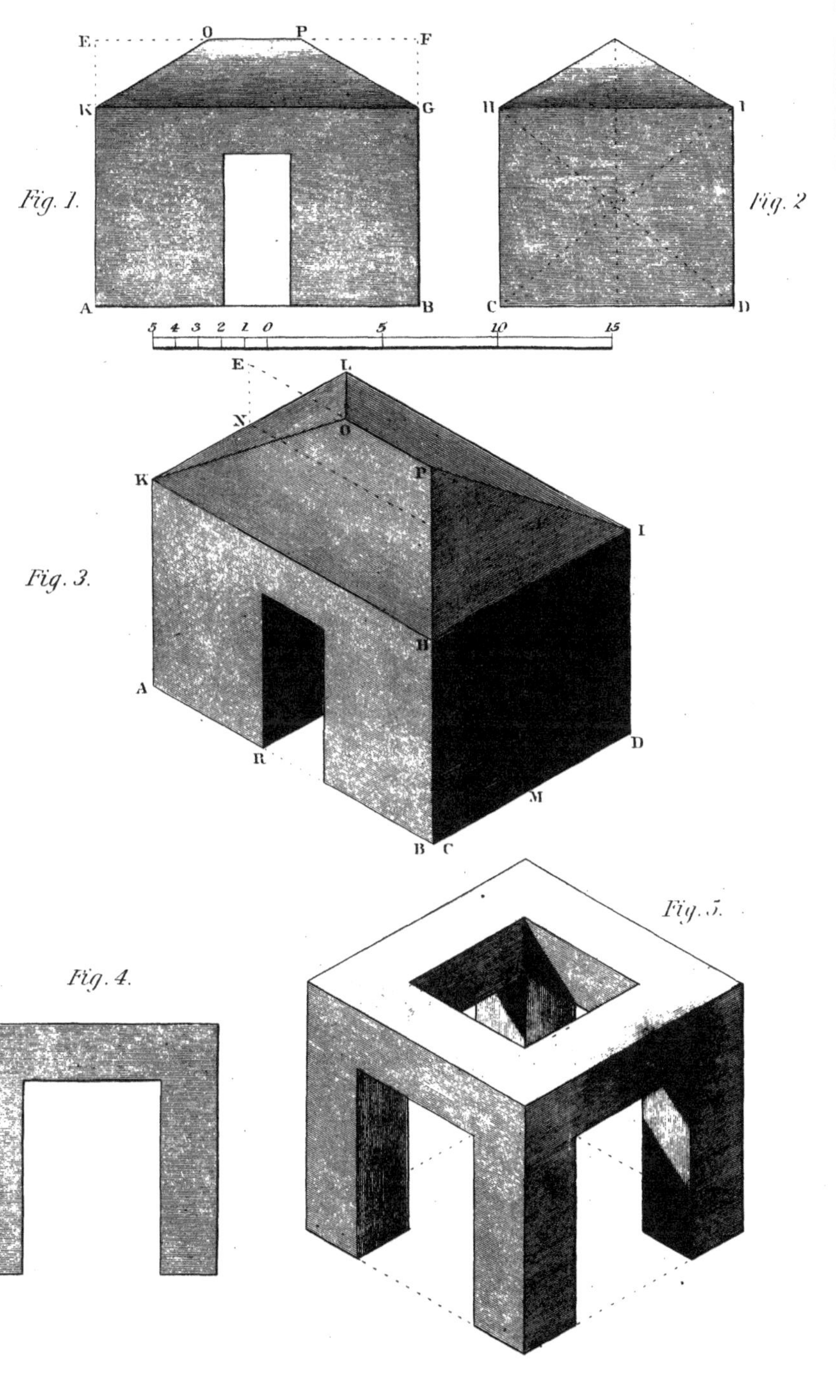

Wm. Minifie.

NOTE 1.—All the lines in this figure, except the diagonals and edges of the chamfer, can be drawn with the triangle and square, as explained in Plate 39.

NOTE 2.—All these lines may be measured by the *same scale*, except the inclined edges of the chamfer, which will require a different scale.

NOTE 3.—The intelligent student will easily perceive from this figure, how to draw a house with a hipped roof, placing the doors, windows, &c., each in its proper place; or how to draw any other rectangular figure. Inclined lines may always be found by a similar process to that we have pursued in drawing the edges of the chamfer.

FIGURE 4

Is the elevation of the side of a cube with a large portion cut out.

FIGURE 5

Is the isometrical drawing of the same, with the top of the cube also pierced through. The mode pursued is so obvious, that it requires no explanation: it is given as an illustration for drawing FURNITURE, or any other framed object. It requires but little ingenuity to convert fig. 5 into the frame of a table or a foot-stool.

PLATE XLI.

TO DRAW THE ISOMETRICAL CIRCLE.

FIGURE 1

Is the plan of a circle inscribed in a square, with two diameters *A. B* and *C. D* parallel to the sides of the square.

FIGURE 2.

To draw the Isometrical Representation.

1st. Draw the isometrical square, *M. N. O. P*, having its opposite angles 120° and 60° respectively.

2nd. Bisect each side and draw *A. B* and *C. D*.

3rd. From *O* draw *O. A* and *O. D*, and from *M* draw *M. C* and *M. B* intersecting in *Q* and *R*.

4th. From *Q*, with the radius *Q. A*, describe the arc *A. C*, and from *R*, with the same radius, describe the arc *D. B*.

5th. From *O*, with the radius *O. A*, draw the arc *A. D*, and from *M*, with the same radius, describe *C. B*, which completes the oval.

NOTE.—An ISOMETRICAL PROJECTION of a circle would be an ellipsis; but the figure produced by the above method is so simple in its construction and approaches so near to an ellipsis, that it may be used in most cases, besides its facility of construction, its circumference is so nearly equal to the circumference of the given circle, that any divisions traced on the one may be transferred to the other with sufficient accuracy for all practical purposes.

FIGURE 3.

To divide the Circumference of the Isometrical Circle into any number of equal parts.

1st. Draw the circle and a square around it as in fig. 2, the square may touch the circle as in fig. 2, or be drawn outside as in fig. 3.

2nd. From the middle of one of the sides as *O*, erect *O. K* perpendicular to *E. F*, and make *O. K* equal to *O. E*.

3rd. Draw *K. E* and *K. F*, and from *K* with any radius, describe an arc *P. Q*, cutting *K. E* in *P*, and *K. F* in *Q*.

4th. Divide the arc *P* 4 into one-eighth of the number of parts required in the whole circumference, and from *K*, through these divisions, draw lines intersecting *E. O* in 1, 2 and 3.

5th. From the divisions 1, 2 and 3, in *E. O*, draw lines to the centre *P*, which will divide the arc *E. O* into four equal parts.

6th. Transfer the divisions on *E. O* from the corners *E. F. G. H*, and draw lines to the centre *P*, when the concentric curves will be divided into 32 equal parts.

NOTE 1.—If a plan of a circle divided into any number of equal parts be drawn, as that of a cog wheel, the same measures may be transferred to the isometric curve as explained in the note to fig. 2, but if the plan be not drawn, the divisions can be made as in fig. 3.

NOTE 2.—The term ISOMETRICAL PROJECTION has been avoided, as the projection of a figure would require a smaller scale to be used than the scale to which the geometrical plans and elevations are drawn, but as the isometrical figure drawn with the same scale to which the plans are drawn, is in every respect proportional to the true projection, and conveys to the eye the same view of the object, it is manifestly much more convenient for practical purposes to draw both to the same scale.

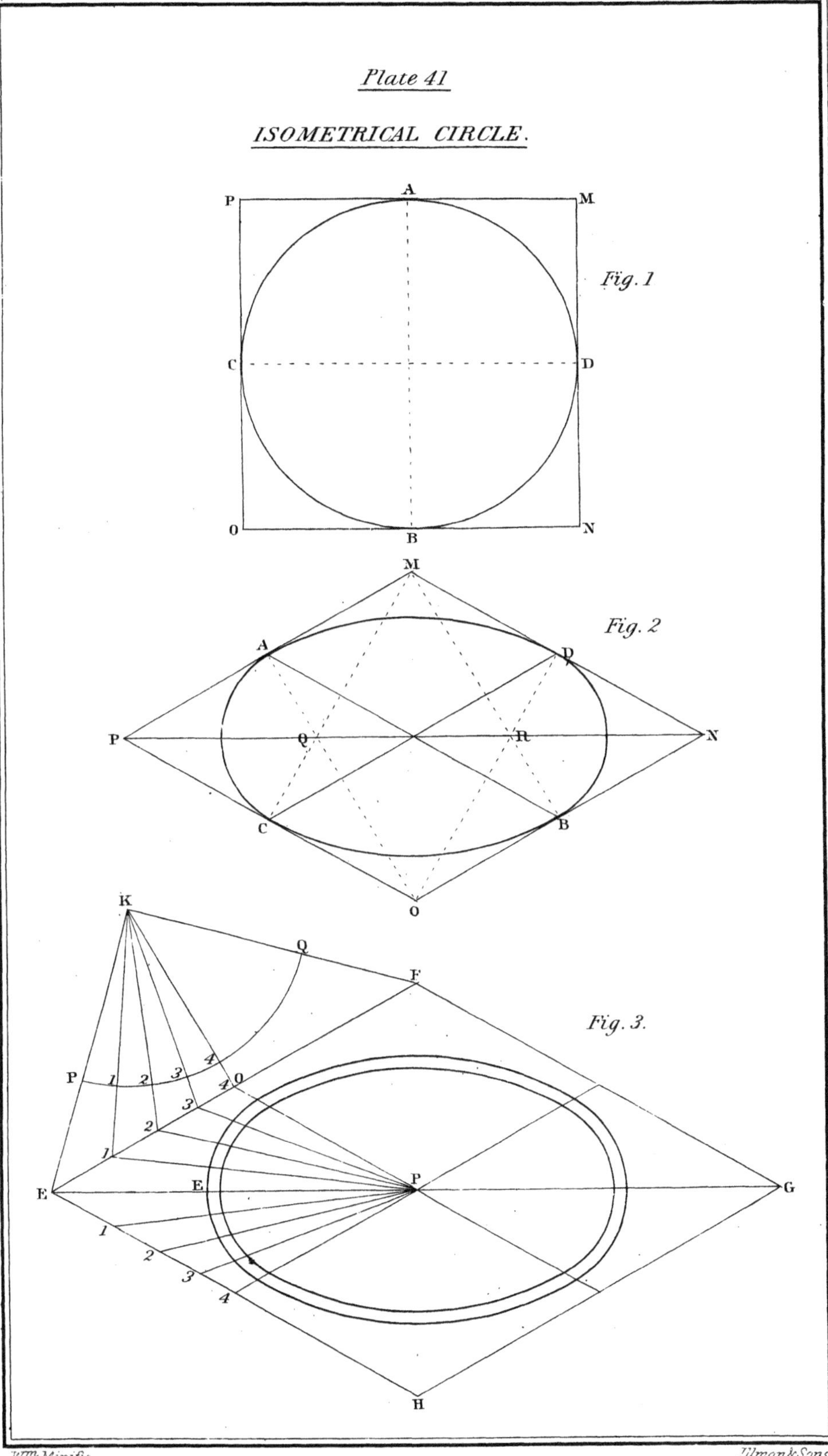
Plate 41
ISOMETRICAL CIRCLE.
P
A
M
Fig. 1
C
D
O
B
N
M
Fig. 2
A
D
P
Q
R
N
C
B
O
K
Q
F
Fig. 3.
P
1
2
3
4
O
4
3
2
1
E
E
P
G
1
2
3
4
H
Wm. Minifie.
Illman & Sons

Note 3.—In Note 2 to fig. 3, Plate 40, allusion has been made to inclined lines requiring a different scale from any of the lines used in drawing the isometric cube: for the mode of drawing those scales as well as for the further prosecution of this branch of drawing, the student is referred to Jopling's and Sopwith's treatise on the subject, as we only propose to give an *introduction* to *isometrical drawing*. Sufficient, however, has been given to enable the student to apply it to a very large class of objects, and it would extend the size of this work too much (already much larger than was intended) if we pursue the subject in full.

PERSPECTIVE.

PLATE XLII.

The design of the art of perspective is to draw on a plane surface the representation of an object or objects, so that the representation shall convey to the eye, the same image as the objects themselves would do if placed in the same relative position.

To elucidate this definition it will be necessary to explain the *manner* in which the image of external objects is conveyed to the eye.

1st. To enable a person to see any object, it is necessary that such object should reflect light.

2nd. Light reflected from a centre becomes weaker in a duplicate ratio of distance from its source, it being only one-fourth as intense at double the distance, and one-ninth at triple the distance, and so on.

3rd. A ray of light striking on any plane surface, is reflected from that surface in exactly the same angle with which it impinges; thus if a plane surface be placed at an angle of 45°, to the direction of rays of light, the rays will be reflected at an angle of 45° in the opposite direction. This fact is expressed as follows, viz: THE ANGLE OF REFLECTION IS EQUAL TO THE ANGLE OF

INCIDENCE. This axiom, so short and pithy, should be stored in the memory with some others that we propose to give, to be brought forward and applied whenever required.

4th. Rays of light reflected from a body proceed in straight lines until interrupted by meeting with other bodies, which by reflection or refraction, change their direction.

5th. REFRACTION of LIGHT. When a ray of light passes from a rare to a more dense medium, as from a clear atmosphere through a fog or from the air into water, it is bent out of its direct course: thus if we thrust a rod into water, it appears broken or bent at the surface of the water; objects have been seen through a fog by the bending of the rays, that could not possibly be seen in clear weather; this bending of the rays of light is called refraction, and the rays are said to be refracted: this effect, (produced however by a different cause) may often be seen by looking through common window glass, when in consequence of the irregularities of its surface, the view of objects without is much distorted.

6th. A portion of light is absorbed by all bodies receiving it on their surface, consequently the amount of light reflected from an object is not equal to the quantity received.

7th. The amount of absorption is not the same in all bodies, but depends on the color and quality of the reflecting surface; if a ray falls on the bright polished surface of a looking-glass, most of it will be reflected, but if it should fall on a surface of black cloth, most of it would be absorbed. White or light colors reflect more of a given ray of light than dark colors; polished surfaces reflect more than those which are unpolished, and smooth surfaces more than rough.

8th. As all objects absorb more or less light, it follows that at each reflection the ray will become weaker until it is no longer perceptible.

9th. Rays received from a luminous source are called direct, and the parts of an object receiving these direct rays are said to be in LIGHT. The portions of the surface so situated as not to receive the direct rays are said to be in SHADE; if the object receiving the direct rays is opaque, it will prevent the rays from passing in that direction, and the outline of its illuminated parts will be projected on the nearest adjoining surface: the figure so projected is called its SHADOW.

10th. The parts of an object in shade will always be lighter than the shadow, as the object receives more or less *reflected light* from the atmosphere and adjoining objects, the quantity depending on the position of the shaded surface, and on the position and quality of the surrounding objects.

11th. If an object were so situated as to receive only a direct ray of light, without receiving reflected light from other sources, the illuminated portion could alone be seen; but for this universal law of reflection we should be able to see nothing that is not illuminated by the direct rays of the sun or by some artificial means, and all beyond would be one gloomy blank.

12th. Rays of light proceeding in straight lines from the surfaces of objects, meet in the front of the eye of the spectator where they cross each other, and form an inverted image on the back of the eye, of all objects within the scope of vision.

13th. The size of the image so formed on the retina depends on the size and distance of the original; the shape of the image depends on the angle at which it is seen.

NOTE.—The size of objects diminishes directly as the distance increases, appearing at ten times the distance, only a tenth part as large; the knowledge of this fact has produced a system of *arithmetical perspective*, which enables the draughtsman to proportion the sizes of objects by calculation.

14th. The strength of the image depends on the degree of illumination of the original, and on its distance from the eye, objects becoming more dim as they recede from the spectator.

15th. To give a better idea of the operation of the eye in viewing an object, let us refer to fig. 1. The circle *A* is intended to represent a section of the human eye, *H* the pupil in front, *K* the crystalline lens in which the rays are all converged and cross each other, and *M* the concave surface of the back of the eye called the *retina*, on which the image is projected.

16th. Let us suppose the eye to be viewing the cross *B. C*, and that the parallelogram *N. O. P. Q* represents a picture frame in which a pane of glass is inserted; the surface of the glass slightly obscured so as to allow objects to be traced on it, then rays from every part of the cross will proceed in straight lines to the eye, and form the inverted image *C. B* on the retina. If with a pencil we were to trace the form of the cross on the glass so as to interrupt the view of the original object, we should have a true perspective representation of the original, which would form exactly the same sized image on the retina; thus the point *b* would intercept the view of *B*, *c* of *C*, *d* of *D* and *e* of *E*, and if colored the same as the original, the image formed from it would be the same in every respect as from the original.

17th. If we move the cross *B. C* to *F. G*, the image formed on the retina would be much larger, as shewn at *G. F*, and the representation on the glass would be larger, the ray from *F* passing through *f*, and the ray from *G* passing through *g*, shewing that the same object will produce a larger or smaller image on the retina as it advances to or recedes from the spectator; the farther it recedes, the smaller will be the image formed, until it becomes so small as to be invisible.

18th. Fig. 2 is given to elucidate the same subject. If we suppose a person to be seated in a room, the ground outside to be on a level with the bottom of the window *A. B*, the eye at *S* in the same level line, and a series of rods *C. D. E. F* of the same height of the window to be planted outside, the window to be filled with four lights of glass of equal size, then the ray from the bottom of all the rods would pass through the bottom of the window; the ray from the top of *C* would pass through the top of the window; from the top of *D* a little farther off, it would pass through the third light; the ray from *E* would pass through the middle, and *F* would only occupy the height of one pane.

19th. Fig. 3. Different sized and shaped objects may produce the same image; thus the bent rods *A* and *C*, and the straight rods *B* and *D* would produce the same image, being placed at different distances from the eye, and all contained in the same angle *D. S. E.* As the bent rods *A* and *C* are viewed edgewise they would form the same shaped image as if they were straight. The angle formed by the rays of light passing from the top and bottom of an object to the eye, as *D. S. E*, is called the VISUAL ANGLE, and the object is said to subtend an angle of so many degrees, measuring the angle formed at *S*.

20th. Of FORESHORTENING. When an object is viewed obliquely it appears much shorter than if its side is directly in front of the eye; if for instance we hold a pencil sidewise at arms length opposite the eye, we should see its entire length; then if we incline the pencil a little, the side will appear shorter, and one of the ends can also be seen, and the more the pencil is inclined the smaller will be the angle subtended by its side, until nothing but the end would be visible. Again if a *wheel* be placed perpendicularly opposite the eye, its rim and hub would shew perfect circles, and the spokes would all appear to be of the same length, but if we incline the wheel a little, the circles will appear to be ellipses, and the spokes appear of different lengths, dependant on the an-

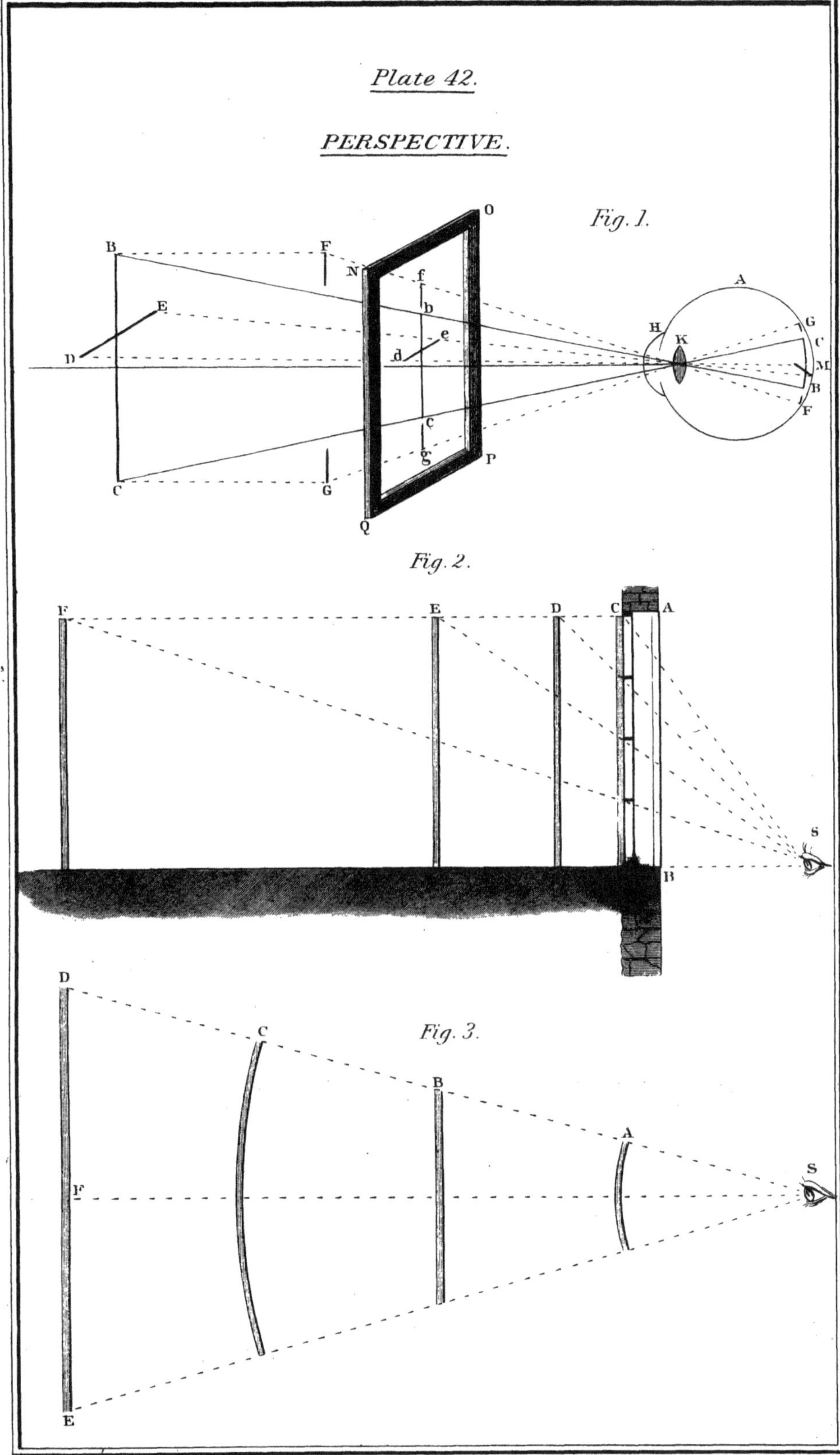

Wm Minifie.　　　　Illman & Sons

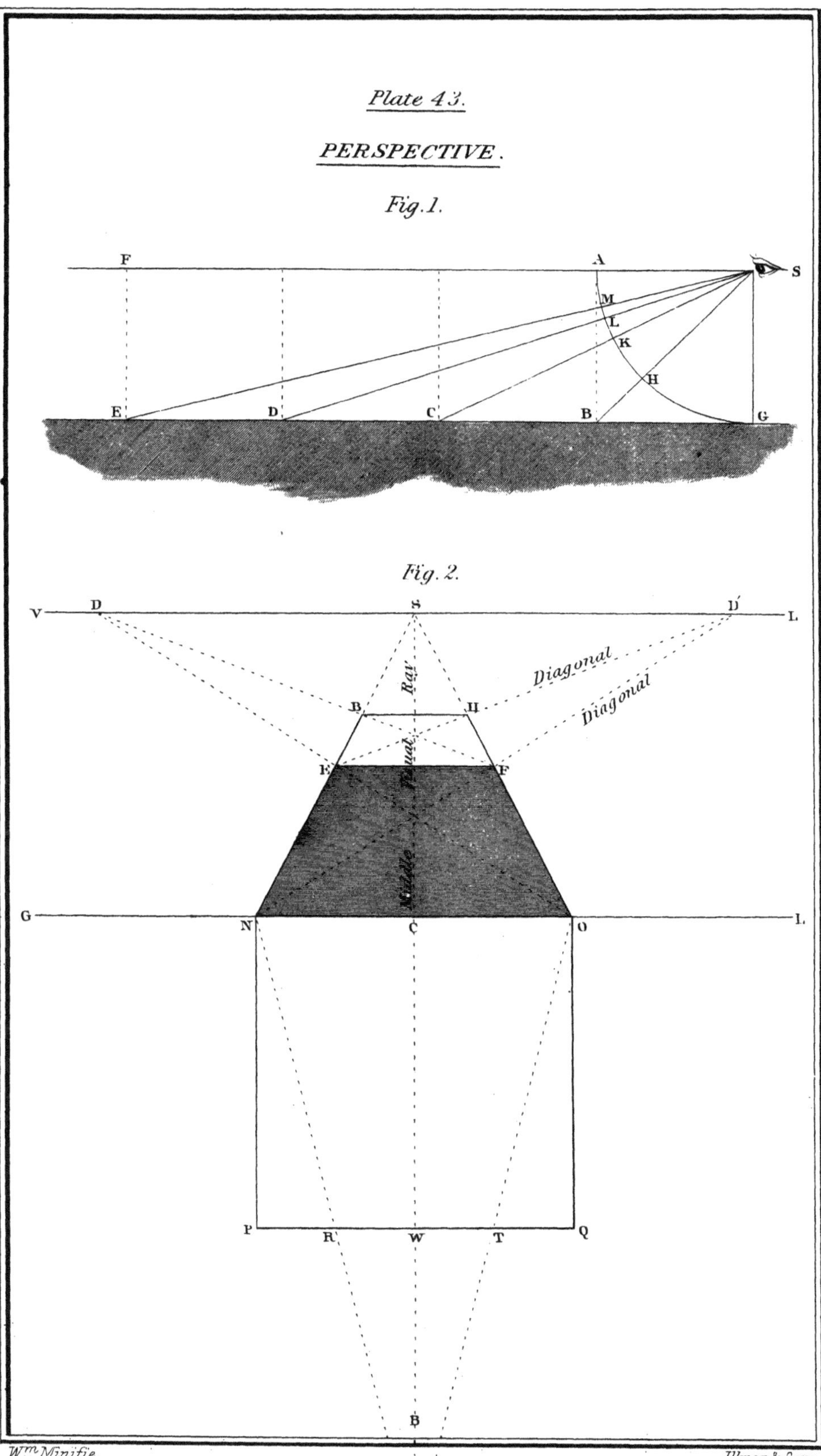
Plate 43.
PERSPECTIVE.
Fig. 1.
F
A
S
M
L
K
H
E
D
C
B
G
Fig. 2.
V
D
S
D′
L
Diagonal
Diagonal
Ray
B
H
Visual
E
F
Middle
G
N
C
O
L
P
R
W
T
Q
B
Wm. Minifie.
Illman & Sons

gle at which they are viewed; the more the wheel is inclined the shorter will be the conjugate diameter of the ellipsis, until the whole would form a straight line whose length would be equal to the diameter, and its breadth equal to the thickness of the wheel. This decrease of the angle subtended by an object, when viewed obliquely, is called *foreshortening*.

PLATE XLIII.

FIGURE 1.

21st. If we suppose a person to be standing on level ground, with his eye at *S*, the line *A. F* parallel to the surface and about five feet above it, and the surface *G. E* to be divided off into spaces of five feet, as at *B. C. D* and *E*, then if from *S*, with a radius *S. G*, we describe the arc *A. G*, and from the points *B. C. D* and *E* we draw lines to *S*, cutting the arc in *H. K. L* and *M*, the distances between the lines on the arc, will represent the angle subtended in the eye by each space, and if we adopt the usual mode for measuring an angle, and divide the quadrant into 90°, it will be perceived that the first space of five feet subtends an angle of 45°, equal to one-half of the angle that would be subtended by a plane that would extend to the extreme limits of vision; the next space from *B* to *C* subtends an angle of about 18 1-2°, from *C* to *D* about 8°, and from *D* to *E* about 4 1-2°, and the angle subtended would constantly become less, until the divisions of the spaces would at a short distance appear to touch each other, a space of five feet subtending an angle so small, that the eye could not appreciate it. It is this foreshortening that enables us in some measure to judge of distance.

22nd. If instead of a level plane, the person at *S* be standing at the foot of a hill, the surface being less inclined would diminish less rapidly, but if on the contrary he be standing on the brow of a hill looking downward, it would diminish more rapidly; hence we derive the following axiom: THE DEGREE OF FORESHORTENING OF OBJECTS DEPENDS ON THE ANGLE AT WHICH THEY ARE VIEWED

23rd. PERSPECTIVE may be divided into two branches, LINEAR and AERIAL.

24th. LINEAR PERSPECTIVE teaches the mode of drawing the lines of a picture so as to convey to the eye the apparent SHAPE or FIGURE of each object from the point at which it is viewed.

25th. AERIAL PERSPECTIVE teaches the mode of arranging the direct and reflected LIGHTS, SHADES and SHADOWS of a picture, so as to give to each part its requisite degree of tone and color, diminishing the strength of each tint as the objects recede, until in the extreme distance, the whole assumes a bluish gray which is the color of the atmosphere. This branch of the art is requisite to the artist who would paint a landscape, and can be better learnt by the study of nature and the paintings of good masters, than by any series of rules which would require to be constantly varied.

26th. Linear perspective, on the contrary, is capable of strict mathematical demonstration, and its rules must be positively followed to produce the true figure of an object.

DEFINITIONS.

27th. The PERSPECTIVE PLANE is the surface on which the picture is drawn, and is supposed to be placed in a vertical position between the spectator and the object—thus in fig. 1, Plate 42, the parallelogram *N. O. P. Q* is the perspective plane.

28th. The GROUND LINE or BASE LINE of a picture is the seat of the perspective plane, as the line *Q. P*, fig. 1, Plate 42, and *G. L*, fig. 2, Plate 43.

29th. The HORIZON. The *natural horizon* is the line in which the earth and sky, or sea and sky appear to meet; the horizon in a perspective drawing is at *the height of the eye of the spectator.* If the object viewed be on level ground, the horizon will be about five feet or five and a half feet above the ground line, as it is represented by *V. L*, fig. 2. If the spectator be viewing the object from an eminence, the horizon will be higher, and if the spectator be lower than the ground on which the object stands, the horizon will be lower; thus the horizon in perspective, means the height of the eye of the spectator, and as an object may be viewed by a person reclining on the ground, or standing upright on the ground, or he may be elevated on a chair or table, it follows that the horizon may be made higher or lower, at the pleasure of the draughtsman; but in a mechanical or architectural view of a design, it should be placed about five feet above the ground line.

NOTE.—The tops of all horizontal objects that are below the horizon, and the under sides of objects above the horizon, will appear more or less displayed as they recede from or approach to the horizon.

30th. The STATION POINT, or POINT of VIEW is the position of the spectator when viewing the object or picture.

31st. The POINT of SIGHT. If the spectator standing at the station point should hold his pencil horizontally at the level of his eye in such a position that the end only could be seen, it would cover a small part of the object situated in the horizon; this point is marked as at *S*, fig. 2, and called the point of sight. It must be remembered that the point of sight *is not the position of a spectator when viewing an object;* but a point in the horizon directly opposite the eye of the spectator, and from which point the spectator may be at a greater or less distance.

32nd. POINTS of DISTANCE are set off on the horizon on either side of the point of sight as at *D. D′*, and represent the distance of the spectator from the perspective plane. As an object may be viewed at different distances from the perspective plane, it follows that these points may be placed at any distance from the point of sight to suit the judgment of the draughtsman, but they should never be less than the base of the picture.

NOTE 1.—Although the height of the horizon, and the points of distance may be varied at pleasure, it is only from that distance and with the eye on a level with the horizon that a picture can be viewed correctly.

NOTE 2.—In the following diagrams the points of distance have generally been placed within the boundary of the plates, as it is important that the learner should see the points to which the lines tend; *they should be copied with the points of distance much farther off.*

33rd. VISUAL RAYS. All lines drawn from the object to the eye of the spectator are called visual rays.

34th. The MIDDLE RAY, or CENTRAL VISUAL RAY is a line proceeding from the eye of the spectator to the point of sight; *external visual rays* are the rays proceeding from the opposite sides of an object, or from the top and bottom of an object to the eye. The angle formed in the eye by the external rays, is called the *visual angle.*

NOTE.—The *perspective plane* must always be perpendicular to the *middle visual ray.*

35th. VANISHING POINTS. It has been shewn at fig. 1 in this plate that objects of the same size subtend a constantly decreasing angle in the eye as they recede from the spectator, until they are no longer visible; the point where level objects become invisible or appear to vanish, will always be in the horizon, and is called the vanishing point of that object.

36th. The POINT of SIGHT is called the PRINCIPAL VANISHING POINT, because all horizontal objects that are parallel to the middle visual ray will vanish in that point. If we stand in the middle of a street looking directly toward its opposite end as in Plate 54, *(the Frontispiece,)* all horizontal lines, such as the tops and bottoms of the doors and windows, eaves and cornices of the houses, tops of chimnies, &c. will tend toward that point to which the eye is directed, and if the lines were continued they would unite in that point. Again, if we stand in the middle of a room looking towards its opposite end, the joints of the floor, corners of ceiling, washboards and the sides of furniture ranged against the side walls, or placed parallel to them, would all tend to a point in the end of the room at the height of the eye.

37th. The VANISHING POINTS of horizontal objects not parallel with the middle ray will be in some point of the horizon, but not in the point of sight. These vanishing points are called *accidental points.*

38th. DIAGONALS. Lines drawn from the perspective plane to the point of distance as *N. D′* and *O. D*, or from a ray drawn to the point of sight as *E. D′* and *F. D*, are called diagonals; all such lines represent lines drawn at an angle of 45° to the perspective plane, and form as in this figure the diagonals of a square, whose side is parallel to the perspective plane.

39th. Of VANISHING PLANES. On taking a position in the middle of a street as described in paragraph 36, it is there stated that all *lines* will tend to a point in the distance at the height of the eye, called the point of sight, or principal vanishing point; this is equally true of *horizontal* or *vertical planes* that are parallel to the middle visual ray: for if we suppose the street between the curb stones, and the side walks of the street to be three parallel horizontal planes as in Plate 54, their boundaries will all tend to the vanishing point, until at a distance, depending on the breadth of the plane, they become invisible. Again, the walls of the houses on both sides of the street are vertical planes, bounded by the eaves of the roofs and by their intersection with the horizontal planes of the side walks, these boundaries would also tend to the same point, and if the rows of houses were continued to a sufficient distance, these planes would vanish in the same point; if the back walls of the houses are parallel to the front, the planes formed by them will vanish in the same point, and if any other streets should be running parallel to the first, their horizontal and vertical planes would all tend to the same point.

NOTE.—A BIRD'S EYE VIEW of the streets of a town laid out regularly, would fully elucidate the truth of the remarks in this paragraph. When the horizon of a picture is placed very high above the tops of the houses, as if the spectator were placed on some very elevated object, or if seen as a *bird* would see it when on the wing, the view is called a bird's eye view; in a representation of this kind the tops of all objects are visible, and the tendency of all the planes and lines parallel to the middle visual ray to vanish in the point of sight, is very obvious.

40th. If we were viewing a room as described in paragraph 36, the ceiling and floor would be horizontal planes, and the walls vertical planes, and if extended would all vanish in the point of sight; or if we were viewing the section of a house of several stories in height, all the floors and ceilings would be horizontal planes, and all the parallel partitions and walls would be vertical planes, and would all vanish in the same point.

41st. When the BOUNDARIES OF INCLINED PLANES are horizontal lines parallel to the middle ray, the planes will vanish in the point of sight; thus the roofs of the houses in Plate 54, bounded by the horizontal lines of the eaves and ridge, are inclined planes vanishing in the point of sight.

42nd. PLANES PARALLEL TO THE PLANE OF THE PICTURE have no vanishing point, neither have any lines drawn on such planes.

43rd. VERTICAL OR HORIZONTAL PARALLEL PLANES running at any inclination to the middle ray or perspective plane, vanish in *accidental points* in the horizon, as stated in paragraph 37; as for example, the walls and bed of a street running diagonally to the plane of the picture, or of a single house as in Plate 53, where the opposite sides vanish in accidental points at different distances from the point of sight, because the walls form different angles with the perspective plane, as shewn by the plan of the walls *B. D* and *D. C*, fig. 1.

44th. ALL HORIZONTAL LINES DRAWN ON A PLANE, or running parallel to a plane, vanish in the same point as the plane itself.

45th. INCLINED LINES vanish in points perpendicularly above or below the vanishing point of the plane, and if they form the same angle with the horizon in different directions as the gables of the house in fig. 2, Plate 53, the vanishing points will be equidistant from the horizon.

From what has been said we derive the following AXIOMS; their importance should induce the student to fix them well in his memory:

1st. The ANGLE OF REFLECTION OF LIGHT is equal to the angle of incidence. See paragraph No. 3, page 81.

2nd. The SHADOW of an object is always darker than the object itself. See paragraph 10, page 82.

3rd. The DEGREE OF FORESHORTENING of objects depends on the angle at which they are viewed. See paragraph 20, page 84.

4th. The APPARENT SIZE of an object decreases exactly as its distance from the spectator is increased. See paragraph 35, p. 87.

5th. PARALLEL PLANES and LINES vanish to a common point. See paragraph 36, page 88.

6th. ALL PARALLEL PLANES whose boundaries are parallel to the middle visual ray, vanish in the point of sight. See paragraph 36, page 88.

7th. ALL HORIZONTAL LINES parallel to the middle ray vanish in the point of sight.

8th. HORIZONTAL LINES AT AN ANGLE OF 45° with the plane of the picture, vanish in the points of distance. See paragraph 38, page 88.

9th. PLANES AND LINES PARALLEL TO THE PLANE OF THE PICTURE have no vanishing point.

PRACTICAL PROBLEMS.

1st. *To draw the perspective representation of the square* N. O. P. Q, *viewed in the direction of the line* W. B, *with one of its sides* N. O *touching the perspective plane* G. L, *and parallel with it.*

1st. Draw the horizontal line *V. L* at the height of the eye.

2nd. From *C*, the centre of the side *N. O*, draw a perpendicular to *V. L*, cutting it in *S*. Then *S* is the point of sight or the principal vanishing point, and *C. S* the middle visual ray.

3rd. As the sides *N. P* and *O. Q* are parallel to the middle ray *C. S*, they will vanish in the point of sight. Therefore from *N* and *O* draw rays to *S;* these are the external visual rays.

4th. From *S*, set off the points of distance *D. D′* at pleasure, equidistant from *S*, and from *N* and *O*, draw the diagonals *N. D′* and

O. D. Then the intersection of these diagonals with the external visual rays determine the depth of the square.

5th. Draw *E. F* parallel to *N. O.* Then the trapezoid *N. O. E. F* is the perspective representation of the given square viewed at a distance from *W* on the line *W. B,* equal to *S. D.*

2nd. *To draw the Representation of another Square of the same size immediately in the rear of* E. F.

1st. From *E,* draw *E. D',* intersecting *O. S* in *H,* and from *F,* draw *F. D,* intersecting *N. S* in *B.*

2nd. Draw *B. H* parallel to *E. F,* which completes the second square; and the trapezoid *N. O. H. B* is the representation of a parallelogram whose side *O. H* is double the side of the given square.

NOTE.—If from *W* on the line *W. B* we set off the distance *S. D,* extending in the example outside of the plate, (which represents the distance from which the picture is viewed,) and from *N* and *O* draw rays to the point so set off, cutting *P. Q* in *R* and *T,* then the lines *R. T* and *E. F* will be of equal length, and prove the correctness of the diagram.

PLATE XLIV.

FIGURE 1.

To draw a Perspective Plan of a Square and divide it into a given number of Squares, say sixty-four.

Let *G. L* be the base line, *V. L* the horizon, *S* the point of sight, and *N. O* the given side of the square.

1st. From *N* and *O,* draw rays to *S* and diagonals to *D. D,* intersecting each other in *P* and *Q,* draw *P. Q.*

2nd. Divide *N. O* into eight equal parts, and from the points of division draw rays to *S.*

3rd. Through the points of intersection formed with those rays by the diagonals, draw lines parallel to *N. O,* which will divide the square as required, and may represent a checker board or a pavement of square tiles.

Of Half Distance.

When the points of distance are too far off to be used conveniently, half the distance may be used; as for example, if we bisect *S. D* in 1-2 *D*, and *N. O* in *C*, and draw a line from *C* to 1-2 *D*, it will intersect *N. S* in *P*, being in the same point as by the diagonal drawn from *O* the opposite side of the square, to the whole distance at *D*.

Note.—Any other fraction of the distance may be used, provided that the divisions on the base line be measured proportionately.

Figure 2.

To draw the Plan of a Room with Pilasters at its sides, the base line, horizon, point of sight, and points of distance given.

Note.—To avoid repetitions, *in the following diagrams we shall suppose the base line, the horizon V. L, the point of sight S, and the points of distance D. D to be given.*

1st. Let *N. O* be the width of the proposed room, then draw *N. S* and *O. S* representing the sides of the room.

2nd. From *N* toward *O* lay down the width of each pilaster, and the spaces between them, and draw lines to *D*, then through the points where these lines intersect the external visual ray *N. S*, draw lines parallel with *N. O* to the line *O. S*.

3rd. From *N* and *O*, set off the projection of the pilasters and draw rays to the point of sight. The shaded parts shew the position of the pilasters.

4th. If from *N* we lay off the distances and widths of the pilasters toward *M*, and draw diagonals to the opposite point of distance, *N. S* would be intersected in exactly the same points.

Note.—Any rectangular object may be put in perspective by this method, without the necessity of drawing a geometrical plan, as the dimensions may all be laid off on the ground line by any *scale of equal parts.*

Figure 3.

To shorten the depth of a perspective drawing, thereby producing the same effect as if the points of distance were removed much farther off.

1st. Let all the principal lines be given as above, and the pilasters and spaces laid off on the base line from *N*.

Plate 44.

PERSPECTIVE.

Fig. 1.

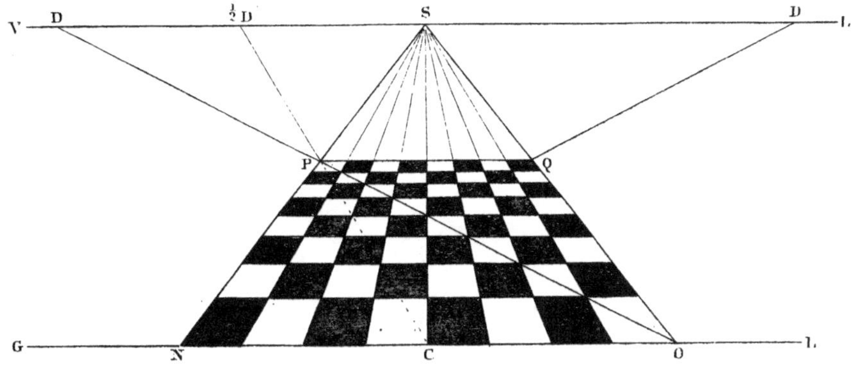

V D ½D S D L

P Q

G N C O L

Fig. 2.

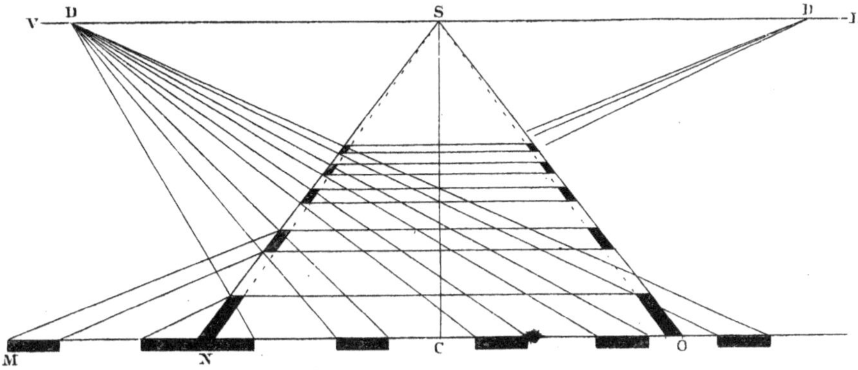

V D S D L

M N C O

Fig 3.

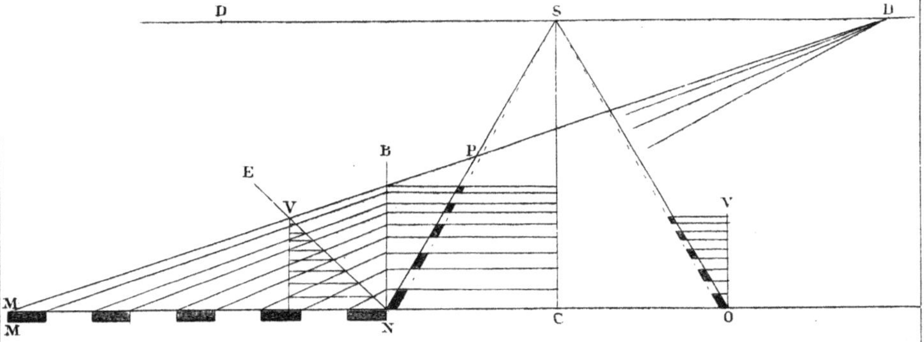

D S D

B P

E V V

M M N C O

Wm Minifie.

Plate 45.

PERSPECTIVE.

Tesselated Pavements.

Fig. 1.

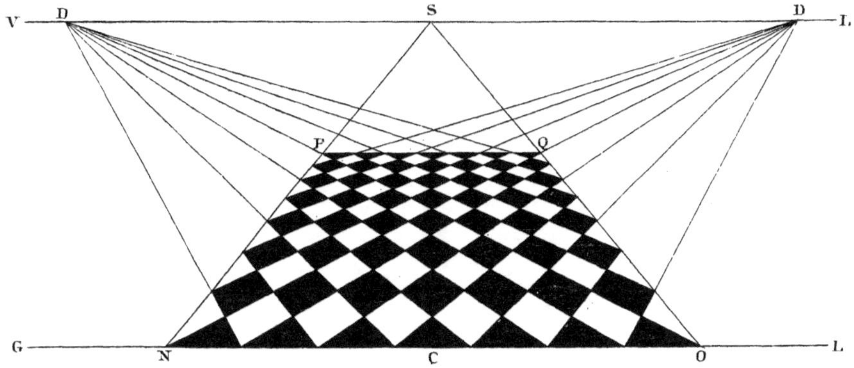

Fig. 2.

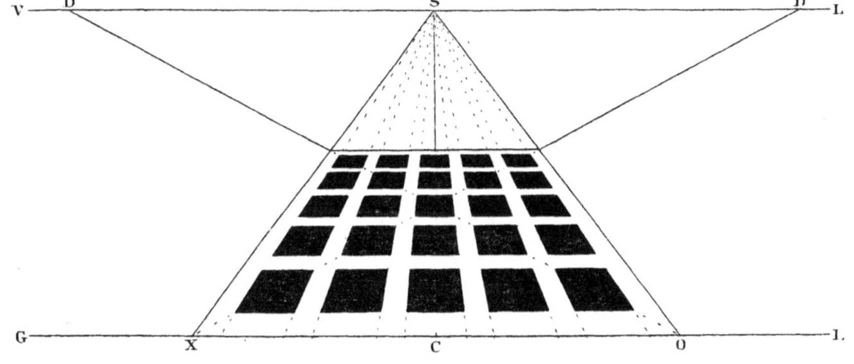

Fig. 3.

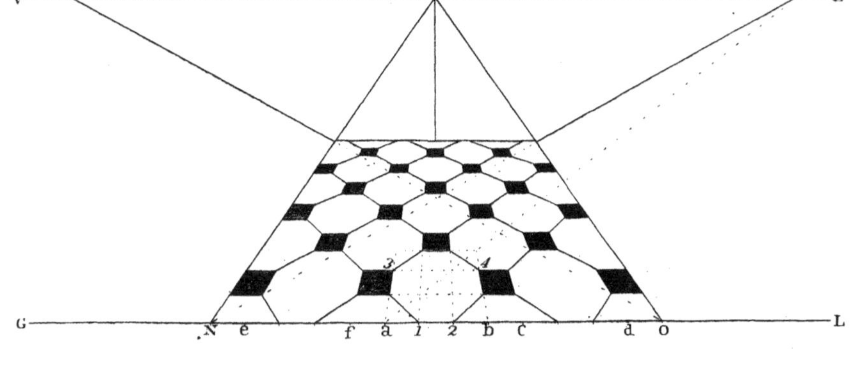

Wm Minns   Hixon & Sons

2nd. From the dimensions on the base line draw diagonals to the point of distance *D*. The diagonal from *M* the outside pilaster will intersect *N. S* in *P*.

3rd. From *N* erect a perpendicular *N. B* to intersect the diagonals, and from those intersections draw horizontal lines to intersect *N. S*.

4th. If from *N* we draw the inclined line *N. E* and transfer the intersections from it to *V. O*, it will reduce the depth much more, as shown at *O. S*.

Most of the foregoing diagrams may be drawn as well with one point of distance as with two.

PLATE XLV.

TESSELATED PAVEMENTS.

FIGURE 1.

To draw a pavement of square tiles, with their sides placed diagonally to the perspective plane.

1st. Draw the perspective square *N. O. P. Q*.

2nd. Divide the base line *N. O* into spaces equal to the diagonal of the tiles.

3rd. From the divisions on *N. O* draw diagonals to the points of distance.

4th. Tint every alternate square to complete the diagram.

FIGURE 2.

To draw a pavement of square black tiles with a white border around them, the sides of the squares parallel to the perspective plane and middle visual ray.

1st. Draw the perspective square, and divide *X. O* into alternate spaces equal to the breadth of the square and borders.

2nd. From the divisions on *X. O* draw rays to the point of sight, and from *X* draw a diagonal to the point of distance.

3rd. Through the intersections formed by the diagonal, with the rays drawn from the divisions on *X. O*, draw lines parallel to *X. O*, to complete the small squares.

Figure 3.

To draw a Pavement composed of Hexagonal and Square Blocks.

1st. Divide the diameter of one of the proposed hexagons *a. b* into three equal parts, and from the points of division draw rays to the point of sight.
2nd. From *a*, draw a diagonal to the point of distance, and through the intersections draw the parallel lines.
3rd. From 1, 2, 3 and 4, draw diagonals to the opposite points of distance, which complete the hexagon.
4th. Lay off the base line from *a* and *b* into spaces equal to one-third of the given hexagon, and draw rays from them to the point of sight; then draw diagonals as in the diagram, to complete the pavement.

PLATE XLVI.

Figure 1.

To draw the Double Square E. F. G. H, *viewed diagonally, with one of its corners touching the Perspective Plane.*

1st. Prolong the sides of the squares as shewn by the dotted lines to intersect the perspective plane.
2nd. From the points of intersection, draw diagonals to the points of distance, their intersections form the diagonal squares.
3rd. The square *A. B. N. O* is drawn around it on the plan and also in perspective, to prove that the same depth and breadth is given to objects by both methods of projection.

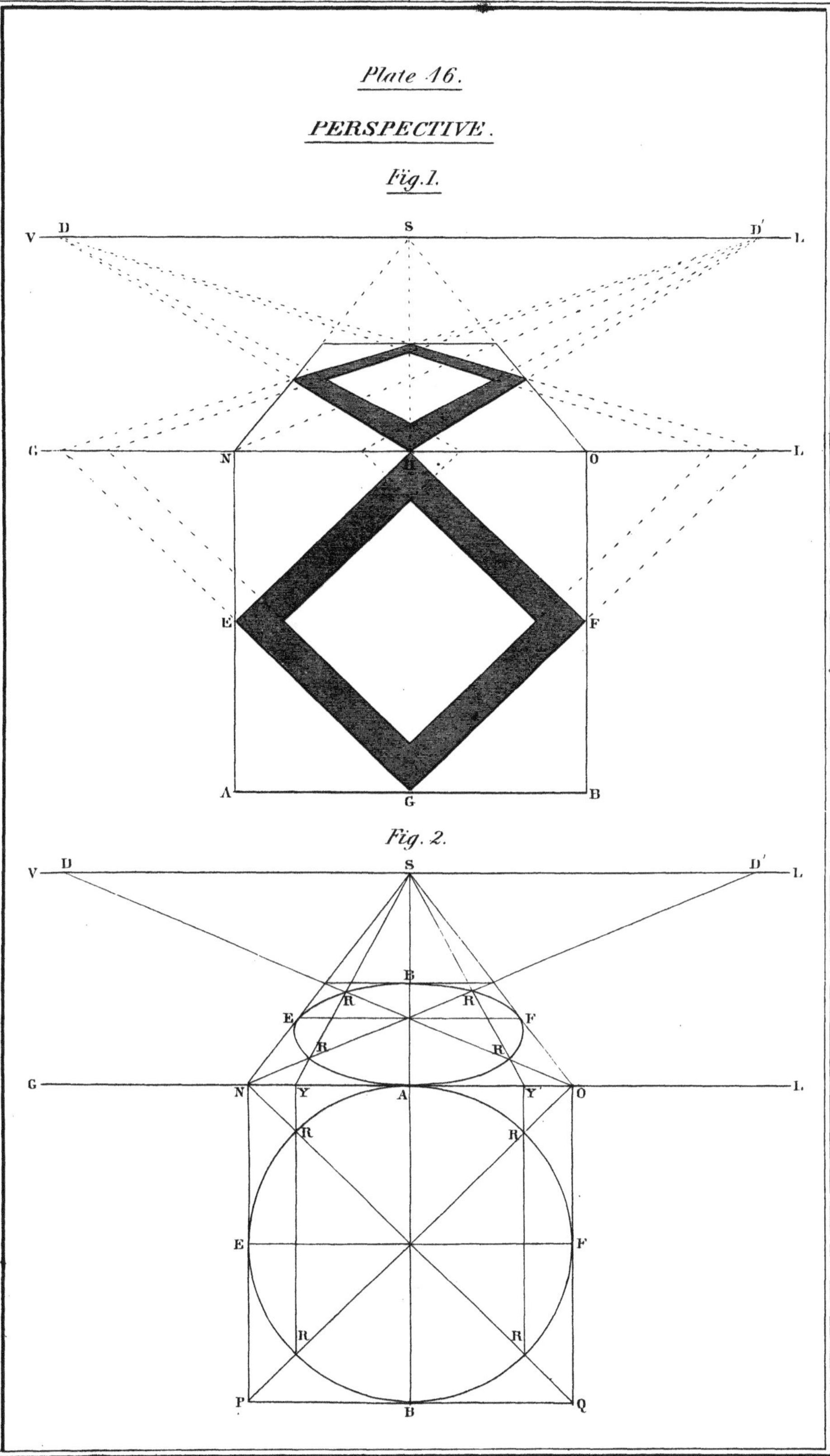

W.m Minifie.

Illman & Sons

Figure 2.

To draw the Perspective Representation of a Circle viewed directly in front and touching the Perspective Plane.

Find the position of any number of points in the Curve.

1st. Circumscribe the circle with a square, draw the diagonals of the square *P. O* and *N. Q*, and the diameters of the circle *A. B* and *E. F*, also through the intersections of said diagonals with the circumference, draw the chords *R. R*, *R. R*, continued to meet the line *G. L* in *Y* and *Y.'*

2nd. Put the square in perspective as before shewn, draw the diagonals *N. D'*, and *O. D*, and the radials *Y. S* and *Y.' S*.

3rd. From *A*, draw *A. S*, and through the intersection of the diagonals draw *E. F* parallel to *N. O*.

4th. Through the points of intersection thus found, viz: *A. B. E. F. R. R. R. R* trace the curve.

Note 1.—This method gives eight points through which to trace the curve, and as these points are equidistant in the plan, it follows that if the points were joined by right lines it would give the perspective representation of an octagon; by drawing diameters midway between those already drawn on the plan, eight other points in the curve may be found. This would give sixteen points in the curve, and render the operation of tracing much more correct.

Note 2.—A circle in perspective may be considered as a polygon of an infinite number of sides, or as a figure composed of an infinite number of points, and as any point in the curve may be found, it follows that every point may be found, and each be positively designated by an intersection; in practice of course this is unnecessary, but the student should remember, that the more points he can positively designate without confusion, the more correct will be the representation.

PLATE XLVII.

LINE OF ELEVATION.

Figure 2

Is the plan of a square whose side is nine feet, each side is divided into nine parts, and lines from the divisions drawn across in opposite directions; the surface is therefore divided into eighty-one squares. *G. L*, fig. 1, is the base line and *D. D* the horizon.

1st.—*To put the plan with its divisions in perspective, one of its sides* N. O *to coincide with the perspective plane.*

Transfer the measures from the side *N. O*, fig. 2, to *N. O* on the perspective plane fig. 1, and put the plan in perspective by the methods before described.

2nd.—*To erect square pillars on the squares N. Q. W, nine feet high and one foot diameter, equal to the size of one of the squares on the plan.*

1st. Erect indefinite perpendiculars from the corners of the squares.
2nd. On *N. A* one of the perpendiculars that touches the perspective plane lay off the height of the column *N. M* from the accompanying scale, then *N. M* IS A LINE OF HEIGHTS on which the true measures of the heights of all objects must be set.
3rd. Two lines drawn from the top and bottom of an object on the line of heights to the point of sight, point of distance, or to any other point in the horizon, forms a scale for determining similar heights on any part of the perspective plan. To avoid confusion they are here drawn to the point *B*.
4th. Through *M* draw *M. C*, parallel to *N. O*, and from *C* draw a line to the point of sight which determines the height of the side of the column, and also of the back column erected on *Q*, and through the intersection of the line *C. S* with the front perpendicular, draw a horizontal line forming the top of the front side of the column *Q*.
5th. To determine the height of the pillar at *W*, 1st. draw a horizontal line from its foot intersecting the proportional scale *N. B* in *Y*; 2nd. from *Y* draw a vertical line intersecting *M. B* in *X*; then *Y. X* is the height of the front of the column *W*. By the same method the height of the column *Q* may be determined as shewn at *R. T*.

3rd.—*To draw the Caps on the Pillars.*

1st. On the line *C. E* a continuation of the top of the front, set off the amount of projection *C. E*, and through *E* draw a ray to the point of sight.
2nd. Through *C* draw a diagonal to the point of distance, and through the point of intersection of the diagonal with the ray

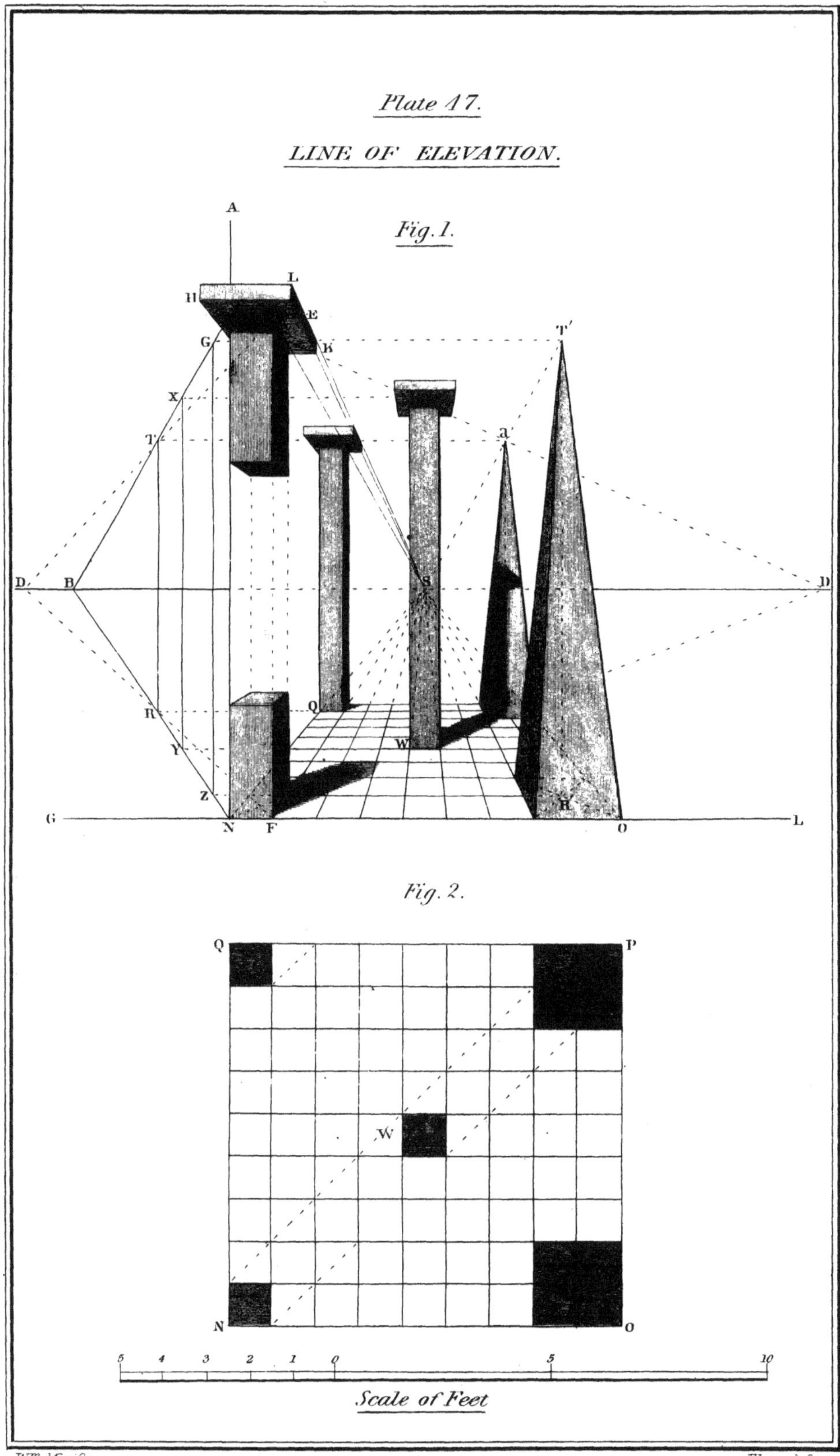

Wm. Minifie. Illman & Sons

last drawn, draw the horizontal line *H* forming the lower edge of the front of the cap.

3rd. Through *M* draw a diagonal to the opposite point of distance, which determines the position of the corners *H* and *K*, from *H* draw a ray to the point of sight.

4th. Erect perpendiculars on all the corners, lay off the height of the front, and draw the top parallel with the bottom. A ray from the corner to the point of sight, will complete the cap.

The other caps can be drawn by similar means.

As a *pillar* is a square *column* the terms are here used indiscriminately.

4th.—*To erect Square Pyramids on* O *and* P *of the same height as the Pillars, with a base of four square feet, as shewn in the plan.*

1st. Draw diagonals to the plan of the base, and from their intersection at *R'* draw the perpendicular *R'. T'.*

2nd. From *R'* draw a line to the proportional scale *N. B*, and draw the vertical line *Z. G*, which is the height of the pyramid.

3rd. Make *R'. T'* equal to *Z. G*, and from the corners of the perspective plan draw lines to *T'*, which complete the front pyramid.

4th. A line drawn from *T* to the point of sight will determine the height of the pyramid at *a*.

NOTE 1.—The point of sight *S* shewn in front of the column *W*, must be supposed to be really a long distance behind it, but as we only see the end of a line proceeding from the eye to the point of sight, we can only represent it by a dot.

NOTE 2.—A part of the front column has been omitted for the purpose of shewing the perspective sections of the remaining parts, the sides of these sections are drawn toward the point of sight, the front and back lines are horizontal. The upper section is a little farther removed from the horizon, and is consequently a little wider than the lower section. This may be taken as an illustration of the note to paragraph 29 on page 87, to which the reader is referred.

NOTE 3.—The dotted lines on the plan shew the direction and boundaries of the shadows; they have been projected at an angle of 45° with the plane of the picture.

PLATE XLVIII.

Figure 1.

To draw a Series of Semicircular Arches viewed directly in front, forming a Vaulted Passage, with projecting ribs at intervals, as shewn by the tinted plan below the ground line.

1st. From the top of the side walls *N. I* and *O. K*, draw the front arch from the centre *H*, and radiate the joints to its centre.

2nd. From the centre *H* and the springing lines of the arch, and from the corners *A* and *M* draw rays to the point of sight.

3rd. From *A* and *M* set off the projection of the ribs, and draw rays from the points so set off to the point of sight.

4th. Transfer the measurements of *A''. B''. C''*, &c., on the plan,to *A'. B'. C'*, &c., on the ground line, and from them draw diagonals to the point of distance, intersecting the ray *A. S* in *B. C. D*, &c.

5th. From the points of intersection in *A. S* draw lines parallel to the base line to intersect *M. S*. This gives the perspective plans of the ribs.

6th. Erect perpendiculars from the corners of the plans to intersect the springing lines, and through these intersections draw horizontal dotted lines, then the points in which the dotted lines intersect the ray drawn from *H* the centre of the front arch, will be the centres for drawing the other arches; *R* being the centre for describing the front of the first rib.

7th. The joints in the fronts of the projecting ribs radiate to their respective centres, and the joints in the soffit of the arch radiate to the point of sight.

Note.—No attempt is made in this diagram to project the shadows, as it would render the lines too obscure. But the front of each projection is tinted to make it more conspicuous.

Plate 48.
ARCHES IN PERSPECTIVE.
Fig. 1.
H
R
I
K
S
D
D
F
E
D
C
B
G
N
A'
B'
C'
M
O
D'
E'
L
A''
B''
C''
D''
E''
F''
Fig. 2.
H
M
J
B
A
L
K
E
C
F
1
2
4
3
S
D
D'
X
W
V
R
T
N
P
Q
O

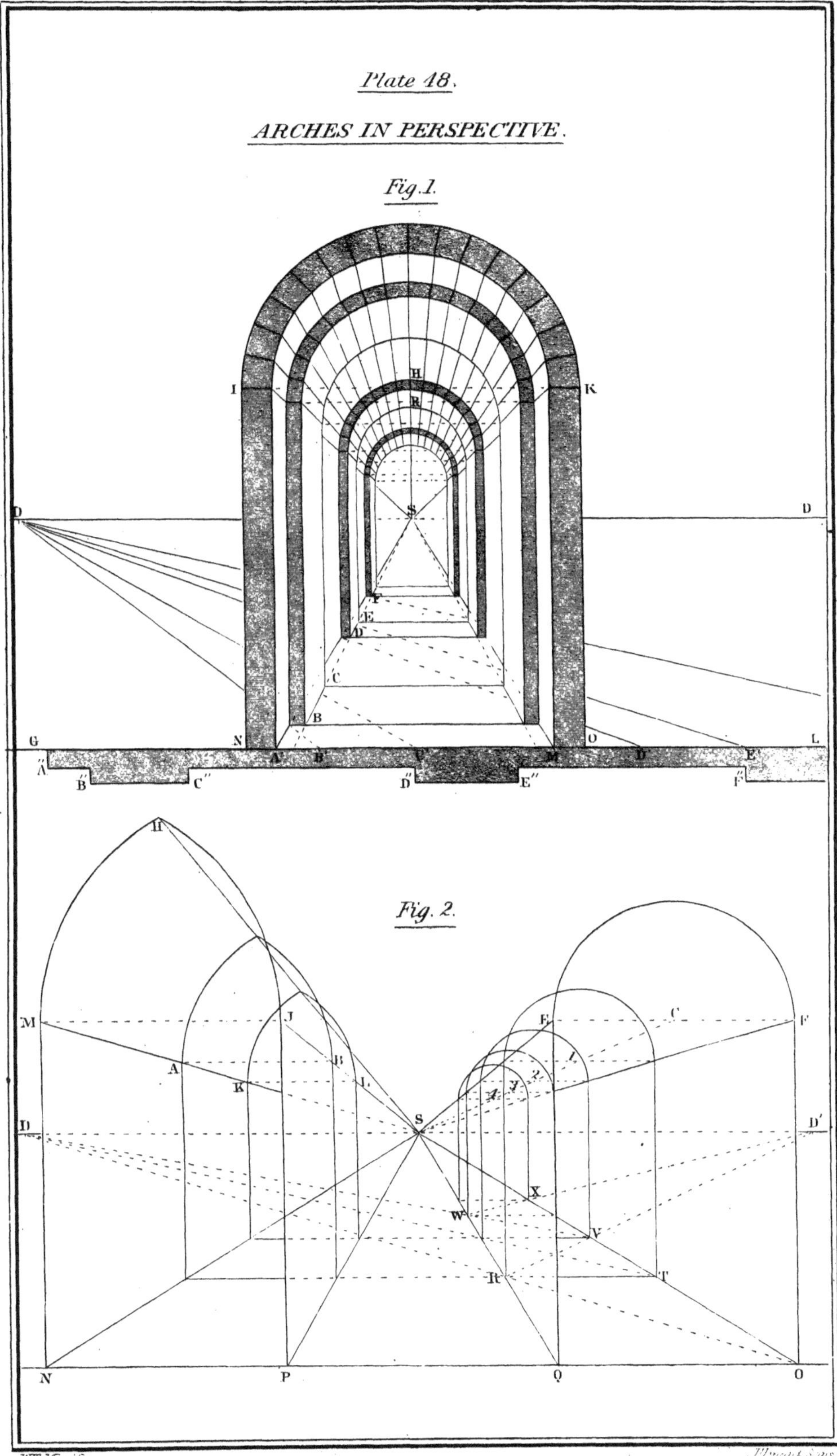

Wm Minifie.

Figure 2.

To draw Semicircular or Pointed Arcades on either side of the spectator, running parallel to the middle visual ray. N. P *and* Q. O *the width of the arches being given, and* P. Q *the space between them.*

1st. From *N. P. Q* and *O* erect perpendiculars, make them all of equal length, and draw *E. F* and *M.* J.

2nd. For the semicircular arches, bisect *E. F* in *C,* and from *E. C. F. O* and *Q,* draw rays to the point of sight.

3rd. From *C,* describe the semicircle *E. F.*

4th. Let the arches be the same distance apart as the width *Q. O,* then from *O* draw a diagonal to the point of distance, cutting *Q. S* in *R,* from *R* draw a diagonal to the opposite point of distance cutting *O. S* in *V,* from *V* draw a diagonal to *D,* cutting *Q. S* in *W,* and from *W* to *D′,* cutting *O. S* in *X.*

5th. Through *R. V. W* and *X,* draw horizontal lines to intersect the rays *O. S* and *Q. S,* and on the intersections erect perpendiculars to meet the rays drawn from *E* and *F.*

6th. Connect the tops of the perpendiculars by horizontal lines, and from their intersections with the ray drawn from *C* in 1, 2, 3 and 4, describe the retiring arches.

7th. For the gothic arches, (let them be drawn the same distance apart as the semicircular,) continue the horizontal lines across from *R* and *V,* to intersect the rays *P. S* and *N. S,* and from the points of intersection erect perpendiculars to intersect the rays drawn from *M* and *J.*

8th. From *M* and *J* successively, with a radius *M. J,* describe the front arch, and from *H* the crown, draw a ray to *S;* from *A* and *B* with the radius *A. B,* describe the second arch, and from *K* and *L,* describe the third arch.

Note.—All the arches in this plate are parallel to the plane of the picture, and although each succeeding arch is smaller than the arch in front of it, all may be described with the compasses.

PLATE XLIX.

TO DESCRIBE ARCHES ON A VANISHING PLANE.

FIGURE 1.

The Front Arch A. N. B, *the Base Line* G. L, *Horizon* D. S, *Point of Sight* S, *and Point of Distance* D, *being given.*

1st. Draw *H. J* across the springing line of the arch, and construct the parallelogram *E. F. J. H.*

2nd. Draw the diagonals *H. F* and *J. E,* and a horizontal line *K. M,* through the points where the diagonals intersect the given arch. Then *H. K. N. M* and *J,* are points in the curve which are required to be found in each of the lateral arches.

3rd. From *F* and *B,* draw rays to the point of sight *S.* Then if we suppose the space formed by the triangle *B. S. F* to be a plane surface, it will represent the vanishing plane on which the arches are to be drawn.

4th. From *B,* set off the distance *B. A* to *Z,* and draw rays from *Z. J* and *C,* to the point of sight.

5th. From *Z,* draw a diagonal to the point of distance, cutting *B. S* in *O;* through *O,* draw a horizontal line cutting *Z. S* in *P;* from *P,* draw a diagonal intersecting *B. S* in *Q;* through *Q,* draw a horizontal line, cutting *Z. S* in *R,* and so on for as many arches as may be required.

6th. From *O. Q. S. U,* erect perpendiculars, cutting *F. S* in *V. W. X. Y.*

7th. Draw the diagonals *J. V, F. I,* &c. as shewn in the diagram, and from their intersection erect perpendiculars to meet *F. S;* through which point and the intersections of the diagonals with *C. S* trace the curves.

FIGURE 2.

To draw Receding Arches on the Vanishing Plane J. S. D, *with Piers between them, corresponding with the given front view, the Piers to have a Square Base with a side equal to* C. D.

1st. From *D* on the base line, set off the distances *D. C, C. B*

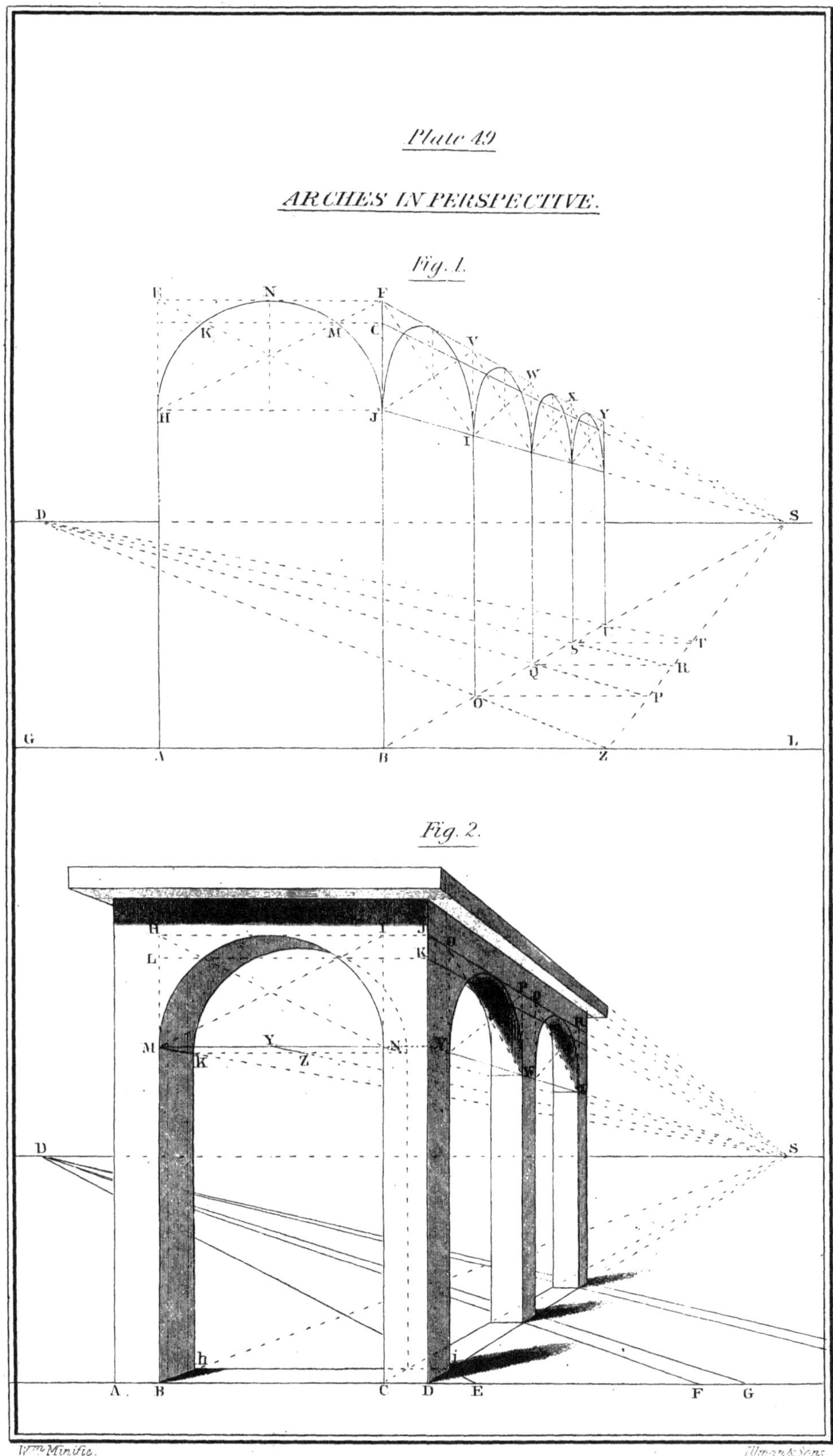
Plate 49
ARCHES IN PERSPECTIVE.
Fig. 1.
E N F K M C V W X Y H J I D S U S T Q R O P G L A B Z
Fig. 2.
H I J K L O P Q R M Y N V K Z W U D S h i A B C D E F G
Wm Minific.
Illman & Sons

and *B. A* to *D. E, E. F* and *F. G*, and from *E. F. G*, &c. draw diagonals to the point of distance to intersect *D. S.*

2nd. From the intersections in *D. S*, erect perpendiculars; draw the parallelogram *M. N. H. I* around the given front arch, the diagonals *M. I* and *H. N*, and the horizontal line *L. K*, prolong *H. I* to *J* and *M. N* to *V.*

3rd. From *B. C. D. M. f. J. K* and *V*, draw rays to the point of sight, put the parallelograms and diagonals in perspective at *O. P V. W* and at *Q. W. R. X*, and draw the curves through the points as in the last diagram.

4th. From *i* where *E. D′* cuts *D. S*, draw a horizontal line cutting *B. S* in *h*, and from *h* erect a perpendicular cutting *M. S* in *k*.

5th. From *Y*, the centre of the front arch, draw a ray to the point of sight, and from *k*, draw a horizontal line intersecting it in *Z*. Then *Z* is the centre for describing the back line of the arch with the distance *Z. k* for a radius.

Note.—The backs of the side arches are found by the same method as the fronts of those arches. The lines are omitted to avoid confusion.

The projecting cap in this diagram is constructed in the same manner as the caps of the pillars in Plate 47.

PLATE L.

APPLICATION OF THE CIRCLE WHEN PARALLEL TO THE PLANE OF THE PICTURE.

V. L is the horizon, and *S* the point of sight.

Figure 1

To draw a Semicircular Thin Band placed above the horizon.

Let the semicircle *A. B* represent the front edge of the band, *A. B* the diameter, and *C* the centre.

1st. From *A. C* and *B*, draw rays to the point of sight.

2nd. From *C* the centre, lay off toward *B*, the breadth of the band *C. E.*

3rd. From *E*, draw a diagonal to the point of distance, intersecting *C. S* in *F*. *Then* F *is the centre for describing the back of the band.*

4th. Through *F*, draw a horizontal line intersecting *A. S* in *K*, and *B. S* in *L*. *Then* F. K *or* F. L *is the radius for describing the back of the band.*

FIGURE 2.

To draw a Circular Hoop with its side resting on the Horizon.

The front circle *A. H. B. K*, diameter *A. B*, and centre *C* being given.

1st. From *A. C* and *B*, draw rays to the point of sight.

2nd. From *C* the centre, lay off the breadth of the hoop at *E*.

3rd. From *E*, draw a diagonal to *D′*, intersecting *C. S* in *F*, and through *F*, draw a horizontal line intersecting *A. S* in *K*, and *B. S* in *L*.

4th. From *F* with a radius *F. L* or *F. K*, describe the back of the curve.

FIGURE 3.

To draw a Cylindrical Tub placed below the Horizon, whose diameter, depth and thickness are given.

1st. From the centre *C* describe the concentric circles forming the thickness of the tub, lay off the staves and radiate them toward *C*.

2nd. Proceed as in figs. 1 and 2 to draw rays and a diagonal to find the point *F*, and from *F* describe the back circles as before; the hoop may be drawn from *F*, by extending the compasses a little.

3rd. Radiate all the lines that form the joints on the sides of the tub toward the point of sight.

FIGURE 4

Is a hollow cylinder placed below the horizon, and must be drawn by the same method as the preceding figures; the letters of reference are the same.

NOTE.—The objects in this Plate are tinted to shew the different surfaces more distinctly without attempting to project the shadows.

Plate 50.

APPLICATION OF THE CIRCLE.

Fig. 1.
Fig. 2.
Fig. 3.
Fig. 4.
A
B
C
E
F
K
L
H
S
V
D
D'

Wm. Minifie.

Illman & Sons

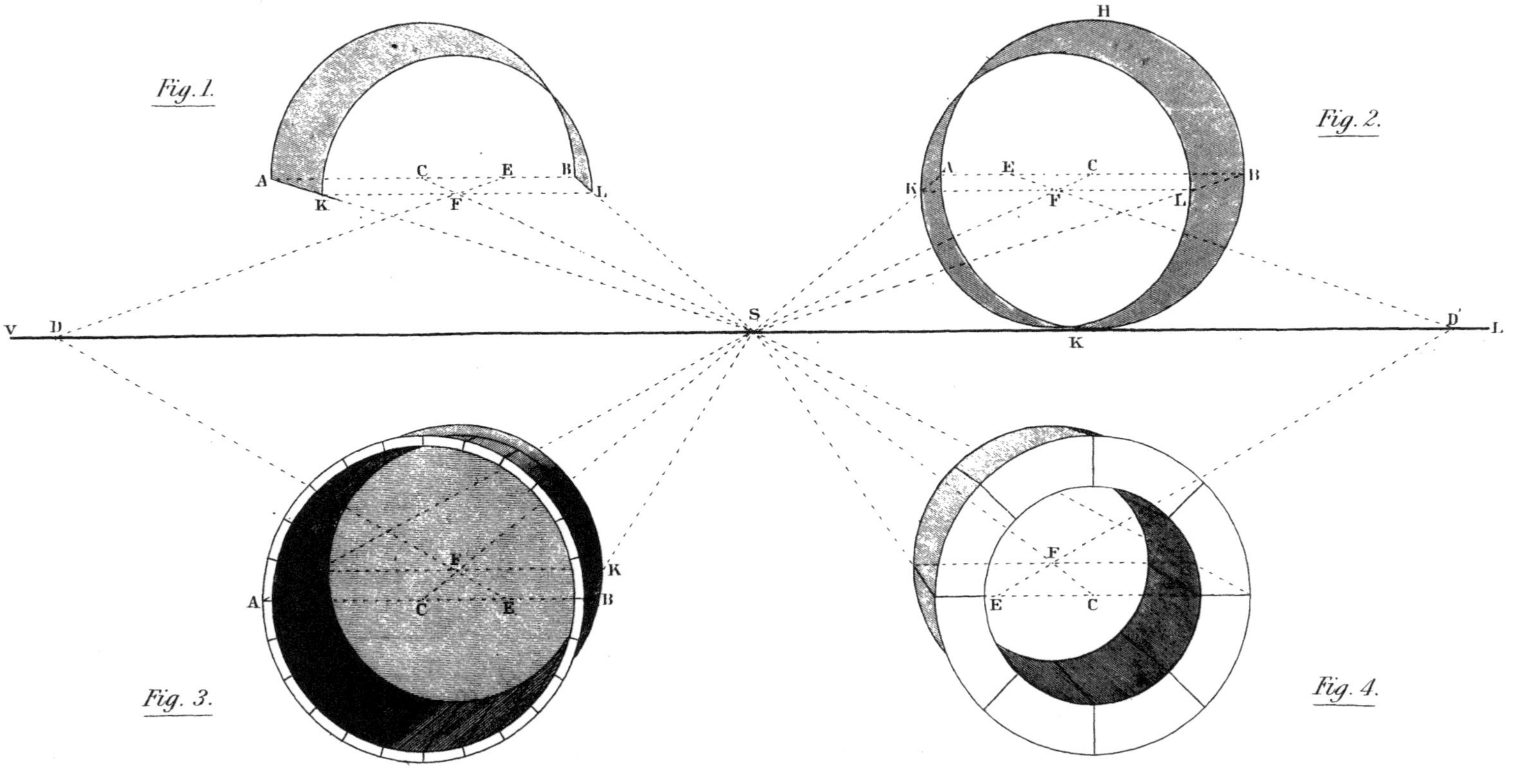

Plate 51.

THE OBJECT AND POINT OF VIEW GIVEN TO FIND THE PERSPECTIVE PLANE AND VANISHING POINTS.

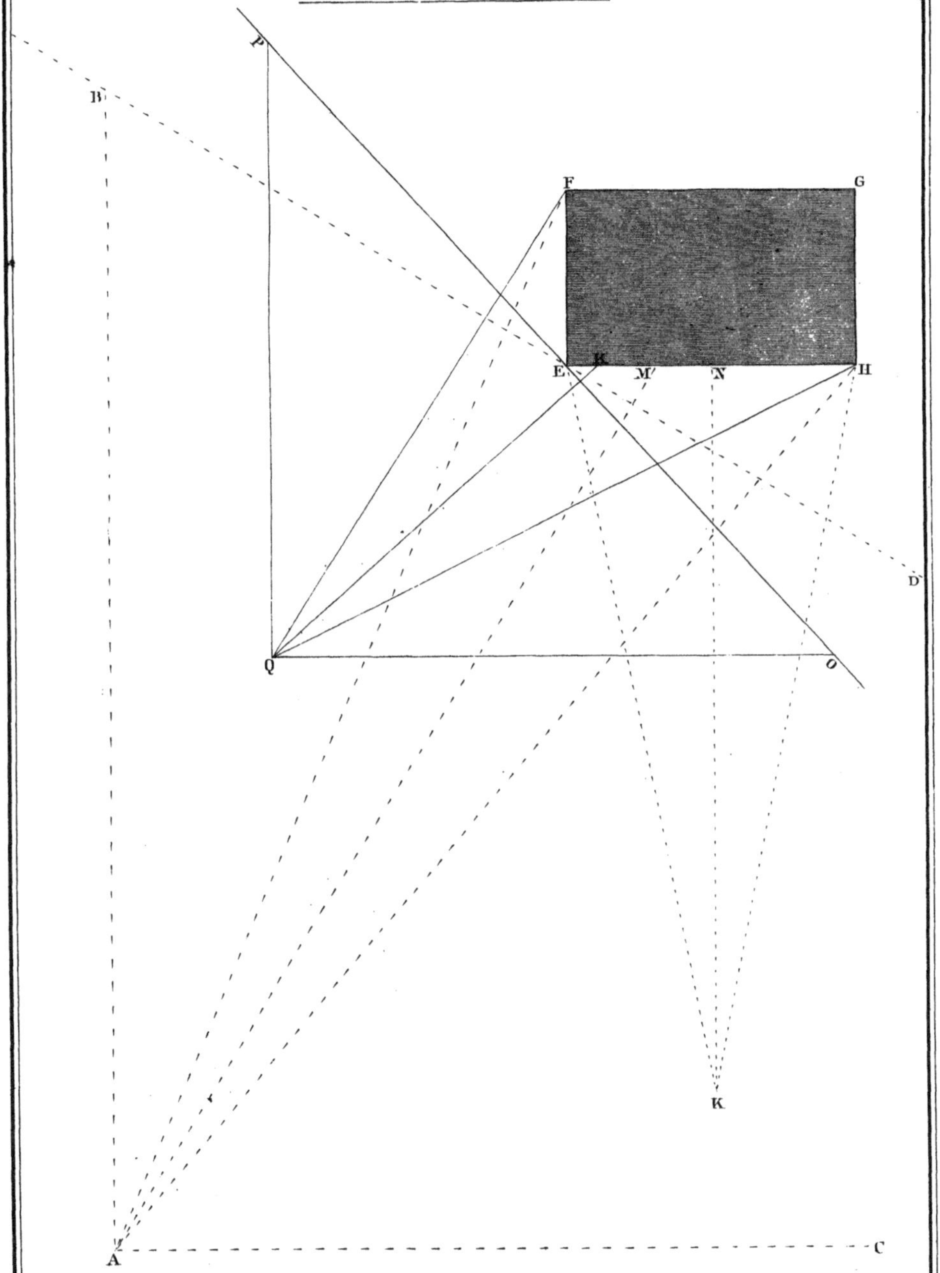

Wm. Minifie.

Weaver & Sons.

PLATE LI.

The object and point of view given, to find the Perspective Plane and Vanishing Points.

Rule 1.—The PERSPECTIVE PLANE must be drawn perpendicular to the middle visual ray.

Rule 2.—The VANISHING POINT of a line or plane is found by drawing a line through the station point parallel with such line or plane to intersect the perspective plane. The point in the horizon immediately over the intersection so found, is the vanishing point of all horizontal lines in said plane, or on any plane parallel to it.

1st. Let the parallelogram *E. F. G. H* be the plan of an object to be put in perspective, and let *Q* be the position of the spectator viewing it, *(called the point of view or station point,)* with the eye directed toward *K, then* Q. K *will be the central visual ray, and* K *the point of sight.* Draw *F. Q* and *H. Q,* these are the external visual rays.

NOTE.—The student should refer to paragraphs 30 and 31, page 87, for the definitions of *station point* and *point of sight.*

2nd. Draw *P. O* at right angles to *Q. K,* touching the corner of the given object at *E,* then P. O *will be the base of the perspective plane.*

NOTE.—This position of the perspective plane, is the farthest point from the spectator at which it can be placed, as the whole of the object viewed must be behind it; but it may be placed at any intermediate point nearer the spectator parallel with *P. O.*

3rd. Through *Q* draw *Q. P* parallel with *E. F,* intersecting the perspective plane in *P, then* P *is the vanishing point of the lines* E. F *and* G. H.

4th. Through *Q* draw *Q. O,* parallel to *E. H,* intersecting the perspective plane in *O, then* O *is the vanishing point for* E. H *and* F. G.

5th. If we suppose the station point to be removed to *A,* then *A. M* will be the central visual ray, *A. F* and *A. H* the external rays, and *B. D* the perspective plane, *B* the vanishing point of

E. F and *G. H,* and the vanishing point of *E. H* and *F. G* will be outside the plate about ten inches distant from *A,* in the direction of *A. C.*

6th. If the station point be removed to *K,* it will be perceived that *E. H* and *F. G* will have no vanishing point, because they are perpendicular to the middle ray, and a line drawn through the station point parallel with the side *E. H* will also be parallel with the perspective plane, consequently could never intersect it.

7th. The sides *E. F* and *G. H* of the plan, would vanish in the point of sight, but if an elevation be drawn on the plan in that position which should extend above the horizon, then neither of those sides could be seen, and the drawing would very nearly approach to a geometrical elevation of the same object.

NOTE.—In the explanation of this plate, the intersections giving the point of sight and vanishing points, are made in the perspective plane, which the student will remember when used in this connection, is equivalent to the base line or ground line of the picture, being the *seat or position of the plane on which the drawing is to be made;* but we must suppose these points to be elevated to the height of the eye of the spectator; in practice, these points must be set off on the horizontal line as described in paragraph 32, page 87.

PLATE LII.

To delineate the perspective appearance of a Cube viewed accidentally and situated beyond the Perspective Plane.

FIGURE 1.

Let *A. B. C. D* be the plan of the cube, *S* the station point, *S. T* the middle visual ray and *B. L* the base line, or perspective plane.

1st. Continue the sides of the plan to the perspective plane as shewn by the dotted lines, intersecting it in *M. E. N* and *O.*

2nd. From the corners of the plan draw rays to the station point, intersecting the perspective plane in *a. d. b. c.*

3rd. Through *S,* draw *S. F* parallel to *A. D,* and *S. G* parallel to *D. C.* *Then* F *is the vanishing point for the sides* A. D *and* B. C; *and* G *is the vanishing point for the sides* A. B *and* D. C.

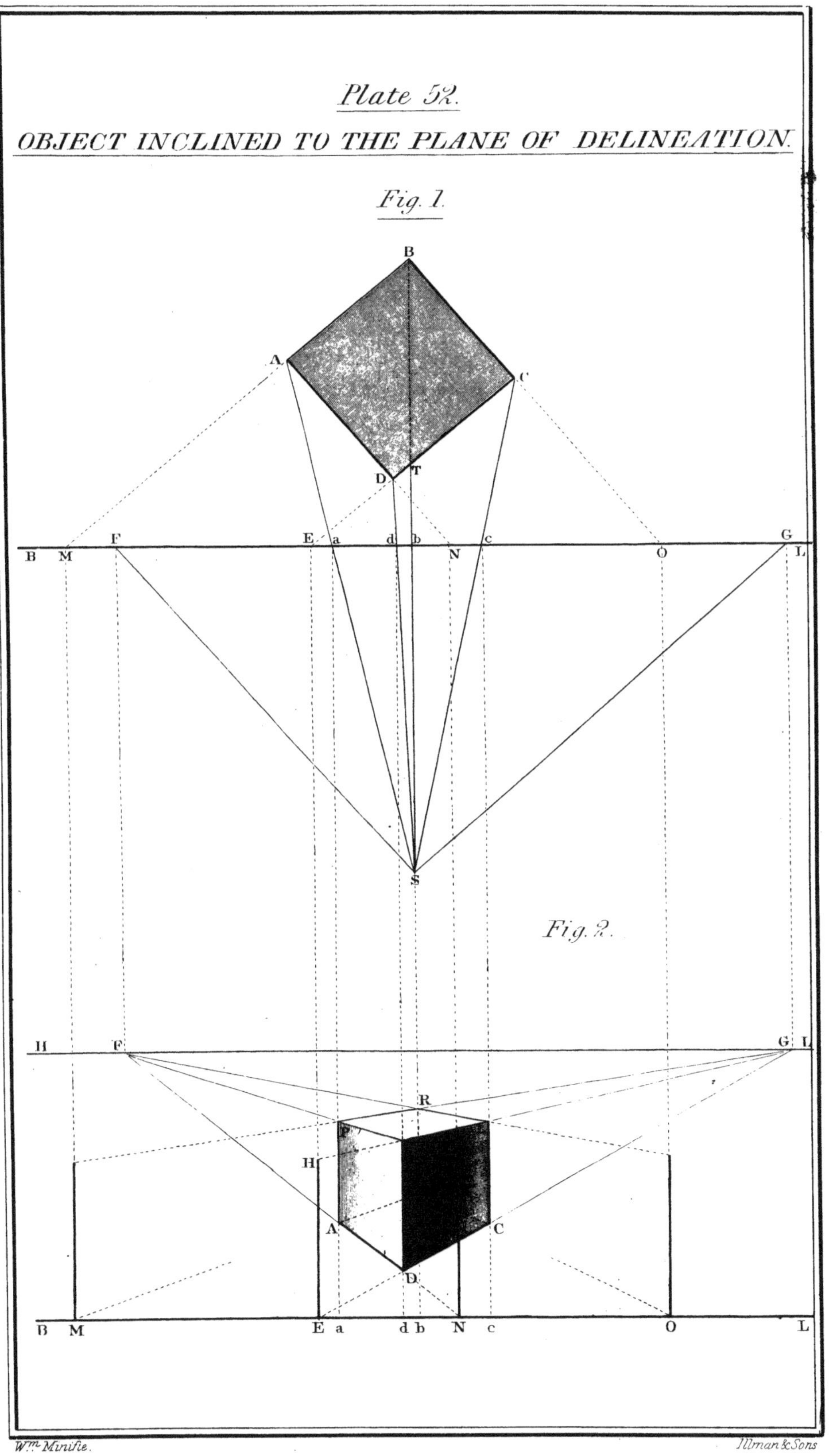
Plate 52.
OBJECT INCLINED TO THE PLANE OF DELINEATION.
Fig. 1.
B
A
C
D
T
F
E
a
d
b
c
G
B
M
N
O
L
S
Fig. 2.
H
F
G
L
R
P
H
A
C
D
B
M
E
a
d
b
N
c
O
L
Wm Minifie.
Illman & Sons

FIGURE 2.

4th. Transfer these intersections from *B. L*, fig. 1, to *B. L*, fig. 2, and the vanishing points *F* and *G* to the horizon, as shewn by the dotted lines.

5th. From *E* and *M*, draw lines to the vanishing point *G*, and from *N* and *O*, draw lines to the vanishing point *F*. *Then the trapezium* A. B. C. D *formed by the intersection of these lines, is the perspective view of the plan of the cube.*

6th. TO DRAW THE ELEVATION. At *M. E. N* and *O* erect perpendiculars and make them equal to the side of the cube.

7th. From the tops of these perpendiculars draw lines to the opposite vanishing points as shewn by the dotted lines, their intersection will form another trapezium parallel to the first, representing the top of the cube.

8th. From *A. D* and *C*, erect perpendicalars to complete the cube.

NOTE.—It is not necessary to erect perpendiculars from all the points of intersection, to draw the representation, but it is done here to prove that the height of an object may be set on any perpendicular erected at the point where the plane, or line, or a continuation of a line intersects the perspective plane; one such line of elevation is generally sufficient.

9th. To draw the figure with one line of heights, proceed as follows: from *A. D* and *C*, erect indefinite perpendiculars.

10th. Make *E. H* equal to the side of the cube, and from *H* draw a line to *G*, cutting the perpendiculars from *D* and *C* in *K* and *L*.

11th. From *K*, draw a line to *F*, cutting *A. P* in *P*; from *L*, draw a line to *F*, and from *P*, draw a line to *G*, which completes the figure.

NOTE.—The student should observe how the lines and horizontal planes become diminished as they approach toward the horizon, each successive line becoming shorter, and each plane narrower until at the height of the eye, the whole of the top would be represented by a straight line. I would here remark, that it would very materially aid the student in his knowledge of perspective, if he would always make it a rule to analyze the parts of every diagram he draws, observe the changes which take place in the forms of objects when placed in different positions on the plan, and when they are placed above or below the horizon at different distances; this would enable him at once to detect a false line, and would also enable him to sketch from nature with accuracy. Practice this always until it becomes a HABIT, and I can assure you it will be a source of much gratification.

PLATE LIII.

TO DRAW THE PERSPECTIVE VIEW OF A ONE STORY COTTAGE, SEEN ACCIDENTALLY.

FIGURE 1.

Let *A*. *B*. *C*. *D* be the plan of the cottage, twenty feet by fourteen feet, drawn to the accompanying scale; the shaded parts shew the thickness of the walls and position of the openings, the dotted lines outside parallel with the walls, give the projection of the roof, and the square *E*. *F*. *G*. *H*, the plan of the chimney above the roof.

Let *P*. *L* be the perspective plane and *S* the station point.

1st. Continue the side *B*. *D* to intersect the perspective plane in *H*, to find the position for a line of heights.

2nd. From all the corners and jambs on the plan, draw rays toward the station point to intersect the perspective plane.

3rd. Through *S* draw a line parallel to the side of the cottage *D*. *C*, to intersect the perspective plane in *L*. This gives the vanishing point for the ends of the building and for all planes parallel to it, viz: the side of the chimney, and jambs of the door and windows.

4th. Through *S* draw a line parallel with *B*. *D*, to intersect the perspective plane, which it would do at some distance outside of the plate; this intersection would be the vanishing point for the sides of the cottage, for the tops and bottoms of the windows, the ridge and eaves of the roof, and for the front of the chimney.

FIGURE 2.

Let us suppose the parallelogram P. L. W. X *to be a separate piece of paper laid on the other, its top edge coinciding with the perspective plane of fig.* 1, *and its bottom edge* W. X *to be the base of the picture, then proceed as follows:*

1st. Draw the horizontal line *R*. *T* parallel to *W*. *X* and five feet above it.

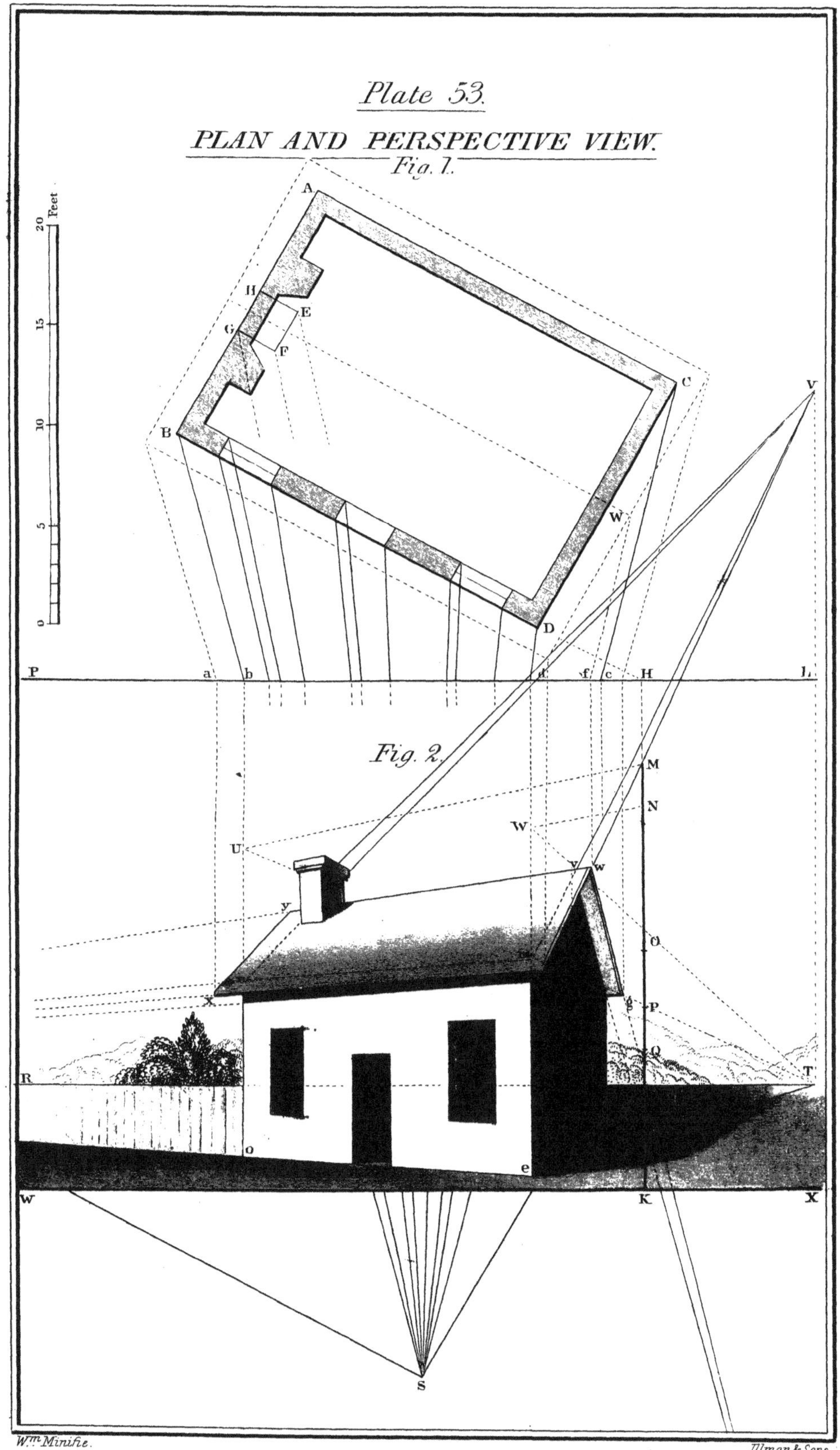

Wm Minifie. Illman & Sons

2nd. Draw *H. K* perpendicular to *P. L* for a line of heights.

3rd. Draw a line from *K* to the vanishing point without the picture, which we will call *Z;* this will represent the line *H. B* of fig. 1, continued indefinitely.

4th. From *b* and *d* draw perpendiculars to intersect the last line drawn, in *o* and *e, which will determine the perspective length of the front of the house.*

5th. On *K. H* set off twelve feet the height of the walls, at *O,* and from *O* draw a line to the vanishing point *Z,* intersecting *d. e* in *m* and *b. o* in *n.*

6th. From *m* and *e* draw vanishing lines to *T,* and a perpendicular from *c* intersecting them in *Y* and *s;* this will give the corner *Y, and determine the depth of the building.*

7th. Find the centre of the vanishing plane representing the end, by drawing the diagonals *m. Y* and *e. s,* and through their intersection draw an indefinite perpendicular *u. v,* which *will give the position of the gable.*

8th. To FIND THE HEIGHT OF THE GABLE, set off its proposed height, say 7′ 0″, from *O* to *N* on the line of heights, from *N* draw a ray to *Z,* intersecting *e. d* in *W,* and from *W* draw a vanishing line to *T* intersecting *u. v* in *v, then* v *is the peak of the gable.*

9th. Join *m. v,* and prolong it to meet a perpendicular drawn through the vanishing point *T,* which it will do in *V, then* V *is the vanishing point for the inclined lines of the ends of the front half of the roof.* The ends of the backs of the gables will vanish in a point perpendicularly below *V,* as much below the horizon as *V* is above it.

10th. FOR THE ROOF. Through *v* draw *v. y* to *Z* without, to form the ridge of the roof, from *f* let fall a perpendicular to intersect *y. v* in *w,* through *w* draw a line to the vanishing point *V* to form the edge of the roof. From *d* let fall a perpendicular to intersect *V. w,* and from the point of intersection draw a line to *Z* to form the front edge of the roof, from *a* let fall a perpendicular to define the corner *x,* and from *x* draw a line to *V* intersecting *w. y* in *y, which completes the front half of the roof;* from *w* draw a line to the vanishing point below the horizon, from *c* let fall a perpendicular to intersect it in g, and through g draw a line to *Z,* which *completes the roof.*

11th. FOR THE CHIMNEY. Set off its height above the ridge at *M,* from *M* draw a line toward the vanishing point *Z,* intersecting *o. b* in *U,* from *U* draw a line to the vanishing point *T,* which gives the height of the chimney, bring down perpendiculars from rays drawn from *G. F* and *E*, fig. 1, and complete the chimney by vanishing lines drawn for the front toward *Z* and for the side toward *T*.

12th For the Door and Windows. Set off their heights at *P. Q* and draw lines toward *Z*, bring down perpendiculars from the rays as before, to intersect the lines drawn toward *Z*; these lines will determine the breadth of the openings. The breadth of the jambs are found by letting fall perpendiculars from the points of intersection, the top and bottom lines of the jambs are drawn toward *T*.

Note 1.—As the bottom of the front fence if continued, would intersect the base line at *K* the foot of the line of heights, and its top is in the horizon, it is therefore five feet high.

Note 2.—The whole of the lines in this diagram have been projected according to the rules, to explain to the learner the methods of doing so, and it will be necessary for him to do so until he is perfectly familiar with the subject. But if he will follow the rule laid down at the end of the description of the last plate, he will soon be enabled to complete his drawing by hand, after projecting the principal lines, but it should not be attempted too early, as it will beget a careless method of drawing, and prevent him from acquiring a correct judgment of proportions.

PLATE LIV.

FRONTISPIECE

Is a perspective view of a street 60 feet wide, as viewed by a person standing in the middle of the street at a distance of 134 feet from the perspective plane, and at an elevation of 20 feet from the ground to the height of the eye. The horizon is placed high for the purpose of shewing the roofs of the two story dwellings.

The dimensions of the different parts are as follows:

1st.—Distances across the Picture.

Centre street between the houses	60	0	feet wide.
Side walks, each	10	0	"
Middle space between the lines of railway	4	6	"
Width between the rails	4	9	"

Depth of three story warehouse	40 feet.
Depth of yard in the rear of warehouse	20 "
Depth of two story dwelling on the right	30 "

Distances from the Spectator, in the Line of the Middle Visual Ray.

From spectator to plane of the picture	134 feet.
From plane of picture to the corner of buildings	50 "
Front of each house	20 "
Front of block of 7 houses 20 feet each	140 "
Breadth of street running across between the blocks	60 "
Depth of second block same as the first	140 "
Depth of houses on the left of the picture, behind the three story warehouses	40 "

To Draw the Picture.

1st. Let *C* be the centre of the perspective plane, *H. L* the horizon, *S* the point of sight.

2nd. From *C* on the line *P. P*, lay off the breadth of the street thirty feet on each side, at *O* and 60, making sixty feet, and from those points draw rays to the point of sight; these give the lines of the fronts of the houses.

3rd. From *O* lay off a point 50 feet on *P. P*, and draw a diagonal from that point to the point of distance without the picture; the intersection of that diagonal with the ray from *O*, determines the corner of the building; from the point of intersection erect a perpendicular to *B*.

4th. From 50, lay off spaces of 20 feet each at 70, 90 and so on, and from the points so laid off draw diagonals to determine by their intersection with the ray from *O*, the depth of each house.

5th. After the depth on *O. S* is found for three houses, the depths of the others may be found by drawing diagonals to the opposite point of distance to intersect the ray 60 *S*, as shewn by the dotted lines.

Note.—As a diagonal drawn to the point of distance forms an angle of 45° with the plane of the picture, it follows that a diagonal drawn from a ray to another parallel ray, will intercept on that ray a space equal to the distance between them. Therefore as the street in the diagram is 60 feet wide and the front of each house is 20 feet, it follows that a diagonal drawn from one side of the street to the other will intercept a space equal to the fronts of three houses, as shewn in the drawing.

6th. Lay off the dimensions on the perspective plane, of the depth of the houses, and the position of the openings on the side of the warehouse, and draw rays to the point of sight as shewn by the dotted lines.

7th. At *O* erect a perpendicular to *D* for a line of heights; on this line all the heights must be laid off to the same scale as the measures on the perspective plane, and from the points so marked draw rays to the point of sight to intersect the corner of the building at *B*. For example, the height of the gable of the warehouse is marked at *A*, from *A* draw a ray toward the point of sight intersecting the corner perpendicular at *B*; then from *B*, draw a horizontal line to the peak of the gable; the dotted lines shew the position of the other heights.

8th. To find the position of the peaks of the gables on the houses in the rear of the warehouses, draw rays from the top and bottom corner of the front wall to the point of sight, draw the diagonals as shewn by the dotted lines, and from their intersection erect a perpendicular, which gives the position of the peak, *the intersection of diagonals in this manner will always determine the perspective centre of a vanishing plane.* The height may be laid off on *O. D* at *D*, and a ray drawn to the point of sight intersecting the corner perpendicular at *C*, then a parallel be drawn from *C* to intersect a perpendicular from the front corner of the building at *E*, and from that intersection draw a ray to the point of sight. The intersection of this ray, with the indefinite perpendicular erected from the intersection of the diagonals, will determine the perspective height of the peak.

9th. The front edges of the gables will vanish in a point perpendicularly above the point of sight, and the back edges in a point perpendicularly below it and equidistant.

10th. As all the planes shewn in this picture except those parallel with the plane of the picture are parallel to the middle visual ray, all horizontal lines on any of them must vanish in the point of sight, and inclined lines in a perpendicular above or below it, as shewn by the gables.

SHADOWS.

1st. The quantity of light reflected from the surface of an object, enables us to judge of its distance, and also of its form and position.

2nd. On referring to paragraph 9, page 82, it will be found that light is generally considered in three degrees, viz: *light*, *shade* and *shadow;* the parts exposed to the direct rays being in light, the parts inclined from the direct rays are said to be in shade, and objects are said to be in shadow, when the direct rays of light are intercepted by some opaque substance being interposed between the source of light and the object.

3rd. The form of the shadow depends on the form and position of the object from which it is cast, modified by the form and position of the surface on which it is projected. For example, if the shadow of a cone be projected by rays perpendicular to its axis, on a plane parallel to its axis, the boundaries of the shadow will be a triangle; if the cone be turned so that its axis would be parallel with the ray, its shadow would be a circle; if the cone be retained in its position, and the plane on which it is projected be inclined in either direction, the shadow will be an ellipsis, the greater the obliquity of the plane of projection, the more elongated will be the transverse axis of the ellipsis.

4th. Shadows of the same form may be cast by different figures: for example, a sphere and a flat circular disk would each project a circle on a plane perpendicular to the rays of light, so also would a cone and a cylinder with their axes parallel to the rays. The sphere would cast the same shadow if turned in any direction, but the flat disk if placed edgeways to the rays, would project a straight line, whose length would be equal to the diameter of the disk and its breadth equal to the thickness; the shadow of the cone if placed sideways to the rays would be a triangle, and of the cylinder would be a parallelogram.

5th. Shadows of regular figures if projected on a plane, retain in some degree the outline of the object casting them, more or less distorted, according to the position of the plane; but if cast upon a broken or rough surface the shadow will be irregular.

6th. Shadows projected from angular objects are generally strongly defined, and the *shading* of such objects is strongly contrasted; thus if you refer to the cottage on Plate 53, you will perceive that the vertical walls of the front and chimney are in *light*, fully exposed to the direct rays of the sun, while the end of the cottage and side of the chimney are in *shade*, being turned away from the direct rays, the plane of the roof is not so bright as the vertical walls, because, although it is exposed to the direct rays of light it reflects them at a different angle, the shadow of the projecting eaves of the roof on the vertical wall forms a dark unbroken line, the edge of the roof being straight and the surface of the front a smooth plane, the under side of the projecting end of the roof is lighter than the vertical wall because it is so situated as to receive a larger proportion of reflected light.

7th. Shadows projected from circular objects are also generally well defined, but the shadings instead of being marked by broad bold lines as they are in rectangular figures, gradually increase from bright light to the darkest shade and again recede as the opposite side is modified by the reflections from surrounding objects, so gradually does the change take place that it is difficult to define the exact spot where the shade commences, the lights and shades appear to melt into each other, and by its beautifully swelling contour enables us at a glance to define the shape of the object.

8th. Double Shadows.—Objects in the interior of buildings frequently cast two or more shadows in opposite directions, as they receive the light from opposite sides of the building; this effect is also often produced in the open air by the reflected light thrown from some bright surface, in this case however, the shadow from the direct rays is always the strongest; in a room at night lit by artificial means, each light projects a separate shadow, the strength of each depending on the intensity of the light from which it is cast, and its distance from the object; the student may derive much information from observing the shading and shadows of objects from artificial light, as he can vary the angle, object and plane of projection at pleasure.

9th. The extent of a shadow depends on the angle of the rays of light. If we have a given object and plane on which it is projected, its shadow under a clear sky will vary every hour of the

Plate 55.

SHADOWS.

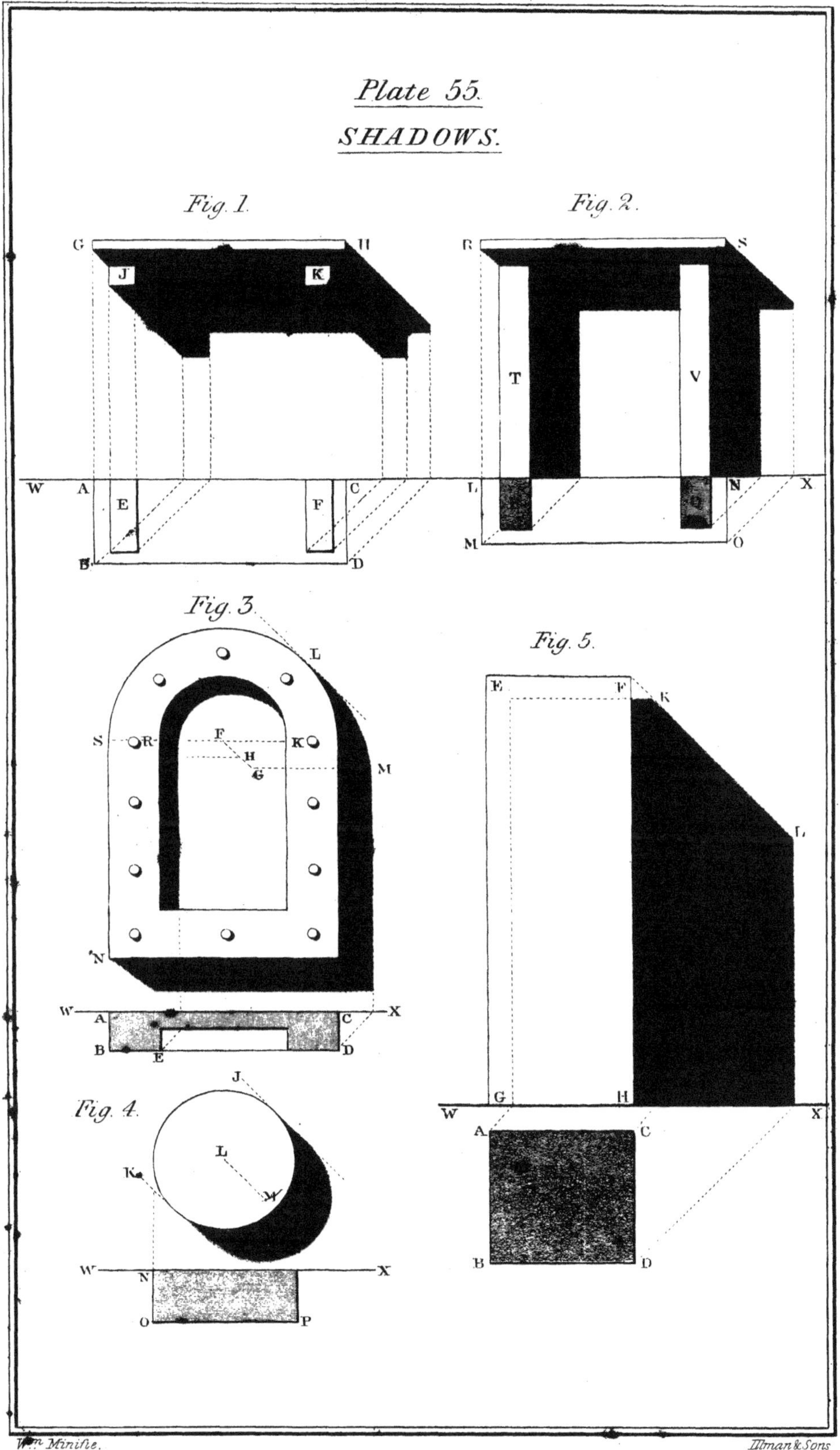

Wm. Minifie.

Illman & Sons

day, the sun's rays striking objects in a more slanting position in the morning and evening than at noon, projects much longer shadows. But in mechanical or architectural drawings made in elevation, plan or section, the shadows should always be projected at an angle of 45°, that is to say, the depth of the shadow should always be equal to the breadth of the projection or indentation; if this rule is strictly followed, it will enable the workman to apply his dividers and scale, and ascertain his projections correctly from a single drawing.

NOTE.—The best method for drawing lines at this angle, is to use with the *T* square, a right angled triangle with equal sides, the hypothenuse will be at an angle of 45° with the sides; with the hypothenuse placed against the edge of the square, lines may be drawn at the required angle on either side.

PLATE LV.

PRACTICAL EXAMPLES FOR THE PROJECTION OF SHADOWS.

FIGURE 1

Is a square shelf supported by two square bearers projecting from a wall. *The surface of the paper to represent the wall in all the following diagrams.*

1st. Let *A. B. C. D* be the plan of the shelf; *A. B* its projection from the line of the wall *W. X; B. D* the length of the front of the shelf, and *E* and *F* the plans of the rectangular bearers.

2nd. Let *G. H* be the elevation of the shelf shewing its edge, and *J* and *K* the ends of the bearers.

3rd. From all the projecting corners on the plan, draw lines at an angle of 45° to intersect the line of the wall *W. X*, and from these intersections erect indefinite perpendiculars.

4th. From all the projecting corners on the elevation, draw lines at an angle of 45° to intersect the perpendiculars from corresponding points in the plan; the points and lines of intersection define the outline of the shadow as shewn in the diagram.

Figure 2

Is a square Shelf against a wall supported by two square Uprights.

L. M. N. O is the plan of the shelf, *P* and *Q* the plans of the uprights, *R. S* the front edge of the shelf, *T* and *V* the fronts of the uprights.

1st. From the angles on the plan draw lines at an angle of 45° to intersect *W. X*, and from the intersections erect perpendiculars.

2nd. From *R* and *S*, draw lines at an angle of 45° to intersect the corresponding lines from the plan.

Figure 3

Is a Frame with a semicircular head, nailed against a wall, the Frame containing a sunk Panel of the same form.

1st. Let *A. B. C. D* be the section of the frame and panel across the middle, and *F* on the elevation of the panel, the centre from which the head of the panel and of the frame is described.

2nd. From *E*, draw a line to intersect the face of the panel, and from *D* to intersect *W. X*, and erect the perpendiculars as shewn by the dotted lines.

3rd. From *N* and *N*,′ draw lines to define the bottom shadow, and at *L* draw a line at the same angle to touch the curve.

4th. At the same angle draw *F. G*, make *F. H* equal to the depth of the panel, and *F. G* equal to the thickness of the frame.

5th. From *H* with the radius *F. R*, describe the shadow on the panel, and from *G* with the radius *F. S*, describe the shadow of the frame.

Note.—The tangent drawn at *L* and the curve of the shadow touch the edge of the frame in the same spot, but if the proportions were different they would not do so; therefore it is always better to draw the tangent.

Figure 4

Is a Circular Stud representing an enlarged view of one of the Nail Heads used in the last diagram, of which N. O. P *is a section through the middle, and* W. X *the face of the frame.*

1st. Draw tangents at an angle of 45° on each side of the curve.

2nd. Through *L* the centre, draw *L. M*, and make *L. M* equal to the thickness of the stud.

3rd. From *M*, with the same radius as used in describing the stud, describe the circular boundary of the shadow to meet the two tangents, which completes the outline of the shadow.

Figure 5

Is a Square Pillar standing at a short distance in front of the wall W. X.

1st. Let *A. B. C. D* be the plan of the pillar, and *W. X* the front of the wall, from *A. C. D* draw lines to *W. X*, and from their intersections erect perpendiculars.
2nd. Let *E. F. G. H* be the elevation of the pillar, from *F* draw *F. K. L* to intersect the perpendiculars from *C* and *D*.
3rd. Through *K*, draw a horizontal line, which completes the outline. The dotted lines shew the position of the shadow on the wall behind the pillar.

PLATE LVI.

SHADOWS—CONTINUED.

Figure 1

Is the Elevation and Fig. 2 *the Plan of a Flight of Steps with rectangular Blockings at the ends, the edge of the top step even with the face of the wall.*

1st. From *A. B. C* and *D*, draw lines at an angle of 45°.
2nd. From *F* where the ray from *C* intersects the edge of the front step, draw a perpendicular to *N*, which defines the shadow on the first riser.
3rd. From *Q* where the ray from *C* intersects the edge of the second step, draw a perpendicular to *M*, which defines the shadow on the second riser.
4th. From *K* where the ray from *A* intersects the top of the third step, draw a perpendicular to *O*, which defines the shadow on the top of that step.

5th. From *L* where the ray from *A* intersects the top of the second step, draw a perpendicular to *H* intersecting the ray drawn from *C* in *H*, which defines the shadow on the top of the second step.

6th. From *P* where the ray from *B* intersects the ground line, draw a perpendicular to intersect the ray drawn from *D* in *E*; this defines the shape of the shadow on the ground.

Figure 3.

To draw the Shadow of a Cylinder upon a Vertical Plane.

Rule.—Find the position of the shadow at any number of points.

1st. From *A* where the tangental ray (at an angle of 45°) touches the plan, draw the ray to *W. X*, and from the intersection erect a perpendicular.

2nd. From *A* erect a perpendicular to *B*, and from *B* draw a ray at 45° with *A. B* to intersect the perpendicular from *A* in *L*. This defines the straight part of the shadow.

3rd. From any number of points in the plan *E. H*, draw rays to intersect the wall line *W. X*, and from these points of intersection erect perpendiculars.

4th. From the same points in the plan erect perpendiculars to the top of the cylinder, and from the ends of these perpendiculars draw rays at 45° to meet the perpendiculars on the wall line; the intersections give points in the curve.

Note 1.—The outlines of shadows should be marked by faint lines, and the shadow put on by several successive coats of India ink. The student should practice at first with very thin color, always keep the camel hair pencil full, and never allow the edges to dry until the whole shadow is covered. The same rule will apply in shading circular objects; first wash in all the shaded parts with a light tint, and deepen each part by successive layers, always taking care to cover with a tint all the parts of the object that require that tint; by this means you will avoid harsh outlines and transitions, and give your drawing a soft agreeable appearance.

Note 2.—The lightest part of a circular object is where a tangent to the curve is perpendicular to the ray as at *P*. The darkest part is at the point where the ray is tangental to the curve as at *A*, because the surface beyond that point receives more or less reflected light from surrounding objects.

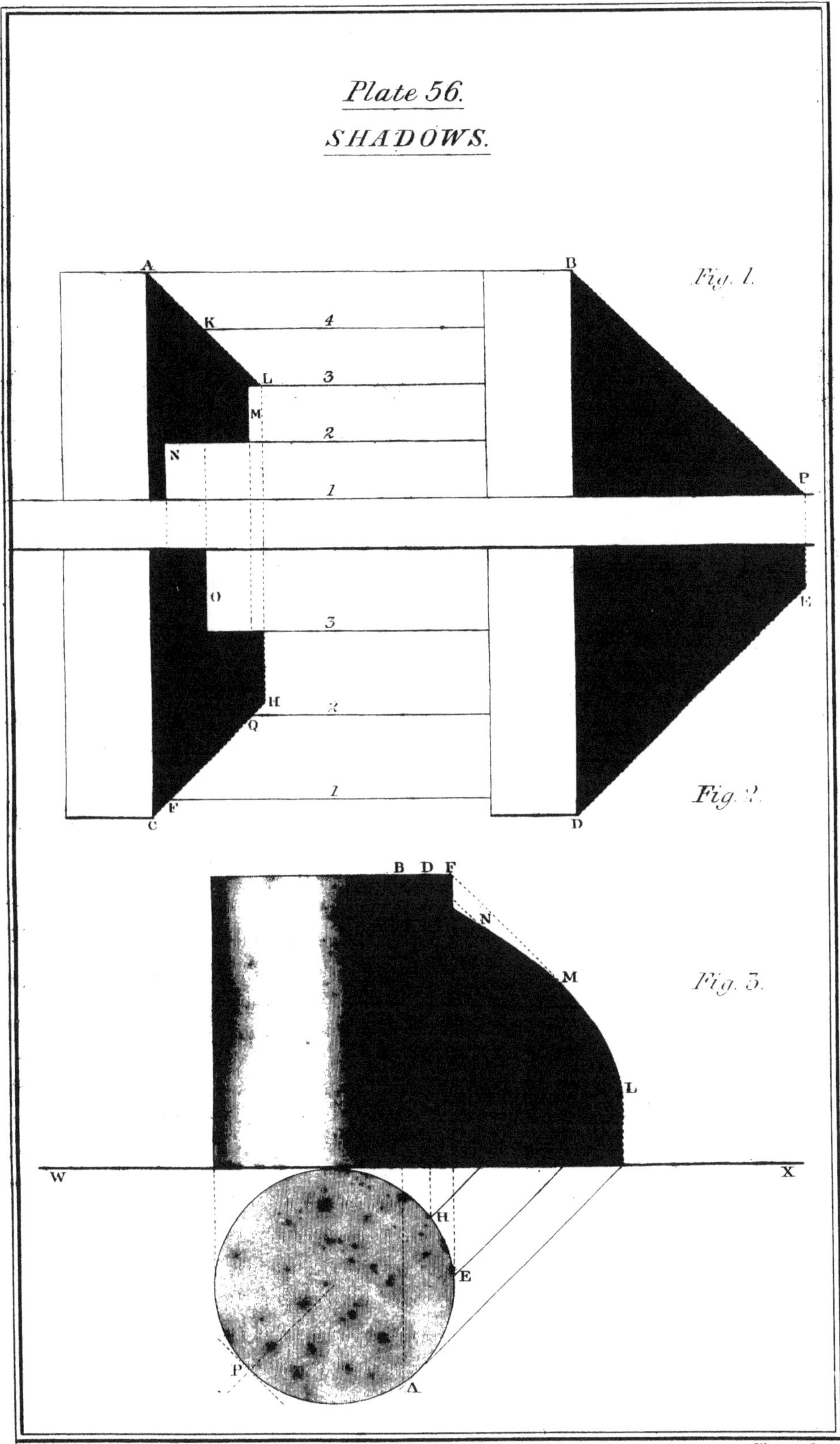

W.m Minifie.

Ullman & Sons

INDEX.

www.ingramcontent.com/pod-product-compliance
Lightning Source LLC
LaVergne TN
LVHW021252110826
845151LV00005BA/1496

* 9 7 8 1 4 2 5 5 2 2 1 2 4 *